International Labour Law

International Labour Law

by Prof. N. Valticos

This book was originally published as a monograph in the International Encyclopaedia for Labour Law and Industrial Relations

1979

Springer-Science+Business Media, B.V.

Cover design: Pieter J. van der Sman

ISBN 978-94-017-4404-1 ISBN 978-94-017-4402-7 (eBook)
DOI 10.1007/978-94-017-4402-7

Originally published by Kluwer, Deventer, The Netherlands in 1979

Foreword

This text was prepared as a monograph for the International Encyclopaedia for Labour Law and Industrial Relations. It is based on a more detailed work which appeared in French in 1970 and in Spanish in 1977. The material was brought up to date and recast to correspond to the type of monographs contained in the Encyclopaedia, which were aimed at providing concise, but reasonably detailed information and analysis of national laws and practice. Thus indications concerning the historical background, important as they may be in the present case, as well as the discussion of a number of theoretical questions, have had to be considerably reduced. However, detailed, up-to-date information is provided on the system of international labour standards and on the substantive provisions of the most important of these international instruments.

As part of the Encyclopaedia for Labour Law and Industrial Relations, the present study will most probably reach those engaged in research in the field of labour law, as well as many employers' organisations and a large section of the trade union movement. However, it has been considered useful to publish the study also in book form to facilitate its use in wider circles such as university teachers and students, diplomats, politicians, international lawyers, and those engaged in daily trade union activities.

Table of Contents

List of Abbreviations

A.J.I.L.	American Journal of International Law.
Ann.	Annuaire Français de droit international.
B.Y.B.I.L.	The British Year Book of International Law.
Intern. Lab. Code	The International Labour Code.[1]
I.L.C.	International Labour Conference.
ILO	International Labour Office.
I.L.R.	International Labour Review.
Minutes G.B.	Minutes of the Governing Body of the ILO.[2]
O.B.	Official Bulletin of the ILO.
Rec. Cours	Recueil des Cours de l'Académie de droit international.
Rec. Proc. Conf.	Record of Proceedings of the ILC.[3]
Rep. Conf. Com.	Report of the Committee on the Application of Conventions and Recommendations of the ILC.
Rep. Com. Exp.	Report of the Committee of Experts on the Application of Conventions and Recommendations.[4]
Rep. D.-G.	Report of the Director-General of the ILO.
Rev. crit.	Revue critique de droit international privé.

1. Reference is made to Volume I.
2. The first number following this abbreviation refers to the session of the Governing Body.
3. The first number following this abbreviation refers to the session of the Conference.
4. Published as Report III (Part 4) submitted to each ordinary session of the International Labour Conference.

Introduction

Chapter I. Historical and General Background

§1. Definition

1. International labour law is understood in the present context as meaning that part of labour law which has an international source. It therefore covers the substantive rules of law which have been established at the international level, as well as the procedural rules relating to their adoption and their implementation. Questions such as that of determining which national law is applicable to given labour relations are quite distinct matters, which are governed by private international law. They will not be dealt with in the present study.

§2. Historical Development

2. Why does international labour law exist? Why was it considered necessary, or useful to adopt at the international level substantive rules on labour matters? One has to consider their historical development[1] in order to understand fully the role of international standards on labour law. In fact, international labour law is almost as old as labour itself, because from the origins of labour law, it was felt that national legislation on labour matters could not be solidly established in individual countries if it was not supported by parallel standards adopted internationally. These standards were considered as a guarantee against a kind of unfair competition exercised by countries with inferior conditions of work. This is why the first moves towards international labour conventions date back to the beginning of the XIXth century. Robert Owen, in England, J. A. Blanqui and Villermé in France and Ducpétiaux in Belgium are considered as the precursors of the idea of international regulation of labour matters, but this idea has been put forward most systematically by David Legrand, an industrialist from Alsace who defended it and developed it in repeated appeals addressed, from 1840 to 1855, to the governments of the main European countries. In the second part of the XIXth century, the idea was first taken up by private associations. Thereafter, a number of proposals to promote it were made in the French and the German Parliaments. The first official initiative came from Switzerland where, following proposals made in 1876 and 1881, and in consultation with the European countries, the Swiss Government suggested the convening of a Conference on the matter in Bern in

May 1890. However, at the last moment, the Emperor of Germany, Wilhelm II, convened a similar Conference in Berlin. That Conference concluded its work by adopting mere wishes which were communicated to governments. However, the move forward continued and it was strengthened in 1897 by the conclusions of two Congresses, one of workers, held in Zurich, and the other of professors, administrators, etc. held in Brussels. The latter was followed by the establishment of an International Association for the Legal Protection of Workers, the seat of which was in Basle. The activity of this private organization was remarkable and it led, in particular, the Swiss Government to convene in Bern, in 1905 and 1906, international Conferences which adopted the first two International Labour Conventions. One of these related to the prohibition of night work for women in industrial employment and the other to the prohibition of the use of white (yellow) phosphorus in the manufacture of matches. The adoption of other draft Conventions was interrupted by the outbreak of the First World War.

1. For a more detailed account of the history of international labour law, see J. Follows, *Antecedents of the International Labour Organization*, Oxford, 1951 and J. Shotwell, *The Origins of the International Labor Organisation*, New York, 1934, Vol. 1.

§3. The Establishment of the International Labour Organization

3. During the First World War, the trade union organizations of both sides, as well as those of neutral countries insisted that their voice be heard at the time of the settlement of peace and that the Peace Treaty contain clauses for improving the condition of workers. Various trade union Congresses expressed a similar desire (at Leeds in 1916, Stockholm in 1917, London in 1918, and Bern in 1917 and 1919). Taking these demands into consideration, the Allied governments, and in particular those of Great Britain and France, elaborated, at the end of the war, drafts aiming at the establishment, by the Peace Treaty, of an international regulation of labour matters. The Peace Conference entrusted the examination of this question to a special commission known as the Commission on International Labour Legislation. The work of that commission led to the inclusion, in the Treaty of Versailles and the other Peace Treaties, of Part XIII, which dealt with labour matters and which provided for the establishment of an International Labour Organization which might adopt conventions and recommendations in this field. Conventions would be binding only to States which ratified them. Proposals made by France and Italy to give conventions binding character as from their adoption were not accepted, but it was provided that governments should submit conventions and recommendations to their 'competent authorities', i.e. as a rule, to their Parliament so that the latter could decide about the effect to be given to them.

§4. The Activity of the International Labour Organization

I. The International Labour Conference

4. In October 1919, the International Labour Conference met in Washington to adopt the first Conventions and to appoint the Governing Body. Since that date, the International Labour Conference has met regularly in general once a year, except during the Second World War. Sometimes it has been held twice a year, one session being devoted to maritime questions. Up to 1978 it had held 64 sessions.

II. The Declaration of Philadelphia

5. At the end of the Second World War, the International Labour Conference adopted in May 1944, in Philadelphia, a Declaration which defined again the aims and purposes of the Organization. This Declaration reaffirmed in particular, that labour is not a commodity, that 'freedom of expression and of association are essential to sustained progress', that 'poverty anywhere constitutes a danger to prosperity everywhere' and that 'the war against want requires to be carried on with unrelenting vigour within each nation, and by continuous and concerted international effort in which the representatives of workers and employers, enjoying equal status with those of governments, join them in free discussion and democratic decision with a view to the promotion of the common welfare'. The Declaration affirmed that 'all human beings, irrespective of race, creed or sex, have the right to pursue both their material well-being and their spiritual development in conditions of freedom and dignity, of economic security and equal opportunity'. It also referred to the social aspect of economic and financial measures (see No. 21 below). The Declaration then defined a number of specific objectives of the ILO, such as full employment and the raising of living standards, facilities for training policies in regard to wages, hours of work and other conditions of work calculated to ensure a just share of the fruits of progress to all, the effective recognition of the right of collective bargaining, the co-operation of management and labour in the continuous improvement of productive efficiency, and the collaboration of workers and employers in the preparation and application of social and economic measures, the extension of social security measures to provide a basic income to all in need of such protection, and comprehensive medical care, etc.

III. The Agreements with the UN and Other International Organizations

6. In 1946, an Agreement was concluded between the United Nations and the ILO. This agreement 'recognizes the ILO as a specialized agency responsible for taking such action as may be appropriate under its basic instrument for the accomplishment of the purposes set forth therein'. It also provides for co-operation and reciprocal representation between the two organizations. Agreements of co-operation have also been concluded by the ILO with other Specialized Agencies of the UN System and with regional Organizations.

IV. The International Labour Standards

7. From 1919 to 1978, the International Labour Conference adopted 151 conventions and 159 recommendations. Some of these instruments were revised to be adapted to changing conception and needs. The conventions and recommendations adopted related to the widest possible variety of matters of labour law and social policy: fundamental human rights (such as freedom of association, abolition of forced labour and elimination of discrimination) employment problems, conditions of work, social policy, social security, industrial relations, work of women, protection of young persons and children, conditions of work of special categories of workers. The general trend of these standards has been the constant broadening of their scope, both as regards the fields covered, the categories of persons protected and the framework within which the matters are treated. Thus a number of these instruments go beyond the traditional field of labour law and touch upon matters of civil liberties and penal law (as in the field of freedom of association and forced labour), of property law (as in the case of indigenous workers) etc. An outline of their content will be given in Part I of the present study. Some illustration will also be given about the ratifications which these instruments have obtained and the system of supervision which has been set up to follow and promote their implementation (Part II).

8. Apart from the ILO standards, an increasing number of bilateral treaties have been concluded in the field of labour. Finally, more recently, various international standards in this field have also been adopted within the framework either of the UN, or of European organizations such as the Council of Europe and the European Communities. The labour law regulations adopted within the framework of the European Communities will not be dealt with in the present study, a special contribution by Professor G. Schnorr being devoted to that question.

§5. The Purpose of International Labour Standards

9. Various arguments have been advanced over the years in support of international labour law, and their related importance has varied from one person to another. One of the oldest ideas which was advanced in favour of international conventions in the field of labour was that of international competition. Later, at the time of the establishment of the ILO, in 1919, the ideas of social justice and of the consolidation of peace came to the fore. Apart from these three main reasons, different other functions and aims were later attributed to international labour standards in the light of the experience that had been gained.

I. International Competition

10. The argument concerning international competition was used mainly throughout the XIXth century and during the first years of the XXth.[1] It was originally developed in answer to those who opposed the adoption of *national* legislation on labour matters on the grounds that such legislation would place the countries concerned in an unfavourable position on the international market, as it would result in higher prices for the goods of these countries as compared with those of their competitors. The reply was, therefore, given that international agreements in the field of labour would avoid international competition from taking place to the disadvantage of workers, by a kind of inhuman 'dumping', and would constitute between employers and between countries, a form of code of fair competition. This argument was put forward for over a century, by theoreticians as well as by workers, employers and statesmen.[2]

1. See Mahaim 'The Historical and Social Importance of International Labor Legislation' in Shotwell, *op. cit*, Vol. I, pp. 13–14 and more generally Valticos *Droit international du travail*, Paris, 1970, Nos. 1, 5, 7, 10, 16 and 135–136.
2. Thus, the then French Minister of Commerce, Millerand, wrote in 1904 to the British Home Secretary that it would be in the interest of the two countries to lead countries such as Belgium into suppressing night work of women (see Delevingne, 'The Pre-War History of International Labor Legislation', in Shotwell, *op. cit*, p. 34).

11. Progressively, however, the argument was used in a less absolute way, especially as it appeared that competition did not prevent the main industrial countries of Europe from adopting the first labour laws. When the ILO was established, the Preamble of Part XIII of the Treaty of Versailles which in fact, was its Constitution, referred to the idea but rather as an additional reason than as the main justification for international legislation. The idea, appearing only after two others had been expressed, was formulated in the following terms:

'. . . the failure of any nation to adopt humane conditions of labour is an obstacle in the way of other nations which desire to improve the conditions in their own countries'.

12. This argument has generally been given less prominence since it has been steadily realized that costs and the competitive value of products depend on many factors other than labour costs (such as the price of raw materials, available resources and capital, the competence of manpower and of management, organization of work, productivity, investment, tax system, available markets, monetary, tariff and customs matters). The economists were themselves rather sceptical about the argument.[1] To give an example, the countries which are the most successful in the world markets are not always those where the conditions of work are the less favourable. From another angle, a view expressed that the competence of the ILO should be limited to cases where the element of international competition came into place, was rejected in 1922 by the Permanent Court of International Justice.[2]

1. See Herbert Feis 'International Labour Legislation in the Light of Economic Theory', *I.L.R.* April 1927, pp. 491–518 and more recently 'Labour Cost as a Factor in International Trade', *I.L.R.* May 1954, pp. 425–446.
2. See P. C. I. J, Series B, Nos. 2 and 3, p. 9.

13. Nonetheless, the argument of international competition remained valid to some extent, particularly as between countries where conditions were similar and were not influenced by tariff barriers. For example, it was for reasons connected with the equalization of costs and competition that the Treaty of Rome, which set up the European Economic Community, dealt with the question of equal remuneration for equal work for men and women workers (Art. 119). Conversely, as between countries in which conditions differ widely, the objective is to secure equivalence rather than uniformity of legislation and costs. Even as between the latter countries, however, the factor of competition is sometimes taken into account. For instance, it has been suggested that, in considering the granting of tariff and commercial advantages to developing countries the acceptance and observance by such countries of fair labour standards would reduce the risk of unfair competition and would facilitate international trade. ILO standards and procedures might be particularly useful in this connection, since they could provide a time-tested and flexible basis for spelling out minimum conditions of work and for promoting their observance in the countries concerned.

14. The element of international competition may also be more or less important according to the subject-matter. Thus, rightly or not, it appeared to be of greater importance in the field of hours of work – and the ratification of the relevant Conventions has suffered from this conception – and in the field of maritime questions.

15. Generally speaking, the factor of international competition, which in its historical context was a relatively valid argument, is today no longer a primary justification for international labour Conventions, except in certain special circumstances. However it remains true that the harmonization of social policy may help to reduce the opportunities for unfair competition and thereby safeguard world markets and facilitate economic integration and the movement of capital, goods and manpower.

II. Contribution to the Consolidation of Peace

16. At the end of the First World War a new argument appeared, namely that injustice in the social field endangers peace in the world and that, therefore, action against such injustice serves the cause of peace. As stated in the Preamble to the Constitution of the ILO '. . . universal and lasting peace can be established only if it is based on social justice; . . . conditions of labour exist involving such injustice, hardship and privation to large numbers of people producing unrest so great that the peace and harmony of the world are imperilled', and the paraphrase *Si vis pacem cole justitiam* was engraved in the foundation stone of the building of the ILO in 1923. The question has sometimes been asked whether the relationship that is stated to exist between social justice and universal peace is really valid or whether it is a mere figure of speech. Albert Thomas, the first Director of the ILO, himself admitted[1] that it would be historically incorrect to accept the formula literally. It should rather be understood in a broad and indirect sense.

1. Albert Thomas, 'Justice sociale et paix universelle', *La Revue de Paris*, 15 March 1924, pp. 241–261. See also Phelan, one of his successors, in 'The contribution of the ILO to Peace', *I.L.R.* June 1949, pp. 607–632.

17. Thus, it has been pointed out that measures of social justice which provide, among other things, for trade union rights, are bound to strengthen democratic regimes, which are more likely than authoritarian governments to be peace loving. Social peace within countries may also sometimes be related to international peace inasmuch as internal tensions may have repercussions abroad. Stress has equally been laid on the positive and dynamic concept of peace, involving the establishment of stable, just and harmonious conditions both within individual countries and between different countries, by eliminating, *inter alia*, rivalry on world markets arising out of too great a disparity between labour conditions. It has also been claimed that the establishment of international labour standards aimed at improving the condition of mankind develops a common sense of solidarity internationally and fosters a climate of mutual collaboration and understanding transcending racial and national differences. The award of the Nobel Peace Prize to the ILO in 1969 tends to show that the link between social justice and the consolidation of world peace is still recognized by a strong current of world opinion.

III. Social Justice

18. The driving force behind the idea of international labour law was not the notion of social justice not only as a factor of peace, but also for its own sake. Thus, the Preamble to the Constitution of the ILO quoted above (para. 16), after having introduced the idea of social justice, went on to say that 'The High Contracting Parties moved by sentiments of justice and humanity, as well as by the desire to secure the permanent peace of the world, agree . . . etc.' Social justice is, thus, in its own right, an objective of international labour law even if little emphasis was laid upon it initially. This was probably due to the fact that it was a great innovation to introduce such a notion in international law, where the only case of international action for improving the welfare of men had been that of slavery. In the field of labour, the humanitarian concern originally appeared in the face of the conditions of great hardship imposed on the workers by development industrialization. It was the mainspring of the movement whose first achievement was the adoption, on both the national and international levels, of measures to protect children from conditions of work which had shocked the public conscience. The expression itself of social justice was introduced in 1919 in the course of the discussions which took place in the Peace Conference when the original Constitution of the ILO was being drafted as part of the Treaty of Versailles. This notion has certainly been the most powerful driving force in the development of international labour law.

19. Of course, since 1919, there has been marked improvement in conditions of work and standards of living in developed countries, although isolated imbalances and pockets of poverty persist in most of them. However, in the greater part of the world, social conditions still involve hardship, and in some cases, are even quite critical. The poorer countries are facing serious problems, such as poverty, unemployment, lack of adequate administrative infrastructure and of essential facilities in the field of health and education, and these problems often lead to importance being attached to the rights of the individual and of groups. The urgency of finding solutions to these problems make it even more important to define clear goals for national development and the welfare of the population, a process in which international standards, used with a proper sense of priorities, could be of considerable help. In this connection reference can be made to the emphasis placed on social development in the Strategy for the Second Development Decade of the United Nations (see below No. 21). Apart from the problems arising from underdevelopment, certain essential freedoms affecting trade union rights are more or less severely restricted or even denied, in almost all parts of the world.

20. More generally, the notion of social justice is constantly evolving to keep pace with rapid technical and social change. A growing need for security and well-being is accompanied by a desire for more freedom, more equality and a greater measure of participation in the management of society, as well as for better 'quality of life' and a substantial improvement in working conditions. The notion of social justice is now understood in such a wide meaning as to go far beyond the elimination of the most crying injustices and what was the original idea of simply protecting the weak. From the onset, Albert Thomas considered that social justice 'meant much more than the removal of social injustice. It meant a possible policy through which the individual might attain his political, economic and moral rights.'[1] It now embraces the general welfare of mankind in the broad sense, as defined by the Declaration of Philadelphia (see No. 6 above). In the same way as it happened for countries at the national level, the notion of social justice developed to mean, at the international level, that the world community is not responsible only for the maintenance of peace and good relations between States, but also for an active contribution to the welfare of mankind.

1. Phelan, *Yes and Albert Thomas*, London 1949, p. 242.

IV. Social and Human Objectives of Economic Development

21. Soon after the establishment of the ILO, in particular during the crisis in the thirties, it appeared that social matters could not be dissociated from the economic problems, and a systematic action was pursued to obtain that economic policy be guided by social consideration. Thus in 1930, Albert Thomas underlined that 'the social factor must take precedence over the economic factor', and these words were repeated by Pope Paul VI when he visited the ILO in 1969.[1] In the middle of the Second World War, in 1941, President Franklin Roosevelt declared to the International Labour Conference that 'economic policy can no longer be an end in itself. It is merely a means for achieving social justice'.[2] The interest of the ILO in economic matters was confirmed, in 1944, by the Declaration of Philadelphia, where it was stated that 'the central aim of national and international policy' should be to attain the social conditions described in the Declaration (see No. 5 above) and that 'all national and international policies and measures, in particular those of an economic and financial character, should be judged' in the light of these social objectives. As years went by, the notions of development and of economic planning became central to national policies, and a new function of international labour law became apparent, that is to emphasize the social and human objectives of development. The concept of development was initially taken as covering mainly the economic aspects of the problem only. It is recognized now that economic growth does not automatically ensure social progress. In 1970, the United Nations General Assembly adopted the International Strategy for the Second United Nations Development Decade which lays equal emphasis on social as well as on economic objectives and which has even squarely placed economics in its social context.[3] There is still, nevertheless, a widespread tendency to give economic development precedence over social considerations. It is, therefore, the function of international labour standards to promote balanced economic and social progress and to contribute the necessary element of precision to international action for social development.

1. Rec. Proc. Conf. 53, 1969, p. 79.
2. Rec. Proc. Conf. 1941, p. 158.
3. See *Freedom by Dialogue – Economic Development by Social Progress – The ILO Contribution*, Rep. D.-G. to the I.L.C. 1971, pp. 5–9.

V. International Movement of Workers and Goods

22. The first, and most obvious, purpose of international labour legislation has, from the very beginning, been the regulation of questions having an international character. This refers principally to migration of workers, which raises a number of complex problems related to working and living conditions of the immigrant workers in the countries of immigration. International standards are also appropriate in respect of the transportation of goods liable to endanger the safety of the workers and of the users generally.

VI. Consolidation of National Labour Legislation

23. It has sometimes been argued that even when the labour legislation or practice of a country has reached a certain level, it may be desirable for that country to ratify the Convention which provides for the corresponding standard, because, even if this did not call for any substantial change, it could contribute to a consolidation of national labour legislation by acting as guarantee against backsliding. Since it is not common for governments to go back on progress made in the social field, this argument may appear to be somewhat academic. There have, however, been cases in which the existence of international commitments based on ratified Conventions has prevented governments from adopting retrograde measures they had contemplated, particularly in times of crisis. In other cases, where retrograde measures had actually been taken, the supervisory machinery of the ILO has intervened to persuade the government concerned to restore the previous position.

VII. Source of Inspiration for National Action

24. Apart from the international commitments to which they may give rise, international labour standards can serve as a general guide and as a source of inspiration to governments by virtue of the authority which attaches to texts adopted by an assembly composed of representatives of governments, employers and workers of nearly all the countries in the world. They may also, for that reason provide a basis for the claims of the workers and guide the policy of employers. International labour standards have thus developed into a kind of international common law, playing a part similar to that played at different periods in history in the field of civil law, first by Roman law and later by certain European Codifications.[1] Those in charge of social policies in various countries have often highlighted this role of international labour law.[2] Such a role is of particular importance at a time when many new countries are engaged in working out a body of labour legislation and when many of the older countries are feeling the need to modernize statutes and structures which are becoming out-of-date. In that way, international standards can contribute both to the formulation of general policies (in the field of employment and more generally of social policy) and to the adoption of specific measures in special technical fields (industrial safety and health, work environment, etc.).

1. See Jenks, 'The *Corpus Juris* of Social Justice', in *Law, Freedom and Welfare*, London 1963, p. 105.
2. See Landy, 'The Influence of international labour standards: possibilities and performance', *I.L.R.* June 1970, pp. 555–604.

§6. International Labour Standards and Technical Co-operation

25. When the ILO was first established, international labour standards were considered as the main, if not the only means at its disposal to reach its objectives. Since, the means of action of the Organization have been diversified and technical co-operation, in particular, has been greatly developed during the past thirty years. Standards and technical co-operation have sometimes been compared and even contrasted. In fact there is no opposition between these two methods. In both cases, the aim is to guide and to stimulate governmental action.[1] The problem is not so much of choosing between them than of combining them in a successful way. Moreover, standards and technical co-operation are interdependent and complementary methods: technical co-operation can be facilitated to a large extent if it is based on well-defined and authoritative standards; conversely, technical co-operation can provide a particularly effective means of promoting the application of standards. For this reason, and because legislation is becoming an increasingly necessary instrument of social policy in all countries, international labour standards, constantly up-dated, remain a necessary source of guidance for government action and hold an important place in the over-all effort of the international community to improve the welfare of men.

1. See Jenks, *Britain and the ILO*, The David Davies Memorial Institute of International Studies, London 1969, pp. 11–12.

Chapter II. The Institutional Framework

26. As the instruments adopted by the ILO are the principal source of international labour law, it is necessary, first of all, to describe the structure of the International Labour Organization. The ILO is an international, intergovernmental organization, composed of States, but its special characteristic is its tripartite structure, i.e. that it comprises representatives not only from governments but also from employers' and workers' organizations in the member countries. We shall, therefore, examine these two main points, then we shall describe the various organs of the ILO and finally the question of its competence. We shall conclude this chapter by referring to the standard-setting activities of the ILO and of other organizations.

§1. The Membership of the ILO

I. States Members and Rules Governing Membership

27. In view of its very objective, the ILO has always aimed at universality in its membership. When it was established by the Treaty of Versailles, the 29 States which signed the Treaty were its first members and they invited 13 other States to join them. Germany and Austria were also admitted by a decision of the first Conference of the ILO, in Washington, in 1919, while they were not members of the League of Nations. In the course of the following years, twenty other States became members of the Organization, most of them (including the USSR in 1934) following their admission to the League of Nations and two (including the United States in 1934) by being admitted without being members of the League. The total membership to the ILO reached 62 States in the thirties but the international crisis, and afterwards the outbreak of the war, led a number of States to withdraw from the ILO, between 1935 and 1942, in most cases following their withdrawal from the League of Nations. The membership fell to 48 in 1942, but as from the end of the Second World War, the number of Member States started again to increase progressively with the readmission of former Members and the admission of newly independent States, generally as a result of the process of decolonization. On 1 July 1978 the number of Member States of the ILO stood at 136. Some of these countries are not members of the UN, while conversely there are some States Members of the UN (most of them small countries having recently achieved independence) which are not Members of the ILO.

28. There are two ways for a State to be admitted to membership in the ILO (Article 1, paras. 2 to 4 of the Constitution of the ILO). First, any State Member of the United Nations may become a Member of the ILO by communicating its formal acceptance of the obligations of the Constitution of the ILO (in fact most of the admissions to membership have followed this procedure); secondly, the Conference of the ILO may admit Members by a vote concurred in by two-thirds of the delegates attending the Session, including two-thirds of the government delegates present and voting.

II. Withdrawal

29. The Constitution of the ILO, as amended in 1945 (Article 1, paragraph 5), provides for the possibility of withdrawal from the Organization. Such withdrawal takes effect two years after the date of the reception of a notice by the State concerned of its intention to withdraw, subject to the Member having at that time fulfilled its financial obligations arising out of its membership. It is also expressly stated that when a State Member has ratified International Labour Conventions, its withdrawal shall not affect the continued validity, for the period provided for in the Conventions 'of all obligations arising thereunder or relatively thereto', that is both of the obligation to implement the Conventions and of the obligations relating to the supervision of such implementation.

30. Apart from the withdrawals which took place between 1935 and 1942, as stated above (No. 27), some countries withdrew from the ILO at a more recent date. In certain of these cases, the withdrawals lasted only one or two years, or the country concerned resumed its participation to the Organization even before the withdrawal took effect. In other cases, the withdrawal is still effective; this is the case for Albania (notice given in 1965), Republic of South Africa (notice given in 1964), Lesotho (notice given in 1969), and the United States (notice given in 1975).

§2. The Tripartite Structure

31. An essential characteristic of the ILO is the fact that it is not composed only of government representatives, but also of representatives of employers' or workers' organizations. This is generally described as the principle of 'tripartism',[1] which is followed in the composition of its various deliberative bodies, as will be described later.[2] This principle also influences, in many respects, the characteristics as well as the content of the instruments which are adopted by the Organization.

1. See Jenks, 'The Significance for International Law of the Tripartite Character of the International Labour Organization', *Transactions of the Grotius Society* (London) Vol. 22, 1936 and the *International Protection of Trade Union Freedom*, London 1957, p. 92–141; Berenstein, *Les organisations ouvrières, leur compétence et leur rôle dans la SDN, notamment dans l'OIT,* Paris, 1936; Bernard Béguin, 'ILO and the Tripartite System', *International Conciliation,* No. 523 (May 1959); Landelius, *'Workers, Employers and Governments'*, Stockholm, 1965; Vogel-Polsky, *Du Tripartisme à l'Organisation internationale du Travail*, Brussels, 1966.
2. See below Nos. 43 ss.

32. In establishing the rule of tripartism, the authors of the ILO Constitution wanted to associate to the government representatives those of the main elements of production, who are directly concerned with the regulation of labour matters. By ensuring such a participation, on an equal footing, of representatives of employers and workers in the decisions which would apply to them – and it had been said, in 1930, that this sort of participation was thus more advanced at the international than at the national level – this principle aimed at inspiring confidence among employers' and workers' representatives, to entrust them with responsibilities and to associate, with a view to achieving social peace, these two parties – often opposed to each other – with governmental action. Tripartism also contributes to avoiding decisions being taken in a purely technocratic spirit and to ensuring a democratic control of the activity of the Organization. The Organization's tripartite structure has been an undeniable source of vigour for the ILO, as it gave it the support not only of the diplomatic representatives of States, but also of the productive forces of nations. The participation of workers brought an element of dynamism. As for employers, if their interest and caution acted at times as a sort of brake, their participation did not generally result in slowing down unduly the legislative action of the Organization. In spite of the delay that divergent interests sometimes involved, the tripartite structure of the ILO gave an increased authority to its decisions, as these were taken with due consideration of the positions of all parties concerned. However, this structure gave rise to a number of difficulties, which sometimes reached a critical stage, in particular when the credentials of employers' or workers' representatives at the International Labour Conference were challenged.

I. Problems Relating to Workers' Representatives

33. As regards the question of workers' representatives, the greatest difficulties were encountered in relation to their designation by countries in which there is trade union pluralism and those where it is considered that the trade union system is not in conformity with the principle of freedom of association.

A. The Problem of Trade Union Pluralism

34. The question of the representation of workers in countries with trade union pluralism arose in the very first years of the ILO's existence. The Organization had to request the opinion of the Permanent Court of International Justice in connection with a case concerning the Netherlands. In that country, there were five trade union organizations, and as these did not agree on the choice of the workers' delegate, the government appointed the representative nominated by three of these organizations which, on aggregate, grouped slightly more members than the other two. One of the latter, which, individually, was numerically stronger than the others, challenged the appointment. The matter was then brought before the Court which considered in 1922[1] that 'the Workers' Delegates represent all workers belonging to a particular Member' and that the intervention of industrial organizations in this connection 'is to ensure, as far as possible, that the governments should nominate persons whose opinions are in harmony with the opinion of employers and workers respectively. If, therefore, in a particular country there exist several industrial organizations representing the working classes, the Government must take all of them into consideration, when it is proceeding to the nomination of the Workers' Delegate and his technical advisers.' The Court observed that 'no suggestion to the effect that only one organization should be represented is anywhere to be found in the Treaty, which on the contrary, expressly refers . . . to the representation of the workers of each particular country'. More generally, the Court felt that 'the aim of each government must, of course, be an agreement with all the most representative organizations . . . , that, however, is an ideal which it is extremely difficult to attain'. 'What is required of the governments is that they should do their best to effect an agreement which, in the circumstances, may be regarded as the best for the purpose of ensuring the representation of the workers of the country'.

1. Advisory Opinion No. 1 of 31 July 1922 (ILO OB, Vol. VI No. 7, 16 August 1922, pp. 291–298).

35. These principles have since been followed by the Credentials Committee of the International Labour Conference and the Conference itself, which has had to decide, over the years, on numerous appeals concerning countries with a pluralism of unions. This happened, in particular, in the case of France after the Second World War. For a number of years there was an agreement only between three of the trade union organizations, and not the fourth, which had individually the largest membership. In such cases, the Committee considered that there had been no infringement of the Constitution by the Government which appointed the Workers' representative in agreement with the three organizations. However, at one stage, the Committee expressed the wish that the government should reach an agreement with all the organizations concerned. Such agreement took place in 1965, when the Government decided to appoint as workers' delegate every year by alternation, a representative of the three most important workers' organizations of the country. This practice was followed also by other countries (such as Belgium, since 1960). In other cases, there have been, at least for a number of years, certain anomalies in countries where the organization which was the most important numerically was excluded for many years from the alternation, as general agreement could not take place between the various representative organizations.

B. The Problem of Countries whose Trade Union System is not Considered to be in Conformity with Freedom of Association

36. A different series of problems arose as regards the representation of workers in countries where it was considered that there was no freedom of association. In some cases, the matter was raised following changes of political regime and the decision of the new authorities to dissolve existing trade union organizations or to deprive them of their means of action. In such circumstances, the Conference decided to invalidate the credentials of the workers delegates from Argentina in 1965 and from Venezuela in 1950. These were exceptional cases.

37. The matter has also arisen in connection with countries whose political and social system does not recognize, in law or in fact, the principles of freedom of association for trade union purposes. Such cases gave rise to ample and heated discussions at the International Labour Conference, and the view of the majority was that the right of delegates to participate to the work of the Conference is not linked to the question of the extent to which freedom of association is observed in the country concerned – as there are other procedures for that[1] – but to the question of whether these delegates were appointed in agreement with the organizations which are the most representative of the workers of the country. It was also argued that in virtue of the principle of universality, States with very different political systems are Members of the Organization and should be able to participate fully in the work of the Conference. The matter was first raised in connection with the workers delegates from Italy, shortly after the establishment of fascism in Italy. After the Second World War, the problem again faced the Conference as regards countries with corporatist systems, such as Spain in 1956. In all these cases the majority of the Conference decided, after long discussions, to reject the proposals to invalidate the delegates. In the case of Italy, the workers' group of the Conference refused to appoint these workers' delegates as members of some technical committees of the Conference, but the Conference itself decided, in 1933 and 1934, to add an Italian worker delegate in some committees. In 1961 and 1962, objections against the credentials of workers' delegates from Portugal were rejected by the Credentials Committee which considered that the question of freedom of association was not within its jurisdiction.

1. See below No. 631 ss.

38. The credentials of workers' delegates from communist countries were also challenged many times.[1] This was done first in 1937 by the International Confederation of Trade Unions against the workers' delegates of the USSR. It was argued that these delegates did not represent free organizations, established by the workers themselves, on the basis of freedom of association, but organizations which were dependent on the same political authorities which controlled the Government. The Credentials Committee, followed by the Conference, was unanimous in recognizing the credentials of the delegates and stated that no evidence has been advanced to show that there existed at that time another organization representative of workers in USSR. After the readmission of the USSR to the ILO in 1954, a certain number of objections against the credentials of worker delegates of that country and of Czechoslovakia were lodged, mainly on the grounds that freedom of association did not exist in these countries and that the trade union organizations were subservient to the State! The majority of the Credentials Committee (i.e. the government and the workers members) referred to the decision of 1937 and considered that, while freedom of association is cited in the ILO Constitution as an objective of the Organization, its existence must not be considered to be a prerequisite to membership or to the exercise of the attributes to membership. The Committee also stated that if in one country only one trade union organization exists, a government is entitled to nominate workers' delegates in agreement with that organization, if it can be presumed actually to represent the majority of the work people in the country concerned. In conclusion the majority of the Committee decided that the objections were not well founded[2] and the Conference followed it by a majority vote.

1. See Jenks, 'The International Protection of Trade Union Rights', in *The International Protection of Human Rights*, ed. by Evan Luard, London, 1967, pp. 126–133.
2. Rec. Proc. Conf. 37, 1954, pp. 439–443.

39. Only in one case, that of Hungary, did the Conference, by a great majority, refuse to admit the workers' delegates, but the reason for this decision, taken in 1957 and in the two following years, was the Soviet intervention of 1956 in Hungary. A similar decision was also taken in respect of the employers delegates from Hungary.

II. Problems Relating to Employers' Representatives

40. The main problem relating to employers' representatives was that of the communist countries. After the USSR became, for the first, time a member of the ILO, in 1934, the Conference asked the Governing Body in 1936, at the request of the employers' group, to examine the question of the representation of States with a socialized economy and the Governing Body in turn requested the International Labour Office to prepare a report on the matter. The report was submitted in 1937 and it was stated in it that 'the qualifications which govern the choice of an employers' delegate may vary at different times and in different places. They are inevitably dependent upon the form of the social regime which exists in any given country . . . No provision requires that this employer be a private individual. The State may undertake that duty and there seems to be no question that in such a case it is the State which should appoint the employer. . .'[1] When the question of the amendments to the ILO Constitution were considered, in 1945 and 1946, one of the reasons adduced not to increase the number of one employers' delegate was that the existing provisions allowed the appointment of a manager of an undertaking of the socialized sector when the USSR was member of the ILO from 1934 to 1940. The Delegation on Constitutional Questions added that if the USSR resumed membership of the ILO 'it would naturally appoint, as employers' delegate, a representative of the socialized management of the USSR'.[2]

1. *Minutes G.B.* 78, 1937, p. 163. During the discussion, Harold Butler, Director of the International Labour Office, referred to the German terms of *Arbeitgeber* and *Arbeitnehmer* and stated that in every country there were employers who 'had one thing in common, which was that they gave work in return for money. This was the essential element in an employer', (*Minutes G.B.*, 79, 1937, pp. 39–40).
2. See I.L.C. 29th Session, Montreal 1946. (Report II–I), *Reports of the Conference Delegation on Constitutional Questions*, p. 91.

41. Serious difficulties arose, however, when the USSR again became member of the ILO, in 1954. The employers' delegates of 32 countries then lodged objections against the credentials of the employers' delegates of the USSR and six other Eastern European countries. This started a controversy which lasted for many years. In short, the minority of the Credentials Committee (i.e. the employers' group representatives) considered that there were no real employers in these countries and that the managers of undertakings were 'merely government agents without a shred of independence', while the fundamental principle of the Organization was that the employers' delegate should represent 'the free association of free Employers'. On the contrary, the majority of the Committee (i.e. the government and workers' representatives) referred to the decision of 1937 and stated that there was nothing in the ILO Constitution which required that the employers should represent private interests or ownership. It stressed that the rôle of the employer must, in its essentials, exist in the structure of any society and that it was not impossible for States with fully socialized economies validly to nominate a delegate representing the employers. It also observed that if this were not so, the aims and purposes of the ILO could not be universally applied. It concluded that the objections against the nomination of these delegates were not well founded.[1] The report of the minority was rejected by 105 votes against 79 with 26 abstentions.[2] Similar objections were raised in the following few years as regards the USSR and some other countries, but with the same results (apart from the case of Hungary – see No. 39 above).

1. See Rec. Proc. Conf. 37, 1954, pp. 432–438.
2. While the matter was under discussion, the Governing Body asked the Director-General, in 1955, to have prepared by a Committee of independent persons, which was established under the chairmanship of Lord McNair, former President of the International Court of Justice, a Report on the independence of employers' and workers' organizations (Geneva, ILO-OB 1956, para. 341, p. 581). The majority of that Committee concluded that 'there has been a shift of emphasis in the nature of the contributions to the work of the ILO to be expected from the employers and workers. Originally employers and workers were represented . . . very largely for the protection and defence of their respective material interests: on the one hand, the interests of private capital and, on the other, the interests of labour . . . the original purpose of the separate representation of employers and workers has in the course of the years taken on wider content and now represents also a combined interest of the two elements in the productivity of industry and in the function or skill of management in industry.'

42. Apart from this question of credentials, the attendance of employers' delegates from communist countries gave rise to the problem of their participation in technical committees of the Conference, as had happened for workers' delegates between the two Wars. As from 1954, the Conference employers' group, which establishes a list of employers' delegates for the appointment of the tripartite Conference Committees, did not include in these lists employers' delegates from communist countries. These delegates appealed to the Conference Selection Committee on the proposal of which, from 1954 to 1958, the Conference admitted them in the Committees as deputy members, i.e. without right to vote. In 1959, the Conference introduced – in spite of the opposition of most employers' delegates – a system designed to ensure equality of treatment to all delegates. By virtue of this system, it is for a Board of independent persons to decide whether a delegate who appealed to it should be added as a voting member of a Conference Committee (but no more than two delegates may be added to each Committee). The decisions of the Appeals Board are final and cannot give rise to any discussion. This system worked effectively from 1959 to 1967. Since 1968, the Employers' group itself placed employers' delegates from communist countries on the lists of employers' members of various Committees, so that the Appeals Board had no appeal to consider.

§3. The Organs of the ILO

43. The ILO comprises three main organs. The International Labour Conference, the Governing Body and the International Labour Office. A certain number of Committees assist it in its work. Moreover, various meetings take place at the regional level. For a number of years the question of the structure of the ILO has been discussed in various bodies of the Organization.

I. The International Labour Conference

44. The International Labour Conference is the principal organ of the ILO.

It frames and adopts Conventions and Recommendations and is responsible for following their application (on the basis of a legal and technical examination made by independent organs and subject to the quasi-judicial procedures provided for in the Constitution[1]). It decides on the admission of new Member States (except in cases of the automatic admission of Members of the United Nations).[2] It votes the programme and budget of the Organization. The Conference meets, in principle, at least once a year. It may hold two sessions in a given year, as in 1976, when the one is the normal one and the other relates to maritime matters.[3]

1. See below No. 620 ss.
2. See above No. 28.
3. See below No. 499.

45. The Conference consists of the delegations of all Member States of the Organization. As a result of the tripartite structure of the Organization, each national delegation should have four members, i.e. two government delegates, one employers' and one workers' delegate. The latter two delegates must be nominated 'in agreement with the industrial organizations, if such organizations exist, which are most representative of employers or work-people . . . in their respective countries' (Article 3 §5 of the Constitution). Every delegate is entitled to vote individually, and it often happens that the employers' and the workers' delegates vote differently from the government delegates of their country. In fact, both the employers' and the workers' delegates at the Conference have established distinct groups which generally review the questions put to the Conference before they are examined by a tripartite body. If, for one reason or another, the national delegation does not comprise a workers' delegate, the employers' delegate has no right to vote and vice versa. In practice the great majority of delegations are constituted on a tripartite basis. Each delegate can be accompanied by technical advisers who can represent him at the various committees which the Conference appoints. There may be no more than two technical advisers for each of the separate matters which are on the agenda of the session (Article 3 §2 of the Constitution). In 1978, the Conference comprised a total of 505 delegates and 1,168 technical advisers.

46. The Conference scrutinizes the credentials of delegates and technical advisers and can refuse, by a two-thirds majority to admit any delegate or technical adviser whom it deems not to have been nominated in conformity with the terms of the Constitution (Article 3 §9 of the Constitution). The credentials of delegates and technical advisers are examined by a Committee of three members (Article 5 and 26 of the Standing Orders of the Conference): one government, one employer and one worker member. The Standing Orders of the Conference define the cases in which objections against the credentials are not receivable. When the Credentials Committee is unanimous about the receivability of the objection, its decision is final and does not call for a discussion at the Conference.

47. The Conference appoints various Committees which initiate the examination of the questions it has before it and submit reports on which it decides at its plenary sittings. These Committees also are constituted on a tripartite basis, apart from the Finance Committee which comprises only government representatives. The Selection Committee, which arranges the programme of the Conference, has a composition analogous to that of the Governing Body. On the other hand, in all other Committees, each of the three groups has an equal number of votes and a system of weighted vote is used when each of the three groups of a commission has a different number of members. At each session, the Conference appoints a Committee for each of the technical items on its agenda, plus a Committee on the Application of Conventions and Recommendations and a Resolutions Committee. It also appoints a Drafting Committee to draft the final text of Conventions and Recommendations.

II. The Governing Body

48. The Governing Body has the responsibility of co-ordinating all the activities of the Organization, of convening the various meetings and of deciding their agenda and their dates. *Inter alia*, it fixes the agenda of the Conference, although the latter can itself decide by a majority of two-thirds to include a subject on its agenda of the following session. The Governing Body appoints the members of various committees. It examines the conclusions of their meetings and decides what effect should be given to them. The Governing Body has important functions in the financial and administrative field and it discusses the draft programme and budget in great detail before it is submitted to the Conference for adoption. Finally, the Governing Body elects the Director-General of the International Labour Office. It meets three times a year and its session, including those of its committees, last for several weeks. Its role is essential to ensure the necessary unity in the diversified activities of the Organization.

49. The Governing Body is elected every three years by the International Labour Conference (Article 7 of the Constitution). It is constituted on a tripartite basis. When the ILO was created, in 1919, the Governing Body had 24 members. Now this number has been increased to 56; 28 of them represent governments, and 14 each the employers and the workers. Ten of the 28 Government members are appointed by the Members of chief industrial importance.[1] The other States are appointed by the Government delegates at the Conference (excluding those of the ten Members mentioned above). The employers' and workers' representatives are elected by the employers and workers representatives at the Conference, respectively. The Governing Body elects a chairman and two vice-chairmen from among its members. One of them must represent a government, and the other two are representatives of the employers and of the workers respectively. The Governing Body also appoints various committees among its members. The important functions assigned to the Freedom of Association Committee will be described later.[2]

1. Up to November 1977, these States were: the United States (which now have withdrawn from the Organization), the USSR, China, the United Kingdom, the Federal Republic of Germany, France, India, Japan, Italy and Canada.
2. See below No. 632.

III. The International Labour Office

50. The International Labour Office is the permanent secretariat of the Organization. It has a Director-General, who is appointed by the Governing Body, and, subject to instructions from the latter, is responsible for the efficient conduct of the International Labour Office. The first Director of the ILO was Albert Thomas (1919–1932) whose strong personality and political experience established a tradition of initiative and dynamism as regards the röle of the Director of the ILO.[1] The following Directors (Directors-General after the Second World War) were Harold Butler (1932–1938), John Winant (1938–1941), Edward Phelan (1941–1948), David A. Morse (1948–1970) and Wilfred Jenks (1970–1973). Since 1974 the Director-General has been Francis Blanchard. The functions of the Director-General and of the staff are exclusively international in character. In the performance of their duties, the Director-General and the staff may not seek or receive instructions from any government or from any other authority external to the Organization. Each Member State of the Organization should respect the exclusively international character of the responsibilities of the Director-General and the staff and should not seek to influence them in the discharge of their responsibilities. The staff of the ILO is bound by Staff Regulations and it can appeal to an Administrative Tribunal in respect of the observance of his contract of employment and of the provisions of the Regulations.[2] On 1 July 1978 the regular staff of the ILO comprised 2,093 officials belong to 102 nationalities. Moreover 662 experts were employed by the ILO for its technical co-operation activities.

1. See Jenks, 'The Continuing Legacy of Albert Thomas' in *Social Policy in a Changing World*, ILO, Geneva, 1976, pp. 69–78.
2. The Administrative Tribunal of the ILO has also been accepted by 18 other organizations.

51. The functions of the ILO are described in general terms by the Constitution of the ILO (Article 10). They include the technical preparation of the work of the Conference and of the Governing Body and the collection and publication of information on labour problems. More particularly, as regards the adoption of international labour standards, the Office prepares the reports on the various items of the agenda of the Conference. For standards which have been adopted, the Office prepares the documentation necessary for the bodies entrusted with the supervision of their application. The Constitution (Article 10, paragraph 2) provides that the Office shall accord to governments at their request all appropriate assistance in connection with the framing of laws and regulations on the basis of the decisions of the Conference and the improvement of administrative practices and systems of inspection, and that it shall carry out the duties required of it in connection with the effective observance of Conventions. The Office also provides governments with assistance in the framework of its technical co-operation programmes which have greatly expanded in the last 30 years.[1] It also has important activities in the field of research, publications and education (mainly workers' education). The ILO has its headquarters in Geneva but it also has established a network of offices in the various regions of the world.

1. See *Technical Co-operation: New Prospects and Dimensions*. Report of the D.-G. to the I.L.C., 1977 (Part I), ILO, Geneva.

52. In addition to the numerous services of the Office, the ILO has established two institutions which function under its auspices: the *International Institute of Labour Studies* and the *International Centre for Advanced Technical and Vocational Training* which has its seat in Turin.

IV. Technical Committees and Meetings

53. Apart from the Committees established by the Conference and the Governing Body among their members and the Committees appointed to supervise the applications of Conventions and Recommendations, a number of other bodies have been created to assist the ILO in its activities: the most important are the Joint Maritime Commission, the Advisory Committee on Rural Development, the Joint Committee on Public Service and the Industrial Committees. For certain matters, the ILO convenes, when necessary, technical meetings of experts.

V. Regional Meetings

54. *Regional Conferences* are held regularly and they group tripartite delegations from the countries of each region, on the same principles as the General Conference. Regional Conferences cannot adopt conventions or recommendations,[1] and they study the labour problems of their region and adopt plans of action or suggestions about the activity of the ILO in this field. There have been eleven Conferences of American States, five African regional Conferences, eight Asian regional Conferences, and two European Regional Conferences. Three Regional Advisory Committees are also associated with the work of the Governing Body concerning their respective regions.

1. On the question of international and regional standards, see below No. 88.

§4. The Competence of the ILO

55. The question of the competence of the ILO has been disputed during the first years of existence of the Organization.[1] It was beyond doubt that, when the

ILO was established, the aim was mainly to regulate conditions of work in industry, and most of the instruments adopted at the first session of the Organization related to such type of labour. When the ILO planned to consider other fields, its competence was disputed in some quarters. The objections were rejected by a great majority of the Conference but in some cases the matter was submitted to the Permanent Court of International Justice.

1. See Hiitonen, *La compétence de l'Organisation internationale du Travail*, Paris, 1929; Jenks 'La compétence de l'OIT. Examen de quatre avis consultatifs rendus par la Cour permanente de Justice internationale', *Revue de droit et de législation comparée*, 1937, pp. 156–183 and 586–623; G. Fischer, *Les rapports entre l'OIT et la Cour permanente de justice internationale*, Geneva, 1945, pp. 319–348.

I. The Question of Agricultural Work

56. The most important case related to the competence of the ILO as regards agricultural matters, to which the Government of France had objections.[1] In its consultative opinion No. 2 of 12 August 1922,[2] the Court referred to the problem of national sovereignty which had been raised in the objections to the ILO's competence and it considered that the question was simply to know what was the precise meaning of the Treaty of Versailles which had established the ILO. It pointed out that the 'comprehensive character of Part XIII is clearly shown in the Preamble' and that 'the language could hardly be more comprehensive'. The Court concluded that 'the competence of the ILO does extend to international regulation of the conditions of labour of persons employed in agriculture'.

1. The case of the competence of the ILO in this field was presented to the Court by Albert Thomas, Director of the International Labour Office, who defended successfully the cause of the Organization against the government of his country.
2. See P.C.I.J. Series B, Nos. 2 and 3, p. 9; O.B. 1922, vol. VI, pp. 339–351.

II. The Question of Means of Production

57. On the other hand, when the question arose as to whether the ILO was competent to deal with matters of agricultural production – which the Director of the ILO had himself formally declined as such – the Court, in its opinion No. 3 of 12 August 1922,[1] concluded that 'the organisation and development of the means of production are not committed to the Organisation', but that 'the Organisation cannot be excluded from dealing with the matters specifically committed to it by the Treaty on the grounds that this may involve in some aspects the consideration of the means or methods of production, or of the effects which the proposed measures would have upon production'. The Court gave, as instances, the fact that protection against sickness, disease and injury may involve the consideration of methods and processes of production, such as the use of white phosphorus. It was also concluded from this reasoning that the ILO could, for several reasons, propose the complete abolition of a given method of production.[2]

1. See P.C.I.J. Series B, Nos. 2 and 3, p. 49; O.B. 1922, Vol. VI, pp. 379–382.
2. Jenks, *op. cit.*, p. 620.

III. The Question of the Personal Work of the Employers

58. The question of the personal work of the employers was raised in relation to a case where the problem was whether, in order to protect workers against night work in the baking industry, an ILO Convention could also provide that the employers themselves should be prohibited from doing the same work. The matter was brought to the Court at the request of the employers' members of the Governing Body of the ILO. In its advisory opinion No. 13 of 23 July 1926,[1] the Court based itself on arguments similar to those of its opinion No. 2. It reaffirmed the exceedingly broad character of the Conference of the ILO, while observing that the Organization has no legislative power and that each Member State is free to adopt or reject any Convention or Recommendation and to object to the inclusion of a particular matter in the Organization's activities. The Court also considered that, if the objects of the Organization defined in Article 427 of the Treaty of Versailles emphasized the importance, from an international point of view, of the welfare of wage-earners, 'this enumeration is neither complete nor final'. Further, the Court referred to cases of national and international practice where the incidental regulation of the personal work of the employers was potentially involved and in which no objection was raised against such regulation. Replying to another objection, it stated that the Treaty made no distinction between principles and provisions to ensure their application, and that the Court concluded unanimously that 'it is within the competence of the ILO to draw up and to propose labour legislation which in order to protect certain classes of workers, also regulates incidentally the same work performed by the employer himself.'

1. I.C.P.J. Series B, No. 13, p. 6; Vol. XI, 1926, pp. 302–316; Jean Morellet, 'The Competence of the ILO: A further decision of the Permament Court of International Justice'; *I.L.R.* Oct. 1926, pp. 459–475.

IV. The Question of Women Holding Positions of Supervision

59. A still more general question was indirectly raised a few years later. The matter as such was not that of the competence of the ILO but merely of the scope of a given Convention and the question put to the Court was whether the Night Work (Women) Convention, 1919 (No. 4) applied to women who hold positions of supervision or management and are not ordinarily engaged in manual work. The more general competence of the ILO to deal with persons who were not engaged in manual work was not challenged, but Judge Anzilotti, in a dissenting opinion, expressed the view that 'the regulation of the conditions of employment of manual workers is the essential and normal task of the Organisation'. In its advisory opinion of 15 November 1932,[1] the majority of the Court replied in the affirmative to the question which was put to it. Referring to the opinion of Anzilotti, the Court stated that 'it is certainly true that the amelioration of the lot of the manual workers was the aim of Part XIII of the Treaty of Versailles' but that 'it is not disposed to regard the sphere of activities of the ILO as circumscribed so closely, in respect of the persons with which it was to concern itself, as to raise any presumption that a labour Convention must be interpreted as being restricted in its operation to manual workers, unless a contrary intention appears'. The Court also stated that 'the limits of the sphere of the ILO are not fixed with precision or rigidity' and that the text 'of Part XIII does not support the view that it is workers doing manual work – to the exclusion of other categories of workers – with whom the ILO was to concern itself'.

1. I.C.P.J, Series A/B, 1932, No. 50, p. 365; O.B. Vol. XVII No. 5, 1932, pp. 129–197.

V. More Recent Evolution. The Competence of the ILO as Redefined by the Declaration of Philadelphia

60. The various opinions of the International Court, and especially the first one, settled definitely the question of the wide competence of the ILO. There have, at times, been more limited objections, as in 1926, when the employers' delegates to the Conference questioned the competence of the ILO as regards the transport of migrants but the objection was rejected by the International Labour Conference.

61. The general character of the competence of the ILO was still more clearly underlined after the Second World War by the general nature of the terms of the Declaration of Philadelphia[1] which replaced the 'general principles' of the Treaty of Versailles. The wording of the Declaration of Philadelphia resulted in widening the constitutional foundation of the competence of the Organization from two points of view: as regards the subject matter, that competence was no longer to be limited strictly to conditions of work, but extended more generally to conditions of life, sometimes in co-operation with other international agencies.[2] As regards the persons to be covered, the Organization was henceforth in a position to deal with all categories of workers, i.e. non-manual as well as manual, independent workers as well as wage-earners,[3] civil servants as well as persons working in the private sector. Certain Conventions, in particular in the field of human rights, expressly use terms such as 'workers and employers without distinction whatsoever'.[4] Furthermore, in a number of fields, such as social security, forced labour or discrimination, ILO Conventions cover not only workers of all categories but can extend to the entire population.

1. See above No. 5.
2. See below No. 533 as regards the Indigenous and Tribal Populations Convention, 1957 (No. 107).
3. Thus, as early as 1921 the right of association (agriculture) Convention (No. 11) related generally to 'workers engaged in agriculture'. Much later, in 1958 when the Discrimination (Employment and Occupation) Convention (No. 111), the Swiss Government was of the opinion that this instrument should not cover independent workers, as this was outside the scope of relations between employers and workers, but the text finally proposed and adopted did cover independent persons and the point was not pressed.
4. Freedom of Association Convention, 1948 (No. 87), Article 2.

62. This extension also resulted in ILO Conventions not only dealing with labour law or more generally social law matters, but in the ILO competence covering the wider ground of social and economic policy and to a certain extent, civil rights.[1]

1. See below under freedom of association (No. 183) and forced labour (No. 224).

63. As had been written already in the thirties,[1] the competence of the ILO is not enclosed within rigid limits but it includes all labour matters. In the light of the evolution of social problems, the Organization may have to deal with questions which were not expressly provided for when it was created. It is a 'continuous creation'.[2] Its functions did not appear any longer to be limited to the protection of the underprivileged, but more generally to ensuring the co-ordination of social policy throughout the world.

1. Scelle, *L'Organisation internationale du Travail et le BIT*, Paris, 1930.
2. Morellet, *op. cit.*, p. 475.

§5. The Standard-Setting Activities of the ILO and Other International Organizations

64. When the ILO was established, its main means of action was the adoption of international Conventions and Recommendations, as appears from the large place devoted to standard-setting in its Constitution. Although the means of action of the ILO have been diversified, in particular by the development of technical co-operation in the last thirty years, standard-setting still plays a key role and practically every year new standards are adopted, while systematic action aims at giving effect to former standards.[1]

1. See below, Part II.

65. More recently, mainly after the Second World War, other organizations, either universal – and in particular the United Nations itself, or regional – mainly European Organizations such as the Council of Europe, and the European Organizations, but also American and Arab – have also adopted a number of international standards related to the field of labour. The following chapter will be devoted to these various sources of international labour law and to the relations between them.

Chapter III. The Sources of International Labour Law

66. The sources of international labour law are mainly to be found in the Conventions and Recommendations adopted by the ILO, but, as has just been said, various instruments adopted by other organizations – such as the United Nations or various regional organizations – also deal with labour matters either as such or from the point of view of human rights. These various instruments differ as regards their legal character; some, such as ILO conventions, the UN Covenants on human rights, the European Social Charter, etc. are designed to create legal obligations for the States which ratify them (and the supra-national regulations of the European Committees have even an immediate effect on Member countries). Other – declarations of principle, recommendations etc. – have no mandatory force but are essentially guides to national action. The distinction is, however, not absolute, as Conventions produce a substantial part of their practical effect as standard-defining as well as obligation-creating instruments. Over the years an important case-law has also been progressively established by the bodies appointed to supervise the application of these standards. Finally, a very important number of bilateral treaties have been concluded to regulate the admission and conditions of work of nationals of each contracting country in the territory of the others.

§1. ILO Sources

67. ILO sources of international labour law can be found in the Constitution itself of the Organization, in the numerous Conventions and Recommendations adopted by it, and in a number of less formal instruments. Apart from these formal sources, reference should be made to the interpretation of the ILO Constitution and Conventions and to what can be described as case-law. A final category comprises the instruments adopted by special Conferences convened by the ILO.

I. The Constitution of the ILO

68. While the Constitution of the ILO contains mainly provisions relating to the organs and the functioning of the Organization, it also lays down a number of general principles which have come to be regarded in certain respects as a direct source of law. Such principles are contained in the Preamble to the Constitution and in the Declaration concerning the Aims and Purposes of the Organization, adopted by the Conference in Philadelphia in 1944 and incorporated in the ILO Constitution in 1946. ILO bodies have frequently drawn legal consequences from them, particularly in the field of freedom of association and in the field of racial discrimination (Apartheid), and States Members of the ILO have been regarded as bound to some extent by these constitutional principles (see *infra* Nos. 631 and 260).

II. Conventions and Recommendations

69. The ILO Conventions and Recommendations are, by far, the main source of international labour law. This is due to their number (from 1919 to 1978, 151 Conventions and 159 Recommendations were adopted) but also to their detailed character and the increasingly broad field which they cover.

A. Nature and Characteristics

70. International labour Conventions and Recommendations differ from the point of view of their legal character: Conventions are instruments designed to create international obligations for the States which ratify them, while Recommendations are not designed to create obligations but to provide guidelines for government action.

71. More particularly international labour Conventions have a number of specific features[1] which can be grouped under three main ideas. Firstly, they are adopted in an institutional framework. Thus the adoption of Conventions does not follow the type of diplomatic negotiation which is usual in the case of treaties, but it is prepared by discussions in an assembly which has many points in common with parliamentary assemblies.[2] This also partly explains the fact that unanimity is not necessary for the adoption of Conventions.[3] The institutional character of these instruments also explains the rules relating to their signature and to the deposit of ratifications. For the same reason, the interpretation of Conventions cannot be given by the States parties to them, but can be given only by the International Court of Justice.[4] Similarly, the revision of a Convention cannot be decided by the States parties to it, but by the General Conference, which is the legislative body of the Organization.

1. As regards the specific character of international labour Conventions, much has been written, especially in the thirties. See in particular Scelle, *op. cit.* pp. 181–185; Jenks, 'Some characteristics of international labour conventions', *Canadian Bar Review*, Vol. XIII, 1935, pp. 448–462 and 'Are International Labour Conventions Agreements between Governments?', *ibid.* Vol. XV, 1973, pp. 574–578; Morellet, 'Un type original de traités, les conventions internationales du travail', *Rev. crit. de. d.i.p*, 1938, pp. 1 et 5.
2. See Valticos, 'Diplomacy in an Institutional Framework: Some Aspects of ILO Practice and Experience', *La Communitá Internazionale*, 1974, pp. 3–21.
3. See below Nos. 73 and 83.
4. See below No. 117.

72. A second characteristic is that, as a consequence of the tripartite structure of the ILO,[1] the International Labour Conference, which adopts Conventions and Recommendations, is not constituted by representatives of governments only, but also of representatives of employers and workers,[2] each delegate being entitled to vote individually. This is one of the reasons why ratification of a Convention cannot be made subject to reservations.[3]

1. See above Nos. 31 ss.
2. See in particular Wilfred Jenks 'The Significance for International law of the Tripartite character of the International Labour Organisation', *op. cit.* pp. 45–81.
3. See below No. 577.

73. Thirdly, the desire to make Conventions particularly effective explains another series of characteristics, such as the rules – which were innovations in international law – that a two-thirds majority is sufficient for the adoption of Conventions and Recommendations and that governments should submit Conventions and Recommendations to their competent authorities, i.e. as a rule to their Parliaments,[1] the obligation of States to supply reports – when requested to do so by the ILO – on Conventions which they have not ratified, as well as on Recommendations,[2] the effects of ratification as regards the application of ratified Conventions to non-metropolitan territories (which went further than the classical 'colonial clause'),[3] the practice of new Member States to confirm the obligations previously accepted on their behalf by the State responsible for their international relations,[4] the provision of Article 1, paragraph 5 of the ILO Constitution according to which the withdrawal of a State from the ILO does not affect the validity of the obligations resulting from a ratified Convention, and the setting up, by specific provisions of the Constitution and by a series of decisions which followed, of a sophisticated system of supervision.[5]

1. See below No. 569 ss.
2. See below No. 575.
3. See below No. 587.
4. See below No. 582.
5. See below No. 606 ss.

74. The various special features of international labour Conventions gave rise, in the early years of the introduction of this type of instrument, to a famous theoretical discussion about the real nature of these Conventions. Georges Scelle,[1] in particular, maintained ILO Conventions were not of a contractual type, but amounted, in a way, to 'international laws', and that the International Labour Conference, which adopted them, was an 'international legislative body'. According to this view, Conventions were legislative instruments, requiring only a 'conditional act', namely ratification – which could be analysed as being simply an accession to a pre-existing act – to acquire the force of an internal law. There is a large amount of truth in the views of Georges Scelle. In fact, international labour Conventions represent a compromise between the notions of contract-making treaties and law-making treaties.[2]

1. Scelle, *op. cit.*, pp. 182–185.
2. See in this connection Albert Thomas, Preface to Georges Scelle's *l'OIT et le B.I.J.* pp. XIV–XV.

75. Thus, international labour Conventions have preserved certain features of traditional treaties. Despite the more radical proposals submitted in 1919 when the system was established by the Peace Conference, a Convention is binding on a State only if it has been ratified by it. Similarly, the influence of the older notion of multilateral treaties can be found in the rule according to which the entry into force of a Convention requires a minimum number of ratifications, though usually not more than two.[1] The same can be said about the rule, established after detailed theoretical discussions around 1930 about the legal effects of the revision of international labour Conventions: according to that rule, when a Convention is revised, the former text continues to be binding on the States which ratified it in its original form until they have ratified it in its revised form.[2]

1. See below No. 583.
2. See below No. 104.

The International Labour Code

76. While the international labour Conventions and Recommendations which were adopted over the years are separate legal instruments, they constitute, from a certain point of view, a comprehensive whole which has often been described as the 'International Labour Code'.[1] The term should not be taken literally, as the various Conventions of which the 'Code' is composed may give rise to independent international obligations and as its content is in constant development and revision. It is, however, justified by the fact that the instruments which constitute the 'Code' form a coherent whole and are, as has been said, all cast to a large extent, in the same mould, although the technique in drafting Conventions has undergone a considerable change over the years. The term 'International Labour Code' has also been given to a methodical and systematic presentation of international labour standards compiled by the International Labour Office.[2]

1. See Jenks 'The *Corpus Juris* of Social justice', in *Law, Freedom and Welfare*, London, 1963, pp. 102–113; See also Wolf, 'L'interdépendance des conventions internationales de travail', *Rec. Cours,* 1967–II, pp. 117–219.
2. *The International Labour Code 1951* (2 vols. ILO, Geneva 1952), which contains a systematic presentation of the standards adopted up to that date.

B. The Procedure for the Adoption of Conventions and Recommendations

1. The Inclusion of Items on the Agenda of the Conference

77. The decision to include the adoption of a Convention or a Recommendation as an item on the agenda of the International Labour Conference is taken, as a rule, by the Governing Body of the ILO in the light of proposals submitted by the Director-General of the International Labour Office. In making such proposals the Director-General places before the Governing Body a brief survey of the legislation in force in the various countries and of the main methods of its application, as regards the various questions among which a choice has to be made. The Conference may also decide itself by a majority of two-thirds to place an item on the agenda of the next Session. In settling the agenda of the Conference, the Governing Body has also to consider suggestions made by governments or by representative organizations of employers and workers or by any public international organization. In past years, some important Conventions[1] were adopted as a result of requests addressed to the ILO by the Economic and Social Council of the United Nations. In the first of these cases, the Council acted following a request from the World Federation of Trade Unions and the American Federation of Labour. The Government of any Member State may object to the inclusion of any item in the agenda of the Conference, and the Conference itself must then decide, by a two-thirds majority, whether the item shali remain on the agenda.

1. The Freedom of Association and Protection of the Right to Organise Convention, 1948 (No. 87) and the Discrimination (Employment and Occupation) Convention, 1958 (No. 111).

78. In some cases, especially when questions are of a technical nature, the Governing Body refers a matter to a preparatory technical Conference,[1] which normally is of tripartite composition. In the case of maritime questions, they are considered in the first place by a joint Maritime Commission (comprising representatives of shipowners and seafarers) and subsequently by a preparatory technical Conference.

1. This happened, e.g. for matters such as fishermen, employment policy, maximum weight to be carried by one person.

2. The Discussion and Adoption by the Conference

79. The procedure followed for the consideration of a draft Convention or Recommendation by the Conference is usually that described as 'double discussion',[1] i.e. that the question is discussed at two successive annual sessions of the Conference. Under the existing rules[2] the International Labour Office first prepares a preliminary report setting out the law and practice in the different countries on the question concerned, together with a questionnaire which is intended to obtain the views of governments as to the international standards which they regard as practicable or desirable. On the basis of the replies received from governments, the ILO draws a further report indicating which are the principal questions which appear to require consideration by the Conference. This report serves as a basis for the first discussion of the question by the Conference.

1. Articles 39–41 of the Standing Orders of the Conference.
2. Articles 39–41 of the Standing Orders of the Conference.

80. During the first discussion, the question is first referred to a special technical committee appointed by the Conference for each of the items on its agenda and constituted on a tripartite basis. The Committee, and then the Conference, decide whether the matter is suitable to form the subject of a Convention or Recommendation and adopt such conclusions as they see fit. Finally, the Conference decides whether the question shall be included in the agenda of its next session.

81. On the basis of this first discussion, the International Labour Office then prepares a proposed draft of a Convention or Recommendation which it forwards to governments for their observations. In the light of such observations a final report incorporating any necessary amendments to the texts is drawn up and sent to governments three months before the session of the Conference at which the second discussion is to be held. The question is then again considered in the first place by a technical committee and the texts adopted by the committee are submitted to the full Conference, which considers them article by article before deciding whether to adopt them as a whole. If approved, the texts are referred to the drafting committee of the Conference, which prepares a final text to be submitted to the Conference for final adoption.

82. In cases of special urgency or where other special circumstances exist, the Governing Body may, by a majority of three-fifths, decide to refer a question to the Conference for a single discussion. This procedure is simpler than the double discussion procedure, but it still entails the preparation of reports, questionnaires and draft texts by the International Labour Office and consultation of governments before the Conference discussion. It is used but rarely, and usually in the case of items that have already been considered by a preparatory technical conference.

83. Whatever procedure is followed, a majority of two-thirds of the votes of the delegates attending the Conference (governments, employers and workers) is required for the adoption of a Convention or Recommendation. When a Convention or Recommendation has been adopted by the Conference two copies are signed by the President of the Conference and by the Director-General of the ILO. Because of the institutional and tripartite structure of the ILO, this formality replaces the practice of signature by the States, which is usual in the case of traditional diplomatic treaties.

84. The authentic texts of Conventions and Recommendations are the English and French versions. An official text is established at the same time in Spanish, a working language of the ILO. A Russian translation is also prepared by the ILO, and German texts are established jointly by the German-speaking States Members of the Organization, in co-operation with the ILO, at translation Conferences held after each session of the Conference. In a number of other countries too, ILO Conventions have been translated into the national language.

85. A procedure similar to that for the adoption of Conventions and Recommendations is followed in the case of revision of these instruments.[1] The Governing Body decides whether it is desirable to place the question of the revision of a Convention or Recommendation in whole or in part on the agenda of the Conference. It does so on the basis of information supplied by the International Labour Office and following consultation with the Governments. The Governing Body has to define exactly the question or questions which it places on the agenda of the Conference in view of the partial or total revision of the instrument under consideration. The Office then submits to the Conference draft amendments drawn up in accordance with the conclusions of the Governing Body. The examination of the draft revision by the Conference follows a procedure analogous to that of the second discussion in the case of a double discussion procedure. In 1965, the Governing Body also adopted a simplified procedure for the technical revision of certain strictly limited provisions of a Convention, but this procedure has not yet been used.

1. See Articles 43 to 45 of the Standing Orders of the Conference; more generally on revision, see below No. 108 ss.

C. The Problems Encountered in Framing Conventions and Recommendations

86. In framing Conventions and Recommendations various problems of substance or form are encountered. They relate in particular to the diversity of national conditions for which the instrument should cater, which in turn raises the question as to whether universal standards are appropriate, what should be the level of the standards and what flexibility clauses should be incorporated in the Conventions. They also relate to the nature of the rights that may be the subject of international standard, to the choice between the form of a Convention or a Recommendation and to the adjustment of instruments to change, which raises the question of their revision.

1. The Diversity of National Conditions

87. Since international labour Conventions and the Recommendations are intended to produce effects – and in the case of the former to create legal obligations – in countries with very different economic, social and political conditions, as well as different constitutional and legal systems, the diversity of the conditions prevailing in the world raises a number of questions.

A. UNIVERSAL OR REGIONAL STANDARDS?[1]

88. The first question would be whether it would not be more appropriate to formulate regional rather than universal standards, since, in spite of sometimes great differences which are to be found between more or less developed countries within the same region, the great regions of the world are, on the whole, more homogeneous than the world community taken as a whole. The idea of regional action in this field has also been encouraged by the very existence of regional organizations, some of which have endeavoured, by such action, to emphasize the identity of the region concerned and to develop the activity of the organization itself. Regional standards undoubtedly have been very useful[2] by supplementing universal standards or dealing with matters of specific interest for the region under consideration (as in the case of the Rhine boatmen or workers occupied in international transport in Europe). However regional standards cannot replace universal standards altogether, as the coexistence of different sets of regional standards would tend to accentuate rather than to reduce existing discrepancies between the different parts of the world. It would also eliminate the spur for emulation and the factor of harmonization provided by universal standards. In the case of coexistence or regional with universal standards, the danger would reside in their overlapping, as a multiplicity of standards would lead to divergencies between them and to both the universal and the regional instruments being discredited. Reference is often made to the meeting in 1972 of the African Advisory Committee of the ILO, in the course of which it was underlined that 'any attempt to adopt standards on a regional basis would be a backward step and would produce anomalies and tensions between different regions' and that 'sub-standards for sub-humans had no place in the ILO'.[3] When, in 1976, the Governing Body of the ILO considered the request of a wide in-depth review of international labour standards, it concluded that 'Conventions should remain universal in character and that the special needs of countries should be taken into account through appropriate provisions in these instruments'.[4] The ILO has therefore approached the matter as one of framing universal standards capable of being applied in differing circumstances.

1. See Valticos 'Normes universelles et normes régionales dans le domaine du travail' in Société française pour le droit international, Colloque de Bordeaux, *Régionalisme et Universalisme dans le droit international contemporain*, Paris, 1977, pp. 289–307; Wolf, 'Y a-t-il un droit social régional?' *eod. lo.* pp. 309–312
2. About these regional standards, see below Nos. 116 and 122 ss.
3. See Minutes G.B. 170, 1967, p. 82, para. 156.
4. See ILO document GB. 199/9/22 (Rev.), Appendix, para. 15.

B. The Level of the Standards

89. As Conventions and Recommendations are generally directed to countries with very different economic, social and political conditions, as well as different constitutional and legal systems, they raise the problem of the appropriate level of the standards which they should set. The Constitution of the ILO already contained a general indication to that effect when it provided that: 'in framing any Convention or Recommendation of general application, the Conference shall have due regard to those countries in which climatic conditions, the imperfect development of industrial organization, or other special circumstances make the industrial conditions substantially different and shall suggest the modifications, if any, which it considers may be required to meet the case of such countries'. Guidelines were also provided in 1946 by a Conference Delegation on Constitutional questions which pointed out[1] that the international standard should not be an obviously impracticable one, or one which can be attained only by a very limited number of countries, as it will not then serve as an immediate target for national action in most countries, though it may come to be regarded as a distant or ultimate objective. On the other hand, it was stated, a standard which represents no substantial advance upon average existing practice is also of very limited utility, as the purpose of standards is not simply to harmonize legislation, but primarily to promote generalized progress. In 1963, the Director-General of the ILO also stressed,[2] in the same connection, that 'the terms of Conventions should, unless they deal exclusively with a simple issue of fundamental principle and contain no detail, be sufficiently flexible in character to be susceptible of application under widely varying national conditions', that a Convention should not contain rigid requirements in regard to matters in respect of which national practice may reasonably vary widely; it should not enter into too much 'administrative detail', but that 'this general approach should not, of course, be carried to the point at which a Convention ceases to be worth having . . . A measure of flexibility the result of which is that a large proportion of the Members of the Organization are not called upon to do more than they are already doing may deprive an international standard of much of its value as a stimulus to further action and achievement'. The problem, is not only to decide, in each case, what the appropriate level of a standard should be. It is, more generally, to avoid that the standard may concern only a more or less limited group of countries because of its level, whatever it may be. The aim, therefore, has increasingly been to frame standards which will be relevant to the greatest number of countries. To this end, various types of flexibility clauses have been devised and included in several Conventions.

1. I.L.C. 29th Session, Montreal, 1946, *Constitutional Questions*, Part I, *Reports of the Conference Delegation on Constitutional Questions* (Report II (1)), ILO, 1946, p. 63.
2. I.L.C. Ref. D.-G. 1963, p. 169.

c. The Flexibility Clauses[1]

90. Some of the earlier Conventions, in particular four of the Conventions adopted in 1919, specified that certain named countries, because of the state of their development, might observe a standard lower than the general standard. This type of clause was soon abandoned and recourse was had to more refined and more diversified clauses of a general character. They can be grouped under various categories.

1. See McMahon, 'The Legislative Technique of the ILO', B.Y.B.I.L., vol. 41, 1965–66, pp. 31–68; Valticos and Wolf, 'L'OIT et les pays en voie de développement; techniques d'élaboration et mise en oeuvre de normes universelles' in Société française pur le droit international, Colloque d'Aix-en-Provence, *Pays en voie de développement et transformation du droit international*, Paris 1974, pp. 127–146.

1. Options Allowed to States as Regards Obligations Undertaken

91. Certain types of flexibility clauses give States the possibility of choosing, at the time of ratification, by means of a formal declaration, the extent of the obligations which they decide to undertake. This is the case for some Conventions consisting of several parts of which ratifying States can accept only one or a minimum number. Naturally, States which make use of such a possibility may, at a later stage, extend their acceptance to other parts of the Convention, and this type of clause thus permits the progressive application of the Convention as a whole. A well-known illustration of this formula has been the Social Security (Minimum Standards) Convention, 1952 (No. 102) which comprises nine parts, at least three of which must be accepted on ratification.[1] A slightly different formula which is used in certain Conventions,[2] allows certain parts of them or annexes to them to be excluded from the ratification. In a different case, a Convention comprises two parts, the one involving strict obligations and the other less strict ones,[3] and States have the option to accept either of these parts at the time of ratification. Finally, another type of clause, which has been used in particular in some Conventions on minimum age[4] and on holidays with pay[5] allows States to specify, at the time of ratification, the exact level of the standard which they undertake to observe and as a rule the standard thus specified by ratifying States may not be lower than a minimum laid down in the Convention.

1. Another example is the Equality of Treatment (Social Security) Convention, 1967 (No. 118).
2. E.g. Labour Inspection Convention, 1947 (No. 81); Migrant Workers' Conventions (No. 97 of 1949 and No. 143 of 1975); Labour Statistics Convention, 1938 (No. 63).
3. Fee-charging Employment Agencies (Revised), 1949 (No. 96) which gives the option between the progressive abolition and the regulation of these agencies.
4. No. 138 of 1973.
5. No. 132 of 1970.

2. *Flexibility in the Formulation of the Standard*

92. The drafting itself of the standard is often flexible enough to give governments a certain amount of latitude in its implementation.

Flexibility as Regards the Scope

93. Sometimes the flexibility resides in the way in which the scope of the Convention is defined, in particular as regards the persons to be covered or the regions in which the Convention must be made applicable. In some cases[1] governments may decide for themselves, subject to certain consultations, what the scope of the Conventions shall be, or they may be permitted to exclude certain categories of persons or undertakings,[2] or again the definition of the persons covered may be based on a specified percentage of the wage earners or the population of the country concerned.[3] Sometimes, exceptions are allowed for certain parts of the country which are sparsely populated or insufficiently developed.[4] In the case of a number of Conventions which cover a particular branch of the economy, such as industry, it is provided that governments may themselves define the line of division separating that branch from others.[5]

1. E.g. various Conventions on minimum wage-fixing machinery (Nos. 26 and 99), on labour inspection (No. 81) and on holidays with pay in agriculture (No. 101).
2. E.g. Conventions of night work (women) (Nos. 41 and 89), holidays with pay (No. 52), protection of wages (No. 95) and maternity protection (No. 103, revised).
3. Many social security conventions (in particular the 1952 social security (minimum standards) (No. 102) Convention.
4. More than ten Conventions (Nos. 24, 25, 62, 63, 77, 78, 81, 88, 94, 95, 96).
5. E.g. The Hours of Work (Industry) Convention, 1919 (No. 1) and the Weekly Rest (Commerce and Office) Convention, 1957 (No. 106).

Flexibility as Regards the Content of the Obligation

94. There are various cases where the formulation of the basic substantive rule itself makes provision for flexibility. This applies in particular to certain 'promotional' conventions, which do not set a definite objective to be attained immediately, but formulate a general policy in a given field to be followed by each country with due regard to its particular circumstances. The most well-known cases in this connection are the Conventions dealing with social policy (No. 117 of 1962), equal remuneration (No. 100 of 1951), equal opportunity and equality of treatment (No. 111 of 1988).

95. This method is generally coupled with the device of including only the fundamental principles in the Conventions and in adopting at the same time a supplementary Recommendation – i.e. a non-binding instrument – containing more detailed suggestions for their implementation. Some sixty Conventions are based on this method.

96. Flexibility may also be attained by the use of general terms such as 'appropriate measures', 'adequate protection', 'sufficient number', or 'appropriate arrangements', or by requiring certain measures to be taken only in so far as they may be 'necessary'. Conventions such as these might be used to provide loopholes for evasion if their application was not, as we shall see (see *infra* Nos. 606 ss), subject to a close system of supervision.

97. Conventions also often allow for *exceptions* to the general rule which they establish. There have been various types of such exceptions. Apart from the exceptions for certain named countries (see above para. 90), which are no longer resorted to, certain Conventions[1] authorize countries which do not yet have any regulations on the subject to ratify on the basis of a standard lower than the general standard. More recently, many of the social security Conventions[2] permit countries 'whose economy and medical facilities are insufficiently developed' to have recourse to specified temporary exceptions. Exceptions are also sometimes permitted on account of special circumstances (materials subject to rapid deterioration, exceptional cases of pressure of work, processes necessarily continuous in character etc.) and adjustment of the standard in respect of night work to climatic conditions is also allowed. Moreover, special arrangements are permitted under certain conditions, or the application of certain Conventions may be suspended in the event of war, *force majeure* or, if in the case of serious emergency, the national interest demands it.

1. E.g. The 1946 Medical Examination (Young Persons) Convention (Nos. 77 and 78) and Night Work (Young Persons) Convention (Non-Industrial Occupations), (No. 79).
2. E.g. Nos. 102 of 1952 and 121 of 1964.

3. Flexibility as Regards the Methods of Application

98. One of the devices which is most frequently used seeks flexibility as regards the methods of application of the standard. Originally, many Conventions provided that effect should be given to them through 'national legislation', but this term has always been interpreted in a very broad sense.[1] Generally, having regard to the fact that the ILO Constitution provides, in Article 19, para. 5(d), that a State which ratifies a Convention shall take 'such action as may be necessary to make effective the provisions of such Convention', custom, administrative measures or, in certain circumstances, collective agreements[2] may, in principle, suffice to give effect to Conventions. It is, moreover, expressly stated in some Conventions, that effect may be given to them by methods appropriate to national conditions and practice, which can be national laws or regulations, collective agreements, arbitral awards, etc. or a combination of these means. Clauses of this type appear in a number of Conventions, such as those, mentioned above, relating to equal remuneration (No. 100 of 1951) and to discrimination in employment (No. 111 of 1968).[3]

1. See *Intern. Lab. Code* 1951, note 43 under Article 380, pp. 307–308.
2. For the application of Conventions by means of collective agreements, see *Intern. Lab. Code*, pp. LXXVI–LXXVIII; Jenks, 'The Application of Conventions by means of Collective Agreements', *Zeitschrift für Auslandisches, Öffentliches Recht und Völkerrecht*, Aug. 1958 (*Festgabe Makarov*), pp. 197–224; Wolf, 'L'application des conventions par voie de conventions collectives'. *Ann.* 1974, pp. 103–114.
3. See also Conventions on weekly rest in commerce and offices (No. 106 of 1957), holidays with pay (No. 132 of 1970), protection of workers' representatives (No. 135 of 1971) and several maritime Conventions (e.g. No. 91 of 1949, No. 109 of 1958 and No. 146 of 1976).

99. Some Conventions have also been deliberately so drafted as to permit their application by means of action by federal authority.[1]

1. See Conventions on Reduction of hours of work in public works (No. 51 of 1936), Labour Clauses in Public Contracts (No. 94 of 1949), Labour Inspection (No. 81 of 1947), Migrant Workers (No. 97 of 1969) and Discrimination in Employment (No. 111 of 1958).

D. The Drafting of the Standard

100. Apart from the diversity of national conditions, there are also other reasons which call for flexibility in the formulation of standards. These are the differences between legal systems – in particular between common law and civil law countries – or between constitutional systems – federal and unitary – so that it is necessary to avoid too strict and detailed drafting and to leave to States a certain choice – as was seen in No. 97 above – as regards the legal methods of application.

E. Results of Flexibility Clauses

101. While there have been cases in which the effort to introduce the necessary flexibility in Conventions has not been completely successful or has gone too far and consequently certain Conventions still contain an element of rigidity or, on the contrary, have been drafted in too loose terms, one may consider that existing ILO Conventions, on the whole, are neither too stringent to be beyond the reach of developing countries nor so flexible as to be devoid of interest for the more advanced ones. It is significant, in this connection, that the average number of ratifications per country naturally is higher for the industrialized States, but that about 60 per cent of the ratifications have been deposited by developing countries and that, in 1977, about three quarters of the ratifications received came from developing countries.

2. The Nature of the Rights which May Be the Subject of International Standards

102. There is a wide difference in the nature of the rights which may be the subject of international standards. Some of these rights lend themselves to immediate application to individuals (such as minimum age, holidays with pay of a specified duration, freedom of association) and they might be considered as self-executing in countries where the constitutional system provides that ratified treaties become automatically part of the law of the land. On the contrary, other rights are more of a programmatic nature, i.e. they consist of a general statement of the objectives aimed at and lay programmes of action, which require measures to be taken by governments, sometimes on a long-term basis, and do not create any direct individual claim for protected persons. This can be said for employment policy, social security, action against discrimination and equal remuneration (if one considers the terms of ILO Convention No. 100).[1]

1. See Jenks, 'Work, Leisure and Social Security as Human Rights in the World Community', *Journal of the International Commission of Jurists*, June 1968, pp. 49–58; Valticos 'The International Labour Organisation. Its Contribution to the Rule of Law and the International Protection of Human Rights', same *Journal*, December 1968, pp. 14–16.

3. The Choice between a Convention and a Recommendation

103. At the time of the drafting and adoption of a new instrument, the question of whether it should take the form of a Convention or a Recommendation is often discussed in view of the differences existing between these two types of instruments from the point of view of their legal character (see above No. 70) and of their respective roles. The Convention certainly is the typical instrument of international labour legislation.[1] When the establishment of the present system of international labour standards was considered by the Peace Conference in 1919, Conventions were the only type of instrument envisaged at the outset of the discussions. The idea of Recommendations was introduced later in the course of these discussions, with a view to meeting the difficulties and objections of the United States. However, it was also realized at that time that Recommendations might serve to deal with certain matters about which the adoption of a Convention would not be possible or appropriate.[2] Later, in 1946, when the ILO Constitution was amended, it was specified in Article 19, para. 1 that it would rest with the Conference to determine whether the proposals before it 'should take the form: (a) of an international Convention, or (b) of a Recommendation to meet circumstances where the subject, or any aspect of it, dealt with is not considered suitable or appropriate at that time for a Convention.'

1. Scelle, *op. cit.* p. 167.
2. See O.B. Vol. I (1919–1920), p. 264.

104. In the light of the above principle the role of Recommendations[1] has become clearer over the years, while still frequently disputed in particular cases. It has often happened that a Recommendation has been considered more appropriate when a subject has not yet been ripe for the adoption of a Convention. Thus, in a number of cases, the adoption of a Recommendation has paved the way for the adoption of a Convention on the same subject, several years later.[2]

1. See I.L.C. 29th Session (Montreal, 1946), Report II (1) *Constitutional Questions*, Part I, Reports of the Conference Delegation on Constitutional Questions, pp. 37–38 (No. 45) and 62–64 (Nos. 73–74). See also Scelle, *op. cit.*, pp. 167–169, Troclet, *Législation sociale internationale*, Brussels, 1952, pp. 517–518, 637–641, Paul Ramadier, 'Conventions and Recommendations de l'OIT', *Droit social* 1951, pp. 598–603.
2. This was the case for the Recommendations on Labour Inspection, 1923 (No. 20) and on Social Security, 1944 (Nos. 67 and 69).

105. A second function of a Recommendation, which has become increasingly important, is to supplement a Convention. Now it is common practice, followed in the case of over 60 Conventions, to adopt, on the same subject, a Convention laying down the basic rules and a Recommendation containing more detailed provisions for their application which might furnish guidelines for governments without the Recommendation having the binding force of a Convention.[1] In some cases, in particular in the field of social security, the supplementary Recommendation sets a higher standard than the Convention.

1. This was the case, for instance, to refer to some of the most important instruments, for the Conventions and the Recommendations on Minimum Wage-Fixing (Convention No. 26 and Recommendation No. 30 of 1928), Employment Service (Convention No. 88 and Recommendation No. 83 of 1948), Equal Remuneration (Convention No. 100 and Recommendation No. 90 of 1951) Discrimination in Employment (Convention and Recommendation No. 111 of 1958) and Employment Policy (Convention and Recommendation No. 122 of 1964).

106. A third function of Recommendations is to deal with matters concerning which the standards laid down have to be of so technical and detailed a character that they may call for frequent adjustment to the situation in different countries, or the nature of which is such that there are wide variations in circumstances and practices from one country to another. Among such subjects reference can be made to industrial relations, training, workers' housing, employment of women with family responsibilities. The form of a Recommendation has been preferred in such cases because strict international obligations could hardly be contemplated in the fields concerned.

107. Generally, however, the Recommendation, as a form of instrument, has often been objected to, generally by the workers, especially when it is envisaged as the only instrument – and not as supplementary to a Convention – to deal with a given subject. The objections are due to the fact that Recommendations are weaker instruments than Conventions. They cannot be the subject of international commitments, nor can their application be supervised as strictly and regularly as that of Conventions.[1] Recommendations have, therefore, frequently been considered as poor relations of Conventions. Nevertheless, they perform a useful function in cases where Conventions would probably not have been adopted or, if adopted, would not have been widely ratified, and where the existence of international standards embodied in a Recommendation may sometimes exercise a substantial influence on national law and practice.[2]

1. See below Nos. 575 and 606 ss.
2. The influence of Recommendation (No. 119) concerning the Termination of the Employment Relationship, 1963 if one of the most obvious instances of the influence of a Recommendation. See *Com. Exp.* 1974 (Part 4B), p. 90; E. Yemin, 'Job Security: influence of ILO Standards and recent trends', *I.L.R.*, Jan–Feb. 1976, pp. 17–33; Kahn-Freund, *Labour and the Law*, 2nd ed., London, 1977, p. 42.

4. The Adjustment to Change. The Revision of Conventions and Recommendations

108. Principles governing revision. The developments which may occur in social needs and conceptions or the difficulties which may be encountered in the implementation of certain standards make it sometimes necessary to revise international labour standards with a view to adjusting them to changing circumstances or to experience. Such revision raises, apart from the procedural questions already referred to above,[1] a more general question of policy: that of deciding how closely revision should seek to adapt the international standard to changes in ideas and needs. Naturally, labour legislation, whether international or national, cannot be a rigid and immutable code. It must be responsive to changing conceptions and even techniques. Therefore, the revision of Conventions should be made possible without having to face insuperable legal obstacles. On the other hand, however, the legal rules laid down by international labour standards must have a minimum of stability and provide a certain measure of security in international relations. They should not be amended too frequently of for considerations which are temporary in nature. In order to reconcile these requirements of change and of stability, the revision procedure has been made subject to time limits and formalities, which, without being excessive, are designed to prevent over-hasty decisions.

1. No. 85.

109. Clauses relating to Revision. The first ILO Conventions contained a clause providing that at least once in ten years the Governing Body of the ILO should present a report on the working of the Convention and consider the desirability of placing on the Agenda of the Conference the question of its revision. This standard clause was modified in 1949 to provide for greater flexibility by enabling the Governing Body to present such reports only when it considered it necessary.[1] Meanwhile, in 1928, when the first ten-year period for the consideration of the possible revision of the Conventions adopted in 1919 was about to expire, the question of the procedure for revision and the effect of revision on the original Convention was the subject of extensive discussion and of wide differences of opinion in the Governing Body. Some employer members of the Governing Body were of the opinion that international labour Conventions were not contracts between States, but 'conditional international laws' and that the new Convention should accordingly replace the original one. The then Legal Adviser of the ILO (Jean Morellet) took the opposite view on the ground that, in spite of their special character, international labour Conventions entailed legal obligations between the States parties to them, and that one Convention could not be automatically substituted for another when the first had been ratified and come into force.

1. Moreover the 1961 Final Articles Revision Convention (No. 116) amended the final articles which were contained in earlier Conventions to adapt them to the new formula.

110. Finally, the solution adopted was to include in the Conventions adopted after 1929 a clause providing:

a. that the adoption of a new revising Convention would not entail the abrogation of the original Convention;
b. that the original Convention should cease to be open to ratification as from the date when the new Convention came into force; and
c. that ratification by a Member State of the new Convention should automatically involve the denunciation by it of the original Convention.

A few years later, in 1933, this clause was refined to allow the International Labour Conference discretion to decide, when adopting a revised Convention, that its entry into force should not have the effect of closing the original Convention to ratification and that its ratification by a State would not automatically entail the denunciation by that State of the original Convention. This latitude may sometimes be useful, especially to keep the earlier Convention open to ratification by States which have not yet reached a stage of development which would allow them to ratify the most recent standard. It has been used in certain cases.[1]

1. See the Employment Injury Benefits Convention, 1964 (No. 121), Article 28.

111. *Use made of revision procedures*. In the light of the principles, rules and procedures described above, some forty Conventions have been formally revised by subsequent Conventions. A number of these revisions have been aimed at making the wording of the original Convention more flexible in order to take account of the difficulties experienced and to facilitate ratification, as in the case of night work of women (apart from the more basic re-examination of the whole principle, which is presently under way). In other cases, on the contrary, revision was designed to raise the earlier standard and provide for greater protection (as in the case of occupational diseases and of minimum age of admission to employment). Sometimes, these two types of operations were combined. Another reason which led to revision was the need to take account of technological changes (thus the first discussion for the revision of Convention no. 32 on dock work has taken place in June 1978). Some Conventions have each undergone more than one revision in the course of years: there were two revisions of the convention concerning night work by women[1] and three revisions of the wages, hours of work and manning on board ship Convention.[2]

1. Convention No. 4 of 1919 revised by Conventions Nos. 41 and 89 of 1934 and of 1948 and the matter is again under consideration, as stated above.
2. Convention No. 57 of 1936 is revised by Conventions Nos. 76, 93 and 109 of 1946, 1949 and 1958.

112. Apart from formal revisions, there have also been cases of the adoption of Conventions which, although not revisions in a technical sense, have supplemented earlier instruments, or dealt with the same subjects from a different angle. This will be explained later in respect of the forced labour Conventions,[1] of the social policy Conventions[2] and of the 1952 Social Security (Minimum Standards) Convention (No. 102).[3]

1. See below Nos. 214 ss.
2. See below No. 409.
3. See below Nos. 418 ss.

113. In the case of Recommendations, formal revision is not as frequent or as necessary as for Conventions, since they do not involve international obligations. However, it may sometimes be useful to state expressly that a new instrument supersedes an earlier one, in order to make it clear to governments that it is the new instrument which should guide their action. Such a course was followed in the case of vocational training Recommendations.[1] It may also be desirable where a Recommendation is supplementary to a Convention and the latter is being revised, to proceed as well with the revision of the Recommendation, as was done in the case of migrant workers.[2]

1. Recommendations No. 117 of 1962 and No. 150 of 1975.
2. Migration for Employment Recommendation (Revised), 1949 (No. 86).

III. Less Formal Instruments

114. The ILO has also laid down standards in certain types of instruments which are less formal than Conventions and Recommendations. This is the case, in the first instance, of *Resolutions* adopted by the International Labour Conference. Some of these resolutions are currently used by the various supervisory bodies of the ILO as guidelines and terms of reference for the appraisal of national situations and the recommendations addressed to governments. This applies in particular to the 1952 Resolution concerning the independence of the trade union movement and to the 1970 Resolution concerning trade union rights and their relation to civil liberties (which were referred to by the Commission of Inquiry in the case of Greece in 1970 and by the Fact-finding and Conciliation Commission in the case of Chile in 1974).[1]

1. See below Nos. 183 and 638.

115. Other types of standards are embodied in the resolutions and conclusions of technical committees of experts and of meetings or bodies set up to deal with particular sectors (industrial committees, etc.) or particular subjects, such as social security and occupational health and safety, multinational enterprises,[1] statistics, etc. or of technical regional conferences and meetings.

1. See below No. 415.

116. These various types of texts vary considerably, first as regards their subject matter: some deal with basic principles while others are of a very practical technical nature. They also differ in respect of the weight they carry. None have the authority of Conventions and Recommendations, but a resolution adopted by the Conference carries more weight than the conclusions of a less comprehensive body. The value of such texts lies mainly in the fact that they are adopted by bodies representative of the interests concerned. Resolutions adopted by the International Labour Conference have also been important in certain cases for the development of the programme of the ILO in certain fields. This was the case as regards labour-management relations, workers' education, rural development and more recently, in 1975, working conditions and environment.

IV. Interpretation

117. The ILO Constitution provides (Article 37) that any question or dispute relating to the interpretation of the Constitution itself or of international labour Conventions must be submitted to the International Court of Justice (formerly the Permanent Court of International Justice). This provision has been resorted to only on a very few occasions, during the early years of the existence of the Organization. As indicated above,[1] the Court was called upon, on four occasions between 1922 and 1932, to give advisory opinions and the first three related exclusively to the question of the competence of the ILO. The fourth, while having also an indirect bearing on that question, referred expressly to the meaning to be attributed to the scope of the Night Work (Women) Convention, 1919 (No. 4).[2]

1. No. 55–59 above.
2. No. 59 above.

118. In 1946, as a result of amendments made to the ILO Constitution, a second paragraph was added to Article 37, with a view to giving greater flexibility to methods of interpretation by providing also for the possibility of appointing a tribunal for the expeditious determination of any dispute or question relating to the interpretation of a Convention. No recourse has so far been had to this provision.

119. Finally, the Director-General of the ILO is frequently consulted by governments as to the interpretation of Conventions and the opinions which he gives, with the proviso that he has no special competence in the matter, are communicated to the Governing Body of the ILO and published in the *Official Bulletin*, and seem to be tacitly accepted. They provide authoritative documentation on the subject and have acquired considerable weight.[1] A very large number of such opinions have been given by the ILO over the years.

1. In this connection, see Jenks, 'The Interpretation of International Labour Conventions by the International Labour Office', *British Yearbook of International Law*, Vol. 20, 1939, pp. 132 and following, and 'The *Corpus Juris* of Social Justice' in *Law Freedom and Welfare*, London, 1963, pp. 121 and following.

120. Lastly, legal opinions on important matters were given in memoranda from the Director-General or the Legal Adviser of the ILO concerning questions connected with the constitutional framework of ILO Conventions, such as the nature of the competent authority contemplated by Article 19 of the Constitution of the ILO[1] and the practice of reservations to multilateral Conventions.[2] In the latter case an ILO memorandum was submitted to the International Court of Justice in the genocide case and it set forth the reasons why international labour Conventions cannot be ratified subject to reservations.[3]

1. See O.B. Vol. XXVI, 1944, pp. 205–221. On this question see below Nos. 569 ss.
2. See O.B. vol. XXXIV, 1951, pp. 274–312.
3. On this question see below No. 577.

V. Case Law

121. In the course of the years, the quasi-judicial bodies which, as will be explained later,[1] have been set up to supervise the implementation of international labour standards, have often had to reach conclusions as to the precise scope and meaning of ILO Conventions, as they were requested to assess the extent to which these Conventions are implemented. A body of case-law has thus been progressively built up.

1. See below Nos. 608 ss, 632 ss.

122. This has been the case, in particular, of the Committee of Experts on the Application of Conventions and Recommendations which, since 1927, has examined every year the reports of governments on the application of Conventions which they have ratified. The interpretative function of the Committee is not based on any explicit authority, but it derives logically from its mandate and the nature of its task. As the Committee itself put it, 'the Committee's terms of reference do not require it to give interpretation of Conventions, competence to do so being vested in the International Court of Justice by Article 37 of the Constitution. Nevertheless, in order to carry out its function of evaluating the implementation of Conventions, the Committee has to consider and express its views on the meaning of certain provisions of Conventions'.[1] Such a function is all the more important as, during the more recent period, a number of international labour Conventions have, in an effort to obtain greater flexibility, been drafted deliberately in general terms,[2] so that the Committee of Experts has had to interpret and define more precisely their meaning and scope. This has happened in particular in the cases of the instruments dealing with forced labour, freedom of association and discrimination in employment.[3]

1. *Rep. Com. Exp.* 1977, p. 11, para. 32.
2. See above Nos. 96 and 100.
3. See the 'general surveys' submitted by the Committee of Experts on forced labour (1962 and 1968), freedom of association (1959 and 1973) and discrimination in employment (1963 and 1971).

123. Particular importance also attaches to the case law established by the Freedom of Association Committee[1] which has dealt with some one thousand cases since it was first set up in 1951. Faced with a wide variety of situations, the Committee, while relying at the outset on the general standards laid down in the ILO Conventions concerning freedom of association, was gradually led to frame principles defining more closely and in some respects supplementing and even extending those expressly embodied in the Conventions. The principles thus established by the Committee refer, in particular, to the right to strike, collective bargaining and the more general civil liberties on which the effective exercise of the right of association depends. The most significant part of this case law has been published.[2]

1. See below No. 633.
2. *Freedom of Association, Digest of Decisions of the Freedom of Association Committee of the Governing Body of the ILO*, Geneva, 2nd edition, 1976.

VI. Instruments Adopted by Special Conferences under the Auspices or with the Co-operation of the ILO

124. In a number of cases, special governmental Conferences have been convened by the ILO outside its institutional framework to deal with questions which concerned only a limited number of countries and therefore were not suitable for regulation by Conventions of a universal character. Special Conferences have also been convened by the ILO jointly with other international organizations in order to deal as a whole with a subject falling within the competence of several international organizations.

125. Among the instruments adopted by Special Conferences of the first type, reference can be made to the *Agreements concerning Rhine Boatmen*, which were adopted in 1950 by an intergovernmental Conference attended by Belgium, France, the Federal Republic of Germany, the Netherlands, Switzerland, the United Kingdom and the United States. The Conference was preceded in 1949 by a special tripartite Conference comprising representatives of Rhine shipowners and boatmen. The Central Commission for Rhine navigation was associated with the various stages of the proceedings. The Governmental Conference adopted two Agreements, one concerning social security, and the other concerning conditions of employment, including hours of work, overtime, rest periods and holidays. These agreements were revised in 1961 and in 1954 and 1963 respectively and came into force a few years after their adoption following their ratification by all the States bordering the Rhine and by Belgium. Another Convention of this type was the *European Convention concerning Social Security for Workers Engaged in International Transport*, which was adopted in 1956 by an intergovernmental Conference convened by the ILO. The Convention was open to signature by governments of European countries Members of the ILO. It came into force in 1958, and an arrangement supplementing it in 1960.

126. Mention should also be made of two Conventions adopted by Conferences convened by other organizations jointly or with the co-operation of the ILO. Thus, the *International Convention on the Protection of Performers, Producers of Phonograms and Broadcasting Organizations* was adopted in Rome in 1961 by a Diplomatic Conference convened jointly by the ILO,

UNESCO and the Bureau of the International Union for the Protection of Literary and Artistic Works. This Convention came into force in 1964. In a different field, a *Recommendation concerning the Status of Teachers* was adopted in October 1966 by a special intergovernmental Conference convened by UNESCO and attended by a delegation of the Governing Body of the ILO and representatives of the International Labour Office.

127. As will be indicated later,[1] the ILO has also been associated with the preparation of instruments adopted by regional organizations such as the Council of Europe and the European Communities.

1. See below No. 134.

§2. United Nations Instruments[1]

128. While the United Nations Organization does not deal with labour matters as such, and recognizes the ILO as the specialized agency responsible for taking appropriate action for the accomplishment of the purposes set out in its Constitution,[2] some UN instruments of more general scope have also covered labour matters. Thus, in respect of *slavery* the 1926 Convention was framed under the auspices of the League of Nations and the supplementary Convention on this subject was adopted in 1956 under the auspices of the United Nations.

1. Apart from the universal instruments adopted in the framework of the UN system, reference should also be made to some instruments, such as the Red Cross Conventions of 12 August 1949 relating to the treatment of prisoners of war and to the protection of civilian persons in the time of war, which also include provisions concerning the employment of these categories of persons (See Wolf, *L'interdependance*, pp. 187–193).
2. This is recognized in the 1946 Agreement between the two organizations.

129. More recently, labour questions have been touched on by the United Nations mainly in the instruments concerning human rights. A number of provisions concerning labour matters are contained in the 1948 *Universal Declaration of Human Rights* and in the two 1966 *International Covenants on Human Rights* which entered into force at the beginning of 1976, when they were ratified by 35 States each.[1] The Covenant on Civil and Political rights includes provisions concerning non-discrimination, forced labour and freedom of association for trade union purposes. The Covenant on Economic, Social and Cultural Rights contains a large number of provisions relating to labour, such as non-discrimination, the right to work, the right to form trade unions, the right to strike, the right to social security, protection of and assistance to family – specifically maternity leave and protection of children and young persons – the right to an adequate standard of living and the right to the highest attainable standard of health.

1. As at 1 July 1978, the Covenants had been ratified by some 50 States each.

130. Because of their comprehensive nature, the Covenants are drafted in general terms, and the various rights relating to labour which they recognize are dealt with in a less precise and detailed way than ILO standards. As regards substance, ILO instruments often provide a greater protection, except on certain points of detail. However, in some fields like agricultural work and occupational safety and health, further development of ILO's standard-setting activity could help to promote the practical implementation of the rights proclaimed in the Covenants. An example in that direction is provided by the more recent Working Environment (Air Pollution, Noise and Vibration) Convention, 1977 (No. 148) and Recommendation (No. 156).

131. A year before the adoption of the Covenants, i.e. in December 1965, the United Nations General Assembly adopted a Convention on the Elimination of All Forms of Racial Discrimination, which came into force in January 1969.[1]

1. See below No. 708.

132. Mention should also be made of the 1951 Convention relating to the Status of Refugees, which came into force in 1954, and which provides that refugees should receive the same treatment as nationals in the field of employment and – subject to certain reservations – of social security. A similar provision appears in the 1954 Convention on the Status of Stateless Persons, which came into force in 1960.

§3. Regional Instruments

133. Since a number of regional organizations, mainly at the European level, were created after the end of the Second World War, these organizations have adopted a number of instruments relating to human rights and, more specifically to labour matters, while, for the reasons given above,[1] the standards framed by the ILO remain universal in character. Regional standard-setting has certainly led to useful results in Europe, although more in the field of human rights than in that of labour.

1. See above No. 88.

I. Council of Europe Instruments

A. European Social Charter

134. Numerous instruments on social questions have been adopted by the Council of Europe. The most comprehensive one is the *European Social Charter*[1] which was drawn up with the technical help of the ILO and signed in 1961 and has so far been ratified by eleven of the twenty Member States of the Council of Europe. Its ratification is subject to acceptance of at least ten of the nineteen articles or 45 of the 72 paragraphs of Part II of the Charter, including a compulsory nucleus of at least five of the seven articles regarded as the most important. The provisions of the European Social Charter have been based to a large extent on the relevant ILO standards,[2] but in view of the comprehensive nature of the instrument they are not drafted with the same degree of detail and precision. As regards substance, the standards set in the Charter are, by and large, equivalent to those contained in ILO Conventions and Recommendations; in some cases they go further or cover matters for which no ILO standards exist, while in other cases they are at a lower level. The most original feature of the Charter is that it recognized the rights of workers and employers to collective action in case of conflicts of interest, including the right to strike, subject to obligations that might arise out of collective agreements previously entered into and to some further restrictions.[3]

1. See in particular Van Asbeck, 'La Charte sociale européenne: sa portée juridique, sa mise en oeuvre', *Mélanges Rolin*, para. 1964, pp. 417–448; Kahn-Freund, 'The European Social Charter' in *European Law and the Individual* ed. by F. G. Jacobs, Amsterdam, 1976, pp. 181–211; Valticos 'La Charte sociale européenne, sa structure, son contenu, le contrôle de son application', *Droit social*, 1963, pp. 466–482; Wiebringhaus, 'La Charte sociale européenne', *Ann*. 1963, pp. 709–721, and the special numbers of *Rassegna del Lavoro* (Rome), October 1961 and of the *Revue de l'Institut de Sociologie* (Belgium), 1966, I, pp. 9–141.
2. For a comparison, see ILO 'The European Social Charter and International Labour Conventions', I.L.R. Nov. and Dec. 1961, pp. 354–375 and 462–477.
3. The machinery established for supervising the implementation of the Charter is examined later (Nos. 709–710).

B. The European Human Rights Convention

135. The European Convention for the Protection of Human Rights and Fundamental Freedom, which was concluded in Rome in 1950 and has been ratified by all the Member States of the Council of Europe, deals essentially with civil and political rights, but it also deals with certain rights falling within the field of international labour law, such as the right not to be required to perform forced or compulsory labour and the right to form trade unions, and it specifies that the rights and freedoms laid down in the Convention shall be enjoyed without discrimination on any ground.

C. Social Security Instruments

136. In the course of years, the Council of Europe has developed a long-term programme in the field of social security with the technical help of the ILO, and this action resulted in the adoption of a number of instruments. After the 1953 two European Interim Agreements on Social Security, which were supplemented by a European Convention concerning Social and Medical Assistance, the basic instrument has been the 1964 *European Code of Social Security*. This Code was based on the ILO Social Security (Minimum Standards) Convention, 1952,[1] but it improved to a certain extent the level of protection provided for its ratification and it was supplemented by a Protocol which itself provided for higher standards. The Code and the Protocol both came into force in 1968. The Code has now been ratified by eleven countries, six of which also accepted the Protocol. At a later stage, in 1972, a *European Convention on Social Security* provided for equality of treatment in respect of social security, as between nationals and aliens, the maintenance of rights acquired abroad and the transfer of benefits from one country to another. It entered into force in March 1977 and has been ratified by four countries.

1. See below No. 420.

II. European Communities Standards

137. While the main purpose of the European Communities is of an economic nature, they have also set themselves a number of social objectives. Provisions of a social character are therefore to be found both in the basic treaties which have established the Communities and in the various acts (regulations, directives and recommendations) provided under the Communities legal system. This question is dealt with in a special contribution by Professor Schnorr[1] and reference is therefore made to this contribution.[2]

1. Labour Law within the European Communities.
2. For former studies of this question, see also Ribas, *La politique sociale des Communautés européennes*, Paris, 1969; *Megret-Louis-Vignes-Waelbroeck, Le droit de la Communauté économique*, vol. 7, Politique sociale, Brussels, 1973, Lyon-Caen et Ribettes-Tillhet, 'Droit du travail dans les Communautés européennes, Juris-classeurs travail, Paris, fascicule 7–3; Lyon-Caen, *Droit social international et européen*, Paris, 4th ed. 1976; Valticos, *Droit international du travail*, pp. 162 ss.

III. Other Regional Instruments

138. In other geographical and political frameworks various instruments have also been adopted about labour matters. Thus the Contracting Parties of the Treaty of Brussels, later the Western European Union, Benelux and the Nordic Council framed a number of instruments which had been adopted earlier than those of the European Communities and were on a narrower basis.

139. In Eastern Europe, the Council for Mutual Economic Assistance established in 1949 was authorized to pass recommendations on matters of economic, scientific and technical co-operation, while decisions are adopted only on procedural and organizational matters. In 1971, the member countries adopted a Comprehensive Programme of socialist economic integration. More particularly in the social field, co-operation is achieved through bilateral agreements.

140. In the American Region, a Social Security Convention prepared with the assistance of the ILO, was adopted in 1967 by the Organization of Central American States (ODECA). As regards the six countries of the Andean group, the Committee of the Agreement of Cartagena adopted in February 1977, an instrument on social security and another one on the migration of workers. From a more general point of view, the Organization of American States adopted in 1948 the American Declaration of the Rights and Duties of Man, which deals in general terms with a number of economic and social rights, and the Inter-American Charter of social guarantees. In 1969, it adopted an American Convention on Human Rights, which contains in particular provisions concerning freedom of association and forced labour. This Convention entered into force in July 1978.

141. In the Middle East, the League of Arab States drew up in 1967, an Arab Convention on Labour Standards[1] which has been influenced by the ILO standards and provides that it shall not affect any Conventions or international treaties that are more favourable to the beneficiaries. More recently, the Arab Labour Organization drafted a number of Conventions on various labour matters.

1. See ILO *Legislative Series*, 1967–Int. 1.

142. In Africa itself, a General Social Security Convention[1] drafted by the African, Malagasy and Mauritius Organization with the assistance of the ILO, was adopted in January 1971.

1. ILO *Legislative series*, 1971–Int. 2.

§4. Bilateral Treaties

I. Labour Treaties

143. Bilateral treaties in the labour field aim at regulating the admission to and conditions of employment in each of the contracting countries of workers who are nationals of the other country. Such treaties are based on the principle of the assimilation of the nationals of each contracting State to the nationals of the other country in which they are resident.[1] The number of bilateral treaties is large and is constantly increasing.[2] Their scope has broadened and they have become considerably diversified. However they follow a number of set patterns.

1. As regards the difference between bilateral treaties and international labour Conventions from the standpoint of reciprocity, see Jean Morellet 'La notion de réciprocité dans les traités de travail et les conventions internationales du travail', *Rev. crit.* 1931, pp. 642–656.
2. A list of the principal international treaties, agreements or arrangements, published in the *Intern. Lab. Code*, Vol. II, pp. 1105–1173, includes more than 850 titles for the period between 1858 and 1953. The most important are listed in the Chronological Index of the *Legislative Series*, a periodic publication of the ILO. There have been several hundred since 1960.

144. Originally, provision concerning labour matters (immigration, etc.) were included in treaties of a more general nature (such as treaties of friendship and trade or navigation treaties). Now, employment questions, particularly where wage-earning employment is concerned, are generally dealt with in special treaties of various kinds. Initially, such treaties applied to limited subjects or groups (immigration, seamen, payment of wages, transfer of savings). Later on, the conclusion of bilateral treaties of a more general type came to be considered necessary when restrictions began to be placed on the employment of aliens and when labour legislation for the protection of workers began to develop. The purpose of such general treaties was henceforth to regulate the conditions of employment of nationals of one contracting country resident in the other and to assimilate them to a certain extent to national workers in respect of conditions of employment and social security.

145. In the development of the bilateral regulation of employment conditions, the labour treaty between France and Italy of 1904 has been an important departure. This treaty did not only prescribe various measures for the protection and assimilation of the nationals of the two contracting countries. It also included an undertaking by Italy to complete the organization of its labour inspection service and to reduce the hours of work of women in industry. The two parties also undertook to publish an annual report on the application of their legislation on the employment of women and children. Then, the French Government, while granting benefits and safeguards to the many Italian workers in France, also sought to ensure that Italian competition should not be favoured by too low a level of employment conditions. This treaty served as a model for the conclusion of several agreements between European countries concerning compensation for industrial accidents, which put the nationals of the contracting countries on an equal footing in this respect and confirmed the principle of the application of the law of the country in which the accident took place.

146. After the First World War, *bilateral Conventions on emigration and immigration* were concluded between various countries. While most of them dealt only with the emigration of individuals, some contained also provisions on organized recruitment. As from that time, the number of bilateral agreements concerning the immigration of foreign workers has multiplied, especially after the Second World War.[1] The matter has also been dealt with in other types of agreements, such as those concerning employment, movement of persons or manpower. The main subject-matter of all such agreements is the recruitment and immigration of workers, and they usually also prescribe equal treatment in various fields for the workers of the contracting parties. Sometimes they also deal with other questions, such as the reuniting of families and vocational training.

1. E.g. the agreements concerning emigration and immigration between France and Poland of 3 September 1919 and between France and Czechoslovakia of 20 March 1920, the Evian Agreement of 1962 which contained provisions regulating the immigration into France of Algerian workers and was followed by an Agreement of 27 December 1968, and the Franco-Portuguese Protocol of 29 July 1971. See also the agreements or Conventions on Migration between the Federal Republic of Germany and Spain on 29 March 1960, between Belgium and Turkey of 16 July 1964, between Spain and Paraguay of 11 January 1965, between Australia and the Netherlands of 20 July 1968 and between the Netherlands and Tunisia of 8 March 1971.

147. In some cases migration has been covered by *labour treaties* of a more general character[1] which also make fuller provision, on the basis of reciprocity, for the granting of complete equality of rights to the nationals of the contracting countries in certain branches of social insurance or social assistance. Bilateral agreements were also concluded for special categories of workers (mine workers, frontier workers, seasonal workers, etc.).

1. E.g. the labour treaty of 30 September 1919 between France and Italy, the treaty of 24 December 1924 between Belgium and France, amended in 1939, the treaty of 1 August 1946 between France and Switzerland.

II. Social Insurance Treaties[1]

148. The development of social insurance and social assistance led to the conclusion of special Conventions in this field. The scope of such Conventions, which was limited at first to matters such as workmen's compensation, was gradually enlarged. Their original subject was equality of treatment as between nationals of the contracting countries, but the Conventions were later extended to cover questions concerning the applicable national legislation and conflict of laws, maintenance of the acquired rights of migrants or rights in the course of acquisition and co-operation between national social security institutions. Bilateral agreements have often been based on the provisions of the relevant ILO Conventions.[2] Some bilateral agreements are confined to one or more branches of social security, while Conventions of a more general kind cover all the contingencies provided for in social security legislation, including unemployment and family dependants. As a rule, and subject to certain qualifications, these Conventions made the law of the country of employment applicable to compensation for social risks. In respect of rights in the course of acquisition, they make it possible for insured persons to totalize the periods of insurance recognized in the two countries and ensure the maintenance of acquired rights to benefit.

1. For more detail see Valticos, *Droit international du travail*, pp. 180–188.
2. In particular, the maintenance of Migrants' Pensions Rights Convention, 1935 (No. 48).

III. Conclusion

149. The great majority of existing bilateral agreements on labour matters relate to social security. Next come those concerning migration, the movement of persons and seasonal workers, social policy, seamen and technical co-operation. Most of these agreements are concluded by European States, on matters such as social security, recruitment, placement and employment of foreign workers. Between Eastern European countries agreements relate to social security and co-operation on social matters.[1] A different type of agreement is that concluded between developed and developing countries[2] – sometimes between a State and former colonies after the latter became independent[3] – on technical co-operation matters.

1. E.g. Agreements of 11 December 1959 between the USSR and Bulgaria concerning social security, Convention of 14 March 1960 between Bulgaria and Rumania concerning co-operation in the field of social problems and Convention of 25 January 1957 between Bulgaria and Czechoslovakia respecting co-operation in the field of social policy, amended on 27 March 1972.
2. Agreements of 9 December 1965 between the Netherlands and Peru and of 2 March 1966 between the Netherlands and the Philippines on questions of training.
3. E.g. the general Convention of 13 October 1962 between Belgium and Rwanda concerning co-operation and technical assistance.

150. Generally speaking, bilateral treaties and agreements still have an important part to play in spite of the multiplication of conventions of world-wide or regional scope. They are particularly useful in making the adjustments necessitated by the variety of national legislations, in supplementing the international standards, in prescribing rules for the implementation of international principles, and in dealing with subjects, such as bilateral co-operation, which are not covered by more general standards. However, bilateral treaties and agreements also have certain defects. They may involve a certain amount of confusion, sometimes be incomplete or make use of out-of-date formulas. They may also, by improving, in a country, the conditions for the nationals of a given State, cause resentment at the treatment of others. Such defects are, nevertheless, mitigated by the multiplication of bilateral arrangements and the fact that the latter are often based on similar models or on multilateral or international conventions which can also, to a certain extent, fill in the gaps in the network of bilateral agreements.

§5. Relations between the Sources

I. The Role of the Various International Sources

151. The role and purpose of the various international sources of labour law varies to a certain degree. The difference is clear between bilateral treaties, on the one hand, and universal or regional standards, on the other. As indicated above, the main purpose of bilateral treaties and agreements is to determine the conditions of entry and of employment in each contracting country for the nationals of the other, while the object of universal Conventions (and to a great extent of regional conventions) is to establish within all countries (or within the countries which belong to the regional organization concerned) and in principle for all workers, whether national or foreign (or citizen of another country member of the regional organization concerned) conditions of employment which conform to the standards which these treaties or conventions lay down.

152. Regional standards are much more similar to universal Conventions, although their application is limited to the nationals of the States which belong to the regional Organization in the framework of which they were adopted – as in the case of European Communities instruments – or to the nationals of the contracting parties (European Social Charter). Although there is some duplication between regional standards and universal Conventions, the practical value of regional standards – mainly at the European level – lies mainly in the possibility which they offer of laying down standards which are more progressive than the world-wide standards, of dealing with the special problems of the region concerned, of securing greater uniformity of law within it, or of providing more extensive reciprocal advantages. Another reason which prompted the adoption of regional standards was the more general desire of some regional organizations to create instruments appropriate to the geographical and political entity which they represent.

II. The Conflict between International Sources

A. Preventive Steps

153. The plurality of international sources of law made it necessary to consider various sorts of steps aiming at preventing the adoption of universal or regional standards which would be in conflict against one another. These steps consist mainly in measures of co-ordination and consultation at the time when standards of common interest are being worked out. Arrangements for this purpose are frequently provided in the agreements between the various organizations of the United Nations System, as well as between each of them and various regional organizations. In fact, such consultation has actually taken place in many cases and in various forms. In particular, the European Organizations have often consulted the ILO or have associated it with their work when preparing instruments on labour matters. Thus, the drafting of the European Social Charter[1] was preceded, in 1958, by discussion at a tripartite Conference of European States who were Members both of the Council of Europe and of the ILO, convened by the ILO at the request of the Council of Europe. This consultation produced positive results, as the unanimous recommendations of that Conference were practically all adopted and embodied in the final text of the Charter. Similarly, the instruments on social security formulated by the Council of Europe and the EEC were prepared with the technical help of the ILO and even on the basis of specific texts drafted by the ILO.

1. See above No. 134.

154. A second device adopted to avoid any conflict is the insertion in the most recent of the instruments concerned, of compatibility clauses stating that there is no contradiction between two successive instruments. Thus the 1966 International Covenants on Human Rights include both a general safeguarding clause[1] and a special clause relating to freedom of association[2] which lay down that nothing in the Covenants shall prejudice the guarantee provided for in the relevant Conventions.

1. Each of these two Covenants provides (Article 5, para. 2) that 'No restriction upon or derogation from any of the fundamental rights recognised or existing in any country in virtue of law, *conventions*, regulations or custom shall be admitted on the pretext that the present Covenant does not recognise such rights or that it recognises them to a lesser extent.'
2. Article 8, para. 3 of the International Covenant on Economic, Social and Cultural Rights provides that 'Nothing in this Article shall authorise States Parties to the International Labour Convention of 1948 concerning Freedom of Association and Protection of the Right to Organise to take legislative measures which would prejudice, or apply the law in such a manner as would prejudice, the guarantees provided for in that Convention'. Article 22, para. 3 of the International Covenant on Civil and Political Rights contains a similar provision.

155. Finally, in order to avoid conflict between the interpretations or findings of the bodies established by the different organizations to supervise the application of instruments dealing with analogous matters, various steps have been taken such as the participation of observers from the other organization concerned, the communication of copies of government reports submitted to that organization and of comments by its supervisory bodies, etc. This is often expressly provided in the instruments themselves (International Covenants on Human Rights, European Social Charter, European Code of Social Security).[1]

1. See in this connection below Nos. 707, 709 and 711.

B. Cases of Conflict

156. As a result of the adoption, by various organizations, of instruments which sometimes deal with the same matters, it may happen that the standards laid down in these instruments differ between themselves in spite of the preventive measures which have just been described. Such differences do not mean that there will necessarily be a conflict between the standards concerned. Two formal conditions must be met for a genuine conflict to arise in such cases. Firstly, the instruments in question must be such as can give rise to international obligations (that is conventions, treaties, etc.) and not mere recommendations, though some confusion may no doubt result from discrepancies even between standards which are only recommended to governments. Secondly, there would really be a conflict if a State were actually bound by two separate instruments laying down contradictory standards. However, in a more general way, the more existence of instruments setting different standards, even if not ratified, may also be a source of confusion, particularly to a State wishing to decide which of the instruments to ratify and implement.

157. The general question of conflict between international standards was originally considered in international law in connection with cases of conflict between bilateral treaties. The criteria adopted in such cases[1] were based sometimes on the assimilation of the treaties to laws or to contracts and sometimes to less formal considerations. They all involve great difficulties in themselves and are, moreover, inadequate in the case of international labour conventions because of the predominantly multilateral and institutional character of these conventions and of the subjects with which they deal.

1. See below No. 162.

158. For the solution of a conflict between instruments on labour matters, the main criterion should be the 'progressive' nature of labour law, whether national or international. The purpose of international labour law is to promote social progress. This being so, a conflict between international labour standards cannot be resolved merely by applying formal criteria. The decisive factor should be the substantive criterion deriving from the purpose and the content of the standard. Consequently, in the event of conflict, preference must be given in principle to the standard which is the most favourable to the workers. This criterion is expressly recognized in respect of the relationship between international and national labour standards, as the ILO Constitution provides (Art. 19, para. 8) that an international standard represents a minimum standard in relation to national legislation, and that the latter may ensure more favourable conditions to the workers.[1] The same principle should logically apply in regard to the relationship between different international labour standards. As a result, there would be no real incompatibility between two international instruments if one of them provides a higher standard of protection than the other. The implementation of the higher standard will necessarily entail implementation of the lower one. This criterion also meets the principle of the independent character of concurrent treaties, in virtue of which a State bound by two (or more) instruments laying down different standards remains bound, in respect of each instrument, by the standard which that instrument prescribes and must therefore discharge the obligations arising out of both.

1. See below No. 586.

159. In considering the possibility of conflict, account should also be taken of the fact that competing international standards generally do not deal with their subject-matter in the same degree of detail. Thus, the International Covenants on Human Rights and the European Social Charter are drafted in more general terms than the specific provisions of ILO Conventions or bilateral treaties. As a result, the criterion of the most specific standard, provided that it is not less favourable to the workers, may also be applicable in accordance with the general principles of law.

160. In case a conflict arises between two different bilateral treaties, which are applicable to the nationals of different States, there is usually no obstacle for the two treaties to be executed concurrently, subject to any problems that might arise in connection with the most favoured clause.

161. In the last resort, there can be a real conflict of concurrent standards only if these differ not in respect of the level of protection provided or of the categories of persons covered, but in respect of the type of protection provided or of the basic principles involved. In fact, such cases are exceptional. If compatibility cannot then be secured by the cumulative implementation of the two instruments concerned and if the principle of the most favourable provision cannot lead to a solution, it will be necessary to have recourse to the criteria of more general application which have been suggested in cases of conflict between treaties in general. The various criteria which have been put forward in this connection include those of the hierarchy of norms, of *lex posterior derogat priori* (and the various other formulae applicable to conflicts between national laws), of the respect of acquired rights, of *pacta sunt servanda*, of good faith, of effectiveness, of the rule which has the greatest positive effect, of the distinction between multilateral and bilateral treaties. All these criteria have limitations.[1] The matter is dealt with to a certain extent in the 1969 Vienna Convention on the Law of Treaties, but the relevant provision (Article 30) does not cover all types of situations.

1. See Rousseau, *Droit international public*, Vol. I, Paris, 1970, pp. 151–163; Valticos, *Droit international du travail*, pp. 188–190.

Chapter IV. Selected Bibliography

162. Collection of Texts and Official Publications of the ILO

- *Constitution of the International Labour Organization and Standing Orders of the International Labour Conference* (ILO, Geneva, 1977).
- *Conventions and Recommendations 1919–1966* (ILO, Geneva, 1966) (The instruments adopted in subsequent years are published in the *Official Bulletin* of the ILO).
- ILO *Official Bulletin* (ILO, Geneva, 1919–. . . .).
- *The International Labour Code 1951* (2 vol., ILO, Geneva, 1952).
- Record of Proceedings of the Sessions of the International Labour Conference.
- Minutes of the ILO Governing Body.
- Reports of the Committee of Experts on the Application of Conventions and Recommendations.
- ILO *Legislative Series*.
- *International Labour Review*.
- *The Impact of International Labour Conventions and Recommendations* (ILO, Geneva, 1976).
- *International Labour Standards – A Workers' Education Manual* (ILO, Geneva, 1978).

Books and Articles

ABDELJAOUAD, A., '*The influence of international labour Conventions on Tunisian legislation*', *I.L.R.*., March 1965, pp. 191–209.

AGO, R., '*La codification du droit international et les problèmes de sa réalisation*', *Recueil d'études en hommage à Paul Guggenheim*, Genève, 1968, pp. 93–131.

Selected Bibliography

Van ASBECK, F. M., *'Quelques aspects du contrôle international non judiciaire de l'application par les gouvernements de conventions internationales'*, *Nederlands Tijdschrift voor Internationaal Recht*, 1959, pp. 27–41.

AYISSI MVODO, V., and LE FAOU, R., *'Influence of international labour standards on the legislation of Cameroon'*, *I.L.R.*, August-September 1973, pp. 163–185.

BADAOUI, A. Z., *'The influence of international labour Conventions on the Arab Labour Standards Convention'*, *I.L.R.*, November 1970, pp. 475–496.

BERENSTEIN, A., *'The influence of international labour Conventions on Swiss legislation'*, *I.L.R.*, June 1958, pp. 495–518.

CASHELL, M., *'Influence on Irish law and practice of international labour standards'*, *I.L.R.*, July 1972, pp. 47–73.

CASSESE, A., *'Il controllo internazionale sul rispetto della libertà sindacale nel quadro delle attuali tendenze in materia di protezione internazionale dei diritti dell'uomo'*, *Communicazione e Studi*, vol. XII, Milan, 1966, pp. 293–418.

DAHL, K. N., *'The influence of ILO standards on Norwegian legislation'*, *I.L.R.*, September 1964, pp. 226–251.

FRIED, E., *Rechtsvereinheitlichung im internationalen Arbeitsrecht*, A. Metzner Verlag, Frankfurter/M.-Berlin, 1965.

'The European Social Charter and international labour standards', *I.L.R.*, November 1961, pp. 354–375, and December 1961, pp. 462–477.

'The influence of international labour Conventions on Nigeria labour legislation', *I.L.R.*, July 1960, pp. 26–43.

IVANOV, S. A. *'International labour Conventions and the USSR'*, *I.L.R.*, April 1966, pp. 401–413.

JENKS, C. W., *'Les fonctions et les formes de la législation internationale du travail'*, *Mélanges Ernest Mahaim*, Sirey, Paris, vol. II–1935, pp. 561–569.

– *The Significance for International Law of the Tripartite Character of the International Labour Organisation*, 22 Trans. Grot. Soc. 45–81, 1936.

– *Are International Labour Conventions Agreements between Governments?* 15 Can. Bar. Rev. 574–578, 1937.

– *'Les instruments internationaux à caractère collectif'*, *Rec. Cours* 69, 1939–III.

– *The International Protection of Trade Union Freedom*, Stevens and Sons, London, 1957.

– *The Application of International Labour Conventions by Means of Collective Agreements*, ZaÖRV 19, 1958 (*Festgabe Makarov*), 197–224.

– *Human Rights and International Labour Standards*, Stevens and Sons, London, F. A. Praeger, New York 1960.

– The *Corpus Juris* of Social Justice, in *Law, Freedom and Welfare*, Stevens and Sons, London, 1963.

– *The International Protection of Trade Union Rights*, in *The International Protection of Human Rights*, edited by Evan Luard, Thames and Hudson, London, 1967.

– *Human Rights, Social Justice and Peace – The Broader Significance of the ILO Experience*, in *International Protection of Human Rights*, *Proceedings of the Seventh Nobel Symposium*, Oslo, September 1967, edited by Asbjörn

Eide and August Schou, Almqvist and Wiksell, Stockholm, 1967, 227–260.
– *Social Justice in the Law of Nations – The ILO Impact after Fifty Years*, Oxford University Press, London-Oxford-New York, 1970.
– *Social Policy in a Changing World, Selected Speeches*, ILO, Geneva, 1976.
JOHNSTON, G. A., *The International Labour Organization*, Europa Publ., London, 1970.
– *'The Influence of international labour standards on legislation and practice in the United Kingdom'*, *I.L.R.*, May 1968, pp. 465–487.
JUVIGNY, P., to *Organization internationale du Travail, Jurisclasseur du travail*, Ed. techniques, Paris, fascicule 11.1.
KAHN-FREUND, O., *'The European Social Charter'*, in *European Law and the Individuals,* edited by F. G. Jacobs, North-Holland Publishing Cy., Amsterdam, 1976, 181–211.
KLOTZ, V., *'Der Einfluss der Übereinkommen der Internationalen Arbeitsorganisation auf die innerstaatliche Gesetzgebung'*, *Bundesarbeitsblatt*, Bonn, 1973, No. 10, pp. 499–504.
LANDY, E. A., *The Effectiveness of International Supervision – Thirty Years of ILO Experience*, Stevens and Sons, London, and Oceana Publ., New York, 1966.
– *'The Influence of International Labour Standards: Possibilities and Performance'*, *I.L.R.*, June 1970, pp. 555–604.
LYON-CAEN, G., *Droit social international et européen*, 4e éd., Dalloz, Paris, 1976.
LYON-CAEN, G., et RIBBETTES-THILLHET, D., *Droit du travail dans les Communautés européennes,* Jurisclasseur du travail, Ed. techniques, Paris, fascicule 7.3.
McMAHON, J. F., *'The legislative techniques of the International Labour Organisation'*, *B.Y.B.I.L.*, Vol. 41, 1965–1966, pp. 1–102.
MORELLET, J., *Un type original de traités: les conventions internationales du travail, Rev. crit.* 1938, pp. 1 s.
MORELLET, J., *'The influence of international labour Conventions on French legislation'*, *I.L.R.*, April 1970, pp. 331–358.
OECHSLIN, J. J., *'Le Code international du travail'*, *Revue française des affaires sociales*, April-June 1969, pp. 55–72.
PESIĆ, R., *'International labour standards and Yugoslav legislation'*, *I.L.R.*, November 1967, pp. 443–467.
PLATA-CASTILLA, A., *'International labour standards and Colombian legislation'*, *I.L.R.*, February 1969, pp. 137–158.
VON POTOBSKY, G., *'Protection of Trade Union Rights: Twenty Years' Work by the Committee on Freedom of Association'*, *I.L.R.*, January 1972, pp. 69–83.
RIBAS, J.-J., *La politique sociale des Communautés européennes*, ed. Eurolibri, Dalloz et Sirey, Paris, 1969.
RIVA-SANSEVERINO, L., *'The influence of international labour Conventions on Italian labour legislation'*, *I.L.R.*, June 1961, pp. 576–601.

SCELLE, G., *L'Organisation internationale du Travail et le BIT*, Rivière, Paris, 1930.
SCHNORR, G., *'The influence of ILO standards on law and practice in the Federal Republic of Germany', I.L.R.*, December 1974, pp. 539–564.
SHOTWELL, J. T., *The origins of the International Labor Organization,* New York, Columbia University Press, 1934, 2 vol.
TROCLET, L.-E., *Législation sociale internationale,* éd. Libr. encyclopédique, Bruxelles, 1952.
– *Eléments de droit social européen*, Ed. de l'Institut de sociologie de l'Université libre de Bruxelles, Bruxelles, 1963.
TROCLET, L.-E., and VOGEL-POLSKY, E., *'The influence of international labour Conventions on Belgian labour legislation', I.L.R.*, November 1968, pp. 389–424.
VALTICOS, N., *Droit international du travail*, vol. 8 of the 'Traité de droit du travail' ed. by Camerlynck, Dalloz, Paris, 1970, and *Supplement (Mise à jour),* 1973.
– *Derecho Internacional del Trabajo*, Tecnos, Madrid, 1977.
– *Un système de contrôle international: la mise en oeuvre des conventions internationales du travail, Rec. Cours* 123, 1961–I, pp. 315–407.
– *Conventions internationales du travail et droit interne, Rev. crit.* 1955, no. 2, pp. 251–288.
– *'The influence of international labour Conventions on Greek legislation', I.L.R.*, June 1955, pp. 593–615.
– *Les conventions internationales du travail devant le juge français, Rev. crit.* 1964. no. 1, pp. 41–72.
– *La Charte sociale européenne. Sa structure, son contenu, le contrôle de son application, Droit social* 1953, pp. 466–482.
– *La Commission d'investigation et de conciliation en matière de liberté syndicale et le mécanisme de protection internationale des droits syndicaux, Ann,* 1967, pp. 445–468.
– *Une nouvelle expérience de protection des droits de l'homme: le groupe d'étude de l'OIT chargé d'examiner la situation en matière de travail et en matière syndicale en Espagne, Ann.* 1970, pp. 567–590.
– *Les systèmes de contrôle non judiciaire des instruments internationaux relatifs aux droits de l'homme, Mélanges offerts à P. Modinos (Problèmes des droits de l'homme et de l'unification européenne)*, Paris, 1968, pp. 331–356.
VALTICOS, P., *Fifty Years of Standard-Setting Activities by the ILO, I.L.R.*, September 1969, pp. 201–237.
– *Universalité des droits de l'homme et diversité des conditions nationales,* in *René Cassin Amicorum discipulorumque Liber,* vol. I, Pedone, Paris, 1969, pp. 383–403.
– *Les normes de l'Organisation internationale du Travail en matière de protection des droits de l'homme*, *Human Rights Journal,* vol. IV–4, 1971, pp. 691–771.
– *La protection internationale de la liberté syndicale vingt-cinq ans après*, Human Rights Journal, vol. VII–1, 1974, pp. 5–39.

– *Les méthodes de la protection internationale de la liberté syndicale, Rec. Cours* 144, 1975–I, pp. 79–138.
– *Un double type d'enquête au Chili, Ann.* 1975, pp. 483–502.
– *L'inspection internationale dans le droit international du travail,* in *L'inspection internationale*, edited by G. Fischer and D. Vignes, Bruylant, Brussels, 1976, pp. 379–437.
– *Les effets des conventions internationales du travail en Suisse, Mémoires de la Faculté de droit de l'Université de Genève*, 1976, pp. 327–345.
– *Droit international du travail et droit interne français, Travaux du Comité français de droit international privé*, 1973–1975, Paris, Dalloz, 1977, pp. 11–37.
– *Normes universelles et normes régionales dans le domaine du travail,* Société française pour le droit international, Colloque de Bordeaux, *Régionalisme et universalisme dans le droit international contemporain*, Paris, 1977, pp. 289–307.
– *Le droit international du travail à l'heure du bilan, Tendances du droit du travail français contemporain – Etudes offertes à G. H. Camerlynck,* Dalloz, Paris, 1978, pp. 3–25.
– *The International Protection of Economic and Social Rights, Rechten van de mens in mundiaal en europees perspectief,* Stichting Ars Aequi, Maarssen (Netherlands), 1978, pp. 142–184.
– *'Mise en parallèle des actions et des mécanismes de contrôle au niveau du Conseil de l'Europe et de l'Organisation internationale du Travail'* in *La Charte sociale européenne*, Brussels, 1978.
VALTICOS, N., and WOLF, F., *L'Organisation internationale du Travail et les pays en voie de développement: techniques d'élaboration et mise en oeuvre de normes universelles,* Société française pour le droit international, Colloque d'Aix-en-Provence, *Pays en voie de développement et transformation du droit international,* Pedone, Paris, 1974, pp. 127–146.
WIEBRINGHAUS, H., *La Charte sociale européenne*, *Ann.*, 1963, pp. 709–721.
– *L'état d'application de la Charte sociale européenne*, Ann. 1973, pp. 928–940.
WOLF, F., *L'interdépendance des conventions internationales du travail*, *Rec. Cours* 121, 1967–III, pp. 117–219.
– *Aspects judiciaires de la protection internationale des droits de l'homme, Human Rights Journal*, vol. IV–4, 1971, pp. 773–838.
– *Les conventions internationales du travail et la succession d'Etat, Ann.* 1961, pp. 742–751.
– *L'application des conventions internationales du travail par voie de conventions collectives*, *Ann*. 1974, pp. 103–114.

Part I. The Content of International Labour Law

163. The present part will deal with the content of international labour law. In view of the great number of instruments concerned and of the detailed character of many of them, it will naturally not be possible to give here more than an outline of the content of these standards. The survey will mainly cover ILO standards but it will also point out standards adopted within the framework of other organizations.[1] The standards described relate to fundamental human rights (as in the case of freedom of association, forced labour and discrimination), employment, wages, general conditions of work (hours of work, weekly rest, annual holidays with pay, hygiene and safety, etc.), social policy, social security, industrial relations, work of women, work of children and young persons, special categories of workers (such as seafarers, agricultural workers and indigenous workers), migrant and foreign workers and labour administration. Mention will also be made of the problems encountered in the framing and application of some of these standards. The ratification figures for the most important of the Conventions concerned will be those applying in December 1978.

1. Apart from those of the European Communities to which a separate contribution by Professor Schnorr is devoted.

Chapter I. Freedom of Association for Trade Union Purposes

§1. General Outline

164. The standards on freedom of association for trade union purposes have a special place in international labour law, as it is an essential means for workers to defend their interests and a particular aspect of the right of association in general, and is therefore considered among the fundamental human rights. Moreover it has a special importance because of the tripartite structure of the ILO.

165. As early as 1919, freedom of association was mentioned in the constitutional provisions of the ILO. The Preamble of Part XIII of the Treaty of Versailles listed the 'recognition of the principle of freedom of association' among the objectives of the Organization, and the General Principles which were enunciated in Article 427 contained a provision on 'the right of association for all lawful purposes by the employed as well as by the employers'. In the years which followed, the ILO tried to confirm this general principle in Conventions dealing more specially with this matter.

166. A first Convention (No. 11) concerning the right of association in agriculture was adopted in 1921, but it provided only that States should 'secure to all those engaged in agriculture the same rights of association and combination as to industrial workers'. This Convention, which is now ratified by 98 States, proved, in certain cases, to be of considerable practical importance, as it resulted in extending to workers in agriculture trade union rights which were previously recognized only to those in industry. However, its scope remained limited since it did not lay down any substantive rule on the content of the right to association and since agricultural workers could enjoy this right only to the extent to which industrial workers enjoyed it.[1]

1. See the opinion to this effect given in 1925 by the International Labour Office and the conclusions, approved by the Governing Body of the ILO in 1938, of the Committee appointed to consider a representation under Article 24 of the Constitution of the ILO (*Intern. Lab. Code*, note 12 under Art. 867).

167. To lead to the adoption of a Convention containing substantive provisions on the right of association, the ILO undertook, in the twenties, a wide-ranging inquiry on the situation in the world in this connection.[1] In 1927, a draft Convention was submitted to the International Labour Conference but this attempt was abandoned.[2]

1. ILO: *Freedom of Association* (Studies and reports, Series A, Nos. 28 to 32), five volumes, ILO, Geneva, 1927–1930.
2. This failure was due directly to two different amendments which were proposed in the course of the discussions: the one aimed at providing for the right not to associate together with the right to associate, and the other at making the establishment of trade unions dependent on the observance of legal formalities; the workers' delegates feared that such a provision might permit the existence of trade unions to be subjected to previous authorization. Apart from these points, more general political considerations, related to the existence of totalitarian regimes in the world, contributed to the failure of the attempts which followed to adopt international instruments on freedom of association.

168. It was only after the Second World War that a new attempt could meet with success. Already in 1944 the Declaration of Philadelphia affirmed that 'freedom of expression and of association are essential to sustained progress', while the principle of freedom of association was maintained in the Preamble of the Constitution. The Declaration also referred to 'the effective recognition of the right of collective bargaining, the co-operation of management and labour in the continuous improvement of productive efficiency, and the collaboration of workers and employers in the preparation and application of social and economic measures.

169. In 1947 a Convention (No. 84) was adopted to provide for the right of association in non-metropolitan territories. It was the first international instrument to contain substantive provisions on the right of association and on the settlement of labour disputes. It has been ratified by four countries and is still applicable to 28 territories.

170. In the same year, the Economic and Social Council of the United Nations, following requests from the World Federation of Trade Unions and from the American Federation of Labour, asked the ILO to place on the agenda of the International Labour Conference the question of trade union rights. As a result the International Labour Conference adopted in 1948 the Freedom of Association and Protection of the Right to Organize Convention (No. 87), which was complemented, the following year, by the Right to Organize and Collective Bargaining Convention (No. 98). These two instruments will be described in greater detail below.[1] In 1950 a special procedure was also established to afford greater international protection in the field of freedom of association,[2] and important case law has been established over the years.[3] In 1961 provisions on freedom of association were also included in the European Social Charter.[4]

1. Nos. 172 ss.
2. See below No. 631 ss.
3. See below No. 633.
4. See below Nos. 208–218.

171. In the ILO itself, various Recommendations dealing mainly with matters of industrial relations were adopted from 1951 to 1967.[1] More recently the ILO Conference adopted in 1971 a Convention and a Recommendation on workers' representatives, in 1975 a Convention and a Recommendation on rural workers' organizations, and in 1978 a Convention and a Recommendation on labour relations in the public service. Various studies have been or will be undertaken about other aspects of freedom of association.

1. See below Nos. 422 ss.

§2. The Freedom of Association and Protection of the Right to Organize Convention, 1948 (No. 87)

172. The Freedom of Association and Protection of the Right to Organize Convention, 1948 (No. 87) is the basic instrument for the international protection of freedom of association.[1] It has been ratified by 91 States. It deals, on the one hand, with the right of employers and workers to establish trade union organizations (which it defines in Art. 10 as 'any organization of workers or employers for furthering and defending the interests of workers and of employers') and, on the other, with the rights and guarantees which such organizations should enjoy.

1. As regards Conventions Nos. 87 and 98, see the general surveys prepared in 1959 and 1973 by the Committee of Experts on the Application of Conventions and Recommendations. See also *Freedom of Association. An International Survey*, ILO, 1975, and Erstling, *The Right to Organise*, ILO, 1977.

I. The Right to Establish Trade Union Organizations

173. The Convention provides (Art. 2) that 'workers and employers, without distinction whatsoever, shall have the right to establish and, subject only to the rules of the organization concerned, to join organizations of their own choosing without previous authorization'.

174. The scope of this provision is very wide, as it refers in particular to workers '*without distinction whatsoever*'. The Convention aimed at excluding any discrimination in trade union matters and it was stated in this connection that 'freedom of association was to be guaranteed not only to employers and workers in private industry, but also to public employees, and without distinction or discrimination of any kind as to occupation, sex, colour, race, creed, nationality or political opinion.[1] The armed forces and the police are the only categories in respect of which the Convention (Art. 9) leaves countries free to determine the extent to which the Convention shall apply.

1. See *Rec. Proc. Conf.* 31, 1948, p. 476.

175. The Convention also provides that the establishment of an occupational organization should not be subject to '*previous authorization*', which means that formalities could be prescribed by law – as is usual in most countries – but they should not be equivalent, in practice, to previous authorization nor constitute an obstacle amounting in fact to prohibition. It is also specified (Art. 7) that the acquisition of legal personality by the occupational organizations shall not be made subject to conditions of such a character as to restrict the application of the Convention.

176. Finally, when it refers to '*organizations of their own choosing*' the Convention requires that there should be freedom of choice as to the organizations which workers, in particular, may wish to establish or to which they may wish to join. Any legal provision which would limit or refuse such freedom of choice at the plant or at the occupational or national level would be at variance with the basic principle of the Convention. Serious difficulties are met, in this connection, especially with the system of trade union monopoly imposed by law which exists in many countries, where the legislation allows for the existence of only one organization for a particular category of workers. Although it is not the purpose of the Convention to make trade union diversity an obligation, the Convention requires this diversity to remain possible.[1]

The system of trade union monopoly is often linked with the economic, social or political conditions or systems of the countries concerned and has been explained by various reasons such as the desire to avoid a multiplicity of unions, especially in the case of newly independent States which refer in particular to a concern to avoid a dispersion of efforts in national development.[2] In communist countries with planned economy, the role of trade unions has undergone a considerable change and the fact that the national Constitution provided that the Communist Party was the leading core of all organizations of working people has been discussed in this connection. More generally, in countries where only a single political party may exist, the political system is bound to influence the organization of trade unions.

1. On this question see *Rep. Com. Exp.* 1973 (Vol. 4B), paras. 68–78, pp. 29–33; and 1977, paras. 63–64, p. 22.
2. About the views according to which freedom of association would be a hindrance to economic development, see Guy Caire, *Freedom of Association and Economic Development*, ILO, Geneva, 1977.

177. Such difficulties arise only to the extent that the single trade union organization is instituted or maintained by legislation and not when it only is a factual situation in which workers or their trade unions join together voluntarily in a single organization. As regards the dangers deriving from a multiplicity of unions, it would not be incompatible with Convention No. 87 that the most representative trade unions be recognized as having certain special rights, principally with regard to collective bargaining, provided that the determination of the most representative trade union organizations is made in an objective and independent manner, that it can be reconsidered periodically and that it does not affect the right of other trade unions to function in a normal way.

II. The Rights and Guarantees of Trade Union Organizations

178. Having dealt with the right of workers and employers to establish trade union organizations, the Convention defines the rights and guarantees which these organizations should enjoy, and specifies that 'the public authorities shall refrain from any interference which would restrict this right or impede the lawful exercise thereof' (Art. 3, para. 2).

179. Among the rights which it recognizes (Art. 3, para. 1) the Convention mentions in the first place *the right of the organizations to draw up their constitutions and rules*. In certain countries the legislation indicates, sometimes in a rather detailed manner, the various subjects which should be dealt with in the rules of trade unions. Such provisions may aim at protecting the rights of individual members. They would be compatible with the Convention only if they conform to the principles of freedom of association and if approval of the rules is not within the discretionary powers of the public authorities.

180. The Convention also provides for *the right of organizations to elect their representatives in full freedom*. In many countries the legislation lays down conditions for the eligibility to trade union office and requirements concerning the election and removal of officers.[1] Problems relating to compatibility with the Convention arise mainly from provisions in regard to nationality, occupational status, political belief or affiliation, penal record and re-election. Provisions requiring trade union officers to be nationals of the country are frequent and their compatibility with the Convention depends to a great extent on how they are applied in practice and which are the local circumstances. As regards provisions which lay down that a person elected must actually be employed in the occupation concerned their purpose has sometimes been explained as being designed to prevent that trade unions be controlled by politicians. However, in many countries, the labour force could not provide qualified leadership entirely from its own ranks. Moreover, a restriction of this kind might encourage acts of interference by employers, such as the dismissal of a worker holding trade union office, which would result in his losing such office. Accordingly a certain flexibility should be introduced in such provisions.

1. See ILO, *Eligibility for trade union office*, Geneva, 1972; B. Gernigon, *Tenure of Trade Union Office*, ILO, Geneva, 1977.

181. Thirdly, the Convention provides for *the right of organizations to organize their administration and activities and to formulate their programmes.* This provision does not affect legislative requirements such as those on the convening of general meetings, etc.the purpose of which is to guarantee the democratic participation of the members and when the application of the rules is mainly left to the members themselves. The question is more complex when the unions are under the obligation to report, in particular on financial matters,[1] to the public authorities on their administration. Legislation giving the administrative authorities the right, at their entire discretion, to investigate the internal affairs of a union would not be in conformity with the Convention. Supervision of union finances by the authorities should not normally exceed periodical reporting requirements. More generally, it would be important that the person to whom the unions might be required to report would enjoy a certain independence and be subject to judicial control.

1. See, more generally, ILO, *The Public Authorities and the Right to Protection of Trade Union Fund and Property*, Geneva, 1974.

182. The right of trade unions to organize their activities raises two important questions, that of the right to strike[1] and that of the *political activities of trade union organizations*. In a number of countries, the law prohibits political activity by trade unions in general terms. The supervisory bodies of the ILO have taken the view that, while this is a complex matter as it is difficult to define a clear line of division between political and trade union activities, a general prohibition of political activities is both incompatible with the Convention and unrealistic in practice. The interpretation which would be given to such a provision could restrict the possibilities of action of the organization. These bodies felt that States should be able, without prohibiting *a priori* and in general terms all political activities by occupational organizations, to entrust to the judicial authorities the task of repressing abuses which might, in certain cases, be committed by organizations which had lost sight of the fact that their fundamental objective should be the economic and social advancement of their members.

1. See below No. 188.

183. In a more general way, the freedom of action of occupational organizations depends to a great extent on the *civil liberties* which are recognized in the country concerned. Freedom is indivisible and cannot be guaranteed only to an isolated sector. The ILO has often stressed the inter-relationship between trade union rights and civil liberties, and in 1970 the International Labour Conference adopted, without opposition, a resolution on this subject, where it stated that the rights conferred upon workers' and employers' organizations must be based on respect for those civil liberties which have been enunciated, in particular, in the Universal Declaration of Human Rights and in the International Covenant on Civil and Political Rights and that the absence of these civil liberties removes all meaning from the concept of trade union rights. In this resolution, the Conference stressed the following rights which it considered essential for the normal exercise of trade union rights:

a. the right to freedom and security of person and freedom from arbitrary arrest and detention;
b. freedom to hold opinions without interference and to seek, receive and impart information and ideas through any media and regardless of frontiers;
c. freedom of assembly;
d. the right to a fair trial by an independent and impartial tribunal;
e. the right to protection of the property of trade union organizations.[1]

1. See on this question Report VII submitted to the 54th Session of the International Labour Conference (1970). See also the report of the Commission of Inquiry established to consider complaints relating to the observance by Greece of the freedom of association Conventions (O.B., Sp. Suppl., Vol. LIV, 1971, No. 2, paras. 280–281) and the report of the Fact-Finding and Conciliation Commission as regards the case of Chile (*The Trade Union Situation in Chile*), ILO, 1975, paras. 538–540). On these complaints see below Nos. 626 and 638.

184. Apart from the rights of occupational organizations, the Convention provides for an additional guarantee (Art. 4) by declaring that workers' and employers' organizations shall *not be liable to be dissolved or suspended by administrative authority*. The purpose of this provision is to ensure that dissolution or suspension are surrounded by the requisite guarantees which are normally ensured by judicial procedure.

185. It is also provided (Art. 5 of the Convention) that occupational organizations shall have the right to establish and join *federations and confederations*, and that any such organizations, federation or confederation shall have the right to affiliate with international organizations of workers and employers. In addition, the rights and guarantees that the Convention provides for occupational organizations shall apply to federations and confederations (Art. 6), in particular as regards the acquisition of legal personality (Art. 7).

186. Finally, in Art. 8, para. 1, the Convention lays down that, in exercising the rights provided for 'workers and employers and their respective organizations, like other persons or organized collectivities, shall respect the law of the land'. However, in order to avoid that such a reference to national law should deprive the Convention of its substance, para. 2 of this Article stresses that 'the law of the land shall not be such as to impair, nor shall it be so applied as to impair, the guarantees provided for in this Convention'.

187. Moreover, in a general provision (Art. 11), the Convention specifies that States which ratify this instrument undertake 'to take all necessary and appropriate measures to ensure that workers and employers may exercise freely the right to organize'.

III. The Right to Strike

188. While Convention No. 87 does not deal expressly with the right to strike, a case law on that matter has been progressively developed by the various supervisory bodies.[1] In the first place, on the basis of Art. 3, 8 and 10 of the Convention, the Committee of Experts has considered[2] that a general prohibition of strikes constitutes a considerable restriction of the opportunities open to trade unions for furthering and defending the interests of their members and of the right of trade unions to organize their activities. The Freedom of Association Committee[3] has also stressed repeatedly, when examining various complaints on the matter, that 'the right to strike by workers and their organizations is generally recognized as a legitimate means of defending their occupational interests'. These two bodies felt, however, that some restrictions on the right of strike are acceptable in certain cases, as in the civil service, in essential services, in emergencies or until existing facilities for negotiation, conciliation and arbitration can be brought to bear, or to fulfil certain procedural conditions. The Freedom of Association Committee has underlined, however, that in such cases where restrictions or prohibition are imposed, there should be adequate guarantees to safeguard the interests of workers who are thus deprived from an essential means of defending their occupational interests. These safeguards should take the form of adequate, impartial and speedy conciliation and arbitration proceedings in which the parties concerned can take part at every stage and in which the awards are binding in all cases on both parties. These awards should be fully and promptly implemented.

1. As regards provisions relating to the strike which can be found in other international instruments, see below No. 205 and No. 211.
2. See *Rep. Com. Exp.* 1973, Vol. 4B, Nos 107–114, pp. 44–47.
3. See *Digest of decisions of the Freedom of Association Committee*, quoted above under para. 123.

§3. The Right to Organize and Collective Bargaining Convention, 1949 (No. 98)

189. The Right to Organize and Collective Bargaining Convention, 1949 (No. 98), which has been ratified by 105 States, provides in the first place (Art. 1) that 'workers shall enjoy adequate protection against acts of anti-union discrimination in respect of their employment'.[1] This provision aims at protecting workers and trade union leaders against victimization by their employers both at the time of taking up employment and in the course of their employment relationship.

1. See more generally in this connection Bartolomei de la Cruz, *Protection against anti-union discrimination*, ILO, Geneva, 1976.

190. Thus the Convention specifies that such protection shall apply more particularly in respect of acts calculated to make the employment of a worker subject to the condition that he shall not join a union or shall relinquish trade union membership. In this connection, the question of the validity of union security arrangements, about which views differ considerably from one country to another, was raised but the Conference Committee which was discussing the draft of this instrument stated, in its report, that Convention No. 98 'could in no way be interpreted as authorizing or prohibiting union security arrangements, such questions being matters for regulation in accordance with national practice'.[1]

1. *Rec. Proc. Conf.* 32, 1949, p. 468.

191. The Convention also provides that the protection shall equally apply in respect of acts calculated to cause the dismissal of or otherwise prejudice a worker by reason of union membership or because of participation in union activities outside working hours or, with the consent of the employer, within working hours.

192. Another aim of the Convention is protection, primarily of trade unions, against acts of interference, although the matter is mentioned in respect of both workers' and employers' organizations. According to Art. 2, 'workers' and employers' organizations shall enjoy adequate protection against any acts of interference by each other or each other's agents or members in their establishment, functioning or administration'. In particular, acts designed to promote the establishment of workers' organizations under the domination of employers' organizations or to support workers' organizations by financial or other means, with the object of placing such organizations under the control of employers or employers' organizations are described as constituting such acts of interference.

193. To ensure respect for the above provisions, Art. 3 provides that machinery appropriate to national conditions shall be established where necessary.

194. Moreover, in order to create conditions for successful voluntary negotiation between employers and workers, it is provided, in Art. 4 of the Convention that 'measures appropriate to national conditions shall be taken, when necessary, to encourage and promote the full development and utilization of machinery for voluntary negotiation between employers or employers' organizations and workers' organizations, with a view to the regulation of terms and conditions of employment by means of collective agreements'.

195. Finally, as regards the scope of the Convention, the same formula is applied as in Convention No. 87 in relation to the armed forces and the police,[1] but the Convention also adds that it does not deal with the position of public servants engaged in the administration of the State and that it should not be construed as prejudicing their rights or status in any way.[2]

1. See No. 174 above.
2. As regards civil servants see No. 202 below.

§4. The Workers' Representatives Convention (No. 135) and Recommendation (No. 143) of 1971

196. Freedom of association cannot be fully implemented if it is not recognized at the plant level as well as at the national or occupational level. This explains the adoption, in 1971, of a Convention (No. 135)[1] and a Recommendation (No. 143) concerning the protection and the facilities to be afforded to workers' representatives in the undertaking. The *Convention* provides that workers' representatives[2] in the undertaking shall enjoy effective protection against any act prejudicial to them, including dismissal, based on their status or activities as a workers' representative or on union membership or participation in union activities, in so far as they act in conformity with existing laws or collective agreements or agreed arrangements. Appropriate facilities should also be afforded to workers' representatives in order to enable them to carry out their functions promptly and efficiently. The Convention contains some clauses of flexibility by stating that account should be taken of the characteristics of the industrial relations system of the country and the needs, size and capabilities of the undertaking concerned, that the granting of such facilities shall not impair the efficient operation of the undertaking concerned, and finally that effect may be given to the Convention through national laws or regulations or collective agreements, or in any other manner consistent with national practice.

1. This Convention has been ratified by 32 States.
2. The Convention defines the term 'workers' representatives' as meaning persons who are recognized as such under national law or practice, whether they are trade union representatives or elected representatives and adds that national laws or regulations, collective agreements, arbitration awards or court decisions may determine the type of workers' representatives which shall be entitled to the protection and facilities. Where there exist in the same undertaking both trade union representatives and elected representatives, measures shall be taken to ensure that the existence of the latter is not used to undermine the position of the trade unions concerned or their representatives and to encourage co-operation between the elected representatives and the trade unions concerned and their representatives.

197. The *Recommendation* lists the various measures which could be taken to ensure effective protection of workers' representatives, such as definition of the reasons justifying termination of their employment; requirement of consultation with, an advisory opinion from, or agreement of an independent body, public or private, or a joint body, before the dismissal becomes final; special recourse procedure open to workers' representatives who consider that their employment has been unjustifiably terminated, or that they have been subjected to an unfavourable change in their conditions of employment or to unfair treatment; provision for an effective remedy in respect of the unjustified termination of employment which, if possible under the law of the country concerned, should include reinstatement; provision for laying upon the employer, in the case of any alleged discriminatory dismissal or unfavourable change of the conditions of employment, the burden of proving that such action was justified; priority with regard to the retention in employment of workers' representatives in case of reduction of the work force. Such a protection should also apply to workers who are candidates for election as workers' representatives and to workers who have ceased to be workers' representatives. Persons who, upon termination of their mandate as workers' representatives in the undertaking in which they have been employed, resume work in that undertaking, should retain or have restored all their rights, including those related to the nature of their job, to wages and to seniority.

198. The Recommendation also lists the facilities to be afforded to workers' representatives. They should be afforded the necessary time off from work, without loss of pay or social and fringe benefits, for carrying out their representation function in the undertaking. They may be required to obtain permission from their supervisor before they take time off from work but such permission should not be unreasonably withheld. Reasonable limits may be set on the amount of time off. Workers' representatives should also be afforded the necessary time off for attending trade union meetings, training courses, seminars, congresses and conferences. Time off for that purpose should be afforded without loss of pay or social and fringe benefits, and the question of who should bear the resulting costs may be determined at the national level.

199. Workers' representatives should be granted access to all work places in the undertaking, where this is necessary to enable them to carry out their representation functions. They should be granted without undue delay access to the management of the undertaking and to management representatives empowered to take decisions, as may be necessary for the proper exercise of their functions. As regards trade union dues, workers' representatives authorized to do so by the trade union should be permitted to collect them regularly on the premises of the undertaking. Workers' representatives acting on behalf of a trade union should be authorized to post trade union notices on the premises of the undertaking in a place or places agreed on with the management and to which the workers have easy access. They should also be permitted to distribute news sheets, pamphlets, publications and other documents of the union among the workers of the undertaking. Such notices and documents should relate to normal trade union activities and their posting and distribution should not prejudice the orderly operation and tidiness of the undertaking. The management should make available to workers' representatives such material facilities and information as may be necessary for the exercise of their functions. Trade union representatives who are not employed in the undertaking but whose trade union has members employed in it should be granted access to the undertaking.

§5. The Rural Workers' Organizations Convention (No. 141) and Recommendation (No. 149) of 1975

200. A Convention and a Recommendation adopted in 1975 dealt more particularly with the right of all rural workers, whether they are wage earners or self-employed, to establish and join organizations of their own choosing without previous authorization. The *Convention*[1] provides that the principles of freedom of association shall be fully respected and reaffirms the main principles of Convention No. 87.[2] It adds that it shall be an objective of national policy concerning rural development to facilitate the establishment and growth, on a voluntary basis, of strong and independent organizations of rural workers as an effective means of ensuring the participation of rural workers, without discrimination, in economic and social development and in the benefits resulting from it. It provides, in particular, for the adoption and implementation by States of policies of active encouragement to these organizations, particularly with a view to eliminating obstacles to their establishment, their growth and the pursuit of their lawful activities.

1. This Convention has been ratified by 13 States.
2. See Nos. 172–187 above.

201. The *Recommendation* contains more detailed provisions about the role of organizations of rural workers and the various means of encouraging their growth. These means comprise legislative and administrative measures, public information, education and training and financial and material assistance.

§6. The Labour Relations (Public Service) Convention (No. 151) and Recommendation (No. 159) of 1978

202. In 1978, a Convention (No. 151) and a Recommendation (No. 159) on Labour Relations in the Public Service[1] dealt in particular with the right to organize of public employees. The provisions concerning the protection against acts of anti-union discrimination are analogous to those of the Right to Organize and Collective Bargaining Convention, 1949 (No. 98).[2] The Convention provides in particular 'that such protection shall apply more particularly in respect of acts calculated to (a) make the employment of public employees subject to the condition that they shall not join or shall relinquish membership of a public employees' organization; (b) cause the dismissal of or otherwise prejudice a public employee by reason of membership of a public employee's organization or because of participation in the normal activities of such organization'. The Convention also provides for complete independence of public employees' organizations from public authorities and from adequate protection against any acts of interference by a public authority in their establishment, functioning or administration, such as acts designed to promote the establishment of public employees' organizations under the domination of a public authority, or to support public employees' organizations by financial or other means, with the object of placing such organizations under the control of a public authority.[3] The Convention also deals with appropriate facilities which should be afforded to the representatives of recognized public employees' organizations to enable them to carry out their functions promptly and efficiently, both during and outside working hours. The granting of such facilities should not impair the efficient operation of the administration or service concerned. The Convention also deals with procedures for determining terms and conditions of employment and with the settlement of disputes (through negotiation between the parties, or through independent and impartial machinery, such as mediation, conciliation and arbitration, established in such a manner as to ensure the confidence of the parties involved). Finally, it provides that public employees shall have, as other workers, the civil and political rights which are essential for the normal exercise of freedom of association, subject only to the obligations arising from their status and the nature of their functions. The Recommendation which complements the Convention adds that the determination of the organizations to be granted the rights provided for under the Convention should be based on objective and pre-established criteria with regard to their representative character, that the procedures for recognition of public employees' organizations should not be such as to encourage the proliferation of organizations covering the same categories of employees. The Recommendation also deals with certain aspects of the procedures for determining terms and conditions of employment. As for the facilities to be afforded to representatives of public employees' organizations, it recommends that regard be had to the Workers' Representatives Recommendation, 1971 (No. 135).[4]

1. See No. 535 below.
2. See No. 190 above.
3. Compare No. 192 above.
4. See No. 197 above.

§7. Fields in which Additional Studies and Standards Have Been Contemplated

203. The 1970 resolution quoted above (No. 183) on trade union rights and their relation to civil liberties suggested that a further study should be made about a certain number of matters with a view to considering further action to ensure respect for trade union rights. It mentioned in particular the following questions: right of trade unions to excercise their activities in the undertaking and other work places; right of trade unions to negotiate wages and all other conditions of work; right of participation of trade unions in undertakings and in the general economy; right to strike; right to participate fully in national and international trade union activities; right to inviolability of trade union premises as well as of correspondence and telephonic conversations; right to protection of trade union funds and assets against intervention by the public authorities; right of trade unions to have access to media of mass communication; right to protection against any discrimination in matters of affiliation and trade union activities; right of access to voluntary conciliation and arbitration procedures; and finally right to workers' education and further training. Work has already been done on certain of these matters, as can be seen from the studies referred to above,[1] and even standards were adopted on the first of these subjects.[2] Further studies are being prepared.

1. See footnotes under Nos. 176, 180, 181 and 189.
2. See above Nos. 196 ss.

§8. Other International Standards

I. Universal Standards

204. In 1948, the *Universal Declaration of Human Rights* provided (Art. 23, § 4) that 'Everyone has the right to form and to join trade unions for the protection of his interests'.

205. A more detailed provision is to be found in the 1966 *International Covenant on Economic, Social and Cultural Rights*, that is Article 8 which provides that the State Parties to the Covenant 'undertake to ensure:

a. The right of everyone to form trade unions and join the trade union of his choice, subject only to the rules of the organization concerned, for the promotion and protection of his economic and social interests. No restrictions may be placed on the exercise of this right other than those prescribed by law and which are necessary in a democratic society in the interests of national security or public order or for the protection of the rights and freedoms of others;
b. The right of trade unions to establish national federations or confederations and the right of the latter to form or join international trade union organizations;
c. The right of trade unions to function freely subject to no limitations other than those prescribed by law and which are necessary in a democratic society in the interests of national security or public order or for the protection of the rights and freedoms of others;
d. The right to strike, provided that it is exercised in conformity with the laws of the particular country.

2. This article shall not prevent the imposition of lawful restrictions on the exercise of these rights by members of the armed forces or of the police or of the administration of the State.
3. Nothing in this article shall authorize States Parties to the International Labour Organization Convention of 1948 concerning Freedom of Association and Protection of the Right to Organize to take legislative measures which would prejudice, or apply the law in such a manner as would prejudice, the guarantees provided for in that Convention.'

This provision is not as detailed as Convention No. 87. Moreover, the restrictions which it authorizes might reduce considerably the extent of the protection which it affords. This applies to the limitations which, contrary to Convention No. 87, are permitted as regards the members of the administration of the State. This is also the case as regards the limitations 'which are necessary in a democratic society in the interests of national security or public order or for the protection of the rights and freedoms of others', for which there is no equivalent in Convention No. 87. However, the obligations arising from that Convention are expressly reserved by the saving clause contained in Art. 8, para. 3 of the Covenant. On the other hand, this Article recognizes the right to strike, but it leaves the conditions of its exercise to the discretion of national legislations.

206. The *International Covenant on Civil and Political Rights*, which was adopted at the same time as the other Covenant, also refers, in general terms, to the right to form trade unions, in the wider framework of freedom of association. Article 22, para. 1 of that Covenant provides that 'Everyone shall have the right to freedom of association, including the right to form and join trade unions for the protection of his interests'. In its paragraph 2, it contains a clause authorizing restrictions in terms similar, though not identical, to that contained in Art. 8, para. 1 (a), second sentence, of the Covenant on Economic, Social and Cultural Rights. The same provision also authorizes restrictions as regards the members of the armed forces and the police, but, contrary to the other Covenant, not of the administration of the State. From this point of view its scope is closer to that of Convention No. 87.

II. European Standards

207. Two instruments of the Council of Europe refer to trade union rights. The first is the *European Convention on Human Rights* of 1950. Article 11 of the European Convention is drafted in terms which are very similar to those which were used later in the International Covenant on Civil and Political Rights referred to in the previous paragraph: that is that the right of everyone 'to form and to join trade unions for the protection of his interests' is mentioned in general terms, in the framework of freedom of association in general, that the Convention authorizes the same type of restrictions 'which are necessary in a democratic society in the interests of national security or public safety, for the prevention of disorder or crime, for the protection of health or morals or for the protection of the rights and freedoms of others', and that the Convention also authorizes restrictions for the members of the armed forces and the police, but equally for members of the administration of the State, contrary to what was finally decided for the International Covenant on Civil and Political Rights.

208. The *European Social Charter* is more specific on the matter. Article 5 deals with the main point of the *right to organize*, though not in as precise a way as ILO Convention No. 87.[1] It provides that: 'With a view to ensuring or promoting the freedom of workers and employers to form local, national or international organizations for the protection of their economic and social interests and to join those organizations, the Contracting Parties undertake that national law shall not be such as to impair, nor shall it be so applied as to impair, this freedom.'

1. See Valticos, 'La Charte sociale européenne', *Droit social*, Sept.-Oct. 1963. p. 471, and 'The European Social Charter and International Labour Standards', *I.L.R.*, Nov. 1961, pp. 363–364.

209. There was some controversy about the exceptions provided by the

Charter. The initial draft provided for exceptions as regards armed forces and the police, as in the case of ILO Convention No. 87,[1] but also included the administration of the State. Following comments by the Tripartite Conference and the Consultative Assembly,[2] the reference to possible exceptions in respect of officials and employees of the State administration was deleted. Moreover the provision about the remaining two possible exceptions was worded in different terms for either case. The final text now reads as follows: 'The extent to which the guarantees provided for in this Article shall apply to the police shall be determined by national laws or regulations. The principle governing the application to the members of the armed forces of these guarantees and the extent to which they shall apply to persons in this category shall equally be determined by national laws or regulations.' The Committee of Experts appointed under the Charter concluded from this wording that the Charter permits a State to limit in any way and even to suppress entirely the freedom to organize of members of the armed forces. On the other hand, a State is only permitted to limit the freedom of organization of the members of the police, but is not justified in depriving them of all the guarantees provided for in the Article.[3] From that point of view the Charter went further than the similar provision in Convention No. 87.

1. See above No. 174.
2. See above No. 153.
3. See Council of Europe, Committee of Independent Experts on the European Social Charter, *Conclusions I*, Strasbourg, 1969–1970, p. 31.

210. Article 6 of the Charter relates to the *right to bargain collectively* and its first provision contain the undertaking by Contracting Parties:
'1. to promote joint consultation between workers and employers;
2. to promote, where necessary and appropriate, machinery for voluntary negotiation between employers or employers' organizations and workers' organizations, with a view to the regulation of terms and conditions of employment by means of collective agreements;
3. to promote the establishment and use of appropriate machinery for conciliation and voluntary arbitration for the settlement of labour disputes.'

211. The most original feature of the Charter is that it was the first international instrument which dealt expressly with the *right to strike*. In accordance with a proposal by the Tripartite Conference,[1] followed by the Consultative Assembly, Article 6, para. 4 of the Charter provides for the recognition of 'the right of workers and employers to collective action in cases of conflicts of interest, including the right to strike, subject to obligations that might arise out of collective agreements previously entered into'. An Appendix to the Charter also adds an understanding that each Contracting Party may 'regulate the exercise of the right to strike by law, provided that any further restrictions that this might place on the right can be justified under the terms of Article 31'. Article 31 relates to restrictions 'necessary in a democratic society for the protection of the rights and freedoms of others or for the protection of public interest, national security, public health, or morals'. While the Charter did not specify whether the recognition of the right to strike means that a strike should not be considered as implying the breach of the contract of employment, the Committee of Experts appointed under the Charter considered that a national rule according to which a strike terminates the contract of employment is not compatible with the respect for the right to strike as envisaged by the Charter.[2]

1. For more details about the discussions in the Tripartite Conference, see 'The European Social Charter and International Labour Standards' quoted above, pp. 364–365.
2. *Conclusions I*, quoted above, p. 39.

212. At the time of the framing of the Charter, a question arose in connection with Article 1, para. 2 which referred to the right of the worker 'to earn his living in an occupation freely entered upon'. The question related to the fact that, as stated above,[1] some countries authorize the so-called trade union security clauses or practices, under which employment in certain occupations may be restricted to workers belonging to a particular trade union, while in other countries such clauses or practices are illegal. The solution followed in this case was similar to that applied by the ILO when Convention No. 98 was adopted.[2] The Appendix to the Charter contains a provision to the effect that Article 1, para. 2 'shall not be interpreted as prohibiting or authorizing union security clause or practice'.

§9. Bilateral Treaties

213. Bilateral treaties sometimes contain clauses which assimilate the nationals of the two Contracting Parties as regards, in particular, various trade union functions which generally are reserved to nationals.

1. See above No. 190.
2. *Op. loc. cit.*

Chapter II. Forced Labour

§1. General Outline

214. While the first international action relating to slavery dates back to the beginning of the 19th century, with the Congress of Vienna, forced labour questions as such were taken up systematically only after the First World War. The international regulation of forced labour followed upon the work of the League of Nations on Mandated Territories and the adoption of the 1926 Slavery Convention. In that year the ILO Governing Body appointed a Committee of Experts on Native Labour whose first task was the study of the systems of forced or compulsory labour existing at that time, especially in countries which were not self-governing. Its work led to the adoption in 1930 of the Forced Labour Convention (No. 29) and two complementary Recommendations (Nos. 35 and 36). While of general application, the Convention related mainly to forms of forced labour which were practised for economic purposes in countries which were under colonial administration and in certain independent States at a similar stage of development. After the Second World War, attention was drawn to systems of forced labour also used as a means of political coercion. The United Nations created therefore, in conjunction with the ILO, an *Ad hoc* Committee of Forced Labour, which was entrusted with carrying out an inquiry into allegations relating to the existence of certain forms of forced labour. The inquiries carried out in 1951–1953 by this Committee and, from 1956 to 1959, by an ILO Committee on Forced Labour revealed the existence in the world of systems of forced labour of a serious nature as a means of political coercion or for economic purposes. They paved the way for the adoption, in 1957, by the International Labour Conference, of a new Convention, the Abolition of Forced Labour Convention (No. 105). The 1930 and 1957 Conventions have been ratified by a very large number of States but their application has given rise to important problems. In relation with some of these problems a Recommendation was adopted in 1970 about Special Youth Schemes. Provisions prohibiting forced labour are also contained in other instruments such as the Employment Policy Convention, 1964 (No. 122) in virtue of which States should formulate and apply an active policy aimed at promoting full productive and *freely chosen*, employment. However, the present chapter will be focused on the Conventions which deal specifically with this matter.

§2. The Forced Labour Convention, 1930 (No. 29)

215. This Convention is the ILO instrument which has obtained the greatest number of ratifications, i.e. 119. It is, moreover, applicable to 35 non-metropolitan territories.[1] Convention No. 29 provided for the progressive suppression of forced labour and, pending its suppression, its use only for public purposes and as an exceptional measure, subject to the conditions and guarantees set forth in detail in the various Articles of the Convention. Forced labour is defined as 'all work or service which is exacted from any person under the menace of any penalty and for which the said person has not offered himself voluntarily'. Certain obligations are not included in the definition of forced labour, such as compulsory military service in the case of 'work of a purely military character', 'normal civic obligations', prison labour (to the extent that it is exacted as a consequence of a conviction in a court of law and provided that the work or service is carried out under the supervision and control of a public authority and that the person is not hired to or placed at the disposal of private individuals, companies or associations), work in cases of 'force majeure' and minor communal services. The Convention provides for the progressive abolition of forced or compulsory labour exacted as a tax and forced and compulsory labour to which recourse is had for the execution of public works by chiefs who exercise administrative functions. It calls for the immediate abolition of forced labour in certain instances: women, men under 18 and over 45 years of age, disabled persons; work for the benefit of private individuals or associations; work underground in mines; work for public purposes which is not of present or imminent necessity and is not a precaution against famine or a deficiency of food supplies; work used as a method of collective punishment. It is forbidden to give persons who do not exercise administrative functions the power to exact forced labour. In all other cases, recourse to forced labour may be authorized provided that the work is of important direct interest for the community called upon to do the work, that the work is of present or imminent necessity, only for public purposes and as an exceptional measure, and subject to certain guarantees designed to protect the health, safety and welfare of the workers involved and ensure the continuance of normal family life and social relationships. Finally various measures must be taken to ensure the effective application of the standards established by the Convention (detailed regulations, complaints procedures, penalties in the event of the illegal exaction of forced labour). It should be added that few countries are now in a position to avail themselves of the transitional provisions of the Convention.

1. The Convention had previously been declared applicable to a much greater number of territories, which have since become independent and in most cases Members of the ILO. In such cases the countries concerned have, as a rule, confirmed the obligations undertaken on their behalf and the declaration was replaced by a ratification (see below No. 582). In certain cases, the States concerned have cancelled modifications subject to which the declarations had been made.

§3. The Abolition of Forced Labour Convention, 1957 (No. 105)

216. The Abolition of Forced Labour Convention, 1957 (No. 105) has been ratified by 102 States and declared applicable to 35 territories. It is couched in general terms and calls for the immediate and complete abolition of any form of forced labour for the following five purposes:

1. as a means of political coercion or education or as a punishment for holding or expressing political views or views ideologically opposed to the established political, social or economic system;
2. as a method of mobilizing and using labour for purposes of economic development;
3. as a means of labour discipline;
4. as a punishment for having participated in strikes;
5. as a means of racial, social, national or religious discrimination.

The general character of the terms of this Convention given rise to certain questions relating to its legal scope. The Committee of Experts on the Application of Conventions and Recommendations has considered that, 'in referring to the use of "any form" of forced labour in the five cases which it listed, the Convention prohibits, in these cases, forced labour resulting from a conviction in a court of law as well as other forms of forced labour'.[1] Apart from this legal question, the application of both Conventions has also given rise to serious problems of substance.

1. See *Rep. Com. Exp*. 1962, pp. 194–195, para. 8–10; *ibid*, 1968, pp. 213–215, para. 83–88, and also pp. 182–183, para. 17–18 (for the contrary view).

§4. Problems of Application of the Forced Labour Conventions

217. The problems of application of the forced labour Conventions have varied according to the periods and the countries. They have been often described and discussed.[1] Initially they were mainly related to problems of labour exacted for economic purposes. More recently difficulties have been experienced in relation with various types of youth services. The application of the provision of the 1957 Convention which prohibit forced labour as a means of political coercion or as a punishment for holding or expressing certain political views has also raised serious questions.

1. See the general surveys made by the Committee of Experts on the Application of Conventions and Recommendations in 1962 and in 1968, and the discussion of the main problems at the International Labour Conference in 1968 *Rec. Proc. Conf.*, 52, 1968, pp. 589–593, paras. 42–60). A new survey will be made by the Committee of Experts in 1979.

I. The Problems of Forced Labour for Economic Purposes

218. When the first forced labour Convention was adopted, in 1930, the principal aim of this instrument was to fight against the forms of forced labour for economic purposes which were practised in colonial territories in order to obtain labour which was not forthcoming spontaneously and this was done within a system of administration which relied to a great extent on traditional tribal relationships. Since that time, radical changes have taken place. Most of the colonial countries have attained independence since the early sixties. The problems of the newly independent States and the changed conditions of the labour market substantially altered the position. While one still finds pieces of legislation providing for compulsory mobilization of labour which are remnants of the past, the situation is no longer characterized by reluctance of populations to offer their services for wage-earning services. On the contrary, most of these countries are faced with problems of rural exodus and therefore of finding employment for large numbers of work-seekers, particularly the young. Certain governments have resorted to various measures of a compulsory character in order to rapidly eliminate the resulting difficulties. Thus many have referred to the needs of economic development to explain legislative measures which gave them wide powers of compulsory assignment or requisition of labour. Such measures, which were not compatible with the ILO Conventions, gave rise to objections by the supervisory bodies of the ILO. The governments concerned often replied by stating that in fact these measures were not applied in practice, and added that they intended to change the legislation in question with a view to bringing it into conformity with the Conventions. More generally, the kind of problems which some governments thought it possible to resolve by authoritarian measures are signs of an imbalance in the utilization of a nation's manpower and the remedy may lie in an over-all employment policy.[1] In any event, in recent years, progress has been achieved in several developing countries in the elimination of legislation providing for compulsory labour for economic purposes.

1. *Rep. Com. Exp.* 1968, p. 237, para. 139.

II. The Various Youth Services

219. While linked to a certain extent with the previous one, a special problem arose with the establishment of various formulae of mobilization of youth which were introduced in particular in newly independent countries. At one stage, a trend was noted to provide for compulsory participation to youth services – or analogous services – created in a number of countries. It should be noted in this connection that when Convention No. 29 was adopted in 1930, it had prohibited, after serious differences of views in the Conference, the use of persons performing compulsory military service for work which will not be of a purely military character. More recently, various forms of national service have been instituted parallel to military service. Thus there may be cases where conscripts in the armed forces can be employed for non-military purposes, as well as cases of national service in units distinct from the army, and cases of service required in relation to or on completion of studies.

220. The objective of such systems was not always of a purely economic character. Frequently they were also designed to promote education and vocational training, thus providing qualifications which would facilitate the future resettlement of those concerned and serve the economy of the countries; they also aimed at allowing unoccupied people to escape unemployment, giving them habits of work, and promoting the creation of productive employment; they also sought to ensure to the entire population the services of young graduates and specialists which it needed. Governments have sometimes felt that some forms of compulsion as regards the participation in such systems were necessary, as transitory or exceptional measures, in order to contribute to a more rapid start of the development of the country. While these various reasons could be understood, emphasis was also put on the risk of abuse which such compulsory measures involved, on the danger that they would progressively lose their transitory and exceptional character and on the fact that, even in terms of efficiency, compulsory schemes could finally prove more costly and less efficient than voluntary schemes.[1]

1. See *The ILO and Human Rights*, Rep. D.-G. to the 52nd Session of the I.L.C., Geneva, 1968, pp. 42–45.

221. These problems, which were relatively new, raised serious difficulties as regards the application of the Forced Labour Conventions.[1] They also called for a more accurate assessment of the objectives pursued by the legislation which introduced the various schemes in question and of the real conditions in which they functioned. The ILO was thus led to undertake special research on these different types of schemes.[2]

1. See *Rep. Comm. Exp.* 1968, pp. 203–208, paras. 63–69, *Rep. Conf. Com.* 1968, pp. 591–592, paras. 51–54.
2. See studies published in the *I.L.R.* in January 1966, May 1966 and, in the issue of April 1967 (pp. 315–326), a general article on the matter by C. Rossillion: 'Youth Services for Economic and Social Development: a General Review'.

222. In view of the importance of the problem, the Conference adopted in

1970 a *Recommendation (No. 136) concerning youth employment and training schemes for development purposes.* The first discussion, in 1969, was long and at times heated. The workers members, as well as a number of governments were opposed to any formula according to which participation in work would not be voluntary, while other governments, and in particular a number of African governments, considered that it could be necessary to provide for the compulsory character of certain programmes, either because of their educational nature or because of the needs of development. Finally a compromise formula was adopted, following a rather close vote. The representatives of a number of African governments expressed reservations about the formula which was adopted, as they considered it to be too rigid and restrictive. While stating that their 'primary interest is in voluntary participation in the schemes' and that they 'are by no means asking for a blank cheque in order to embark on getting cheap and forced labour through the back door', they expressed the desire to provide a safety valve that would permit an element of compulsion in operating special youth schemes, which would be used only in exceptional circumstances when national interests were at stake and required it.[1] On the other hand, the workers' representatives stated that they were not convinced of the need for compulsory participation and believed that 'compulsory schemes can only lead to exploitation and to political and military coercion'.[2]

1. *Rec. Proc. Conf.*, 53, 1969, p. 449.
2. *Op. cit.*, p. 450.

223. The final text of the Recommendation provides as a general principle (para. 7) that 'participation in special schemes should be voluntary; exceptions may be permitted only by legislative action and where there is full compliance with the terms of existing international labour Conventions on forced labour and employment policy'. It states more specifically that 'schemes in respect of which exceptions may be permitted may include:

a. schemes of education and training involving obligatory enrolment of unemployed young people within a definite period after the age limit of regular school attendance;
b. schemes for young people who have previously accepted an obligation to serve for a definite period as a condition of being enabled to acquire education or technical qualifications of special value to the community for development'.

The Recommendation also suggests that 'where such exceptions are so permitted, participants should, to the greatest possible extent, be given a free choice among different available forms of activity and different regions within the country and due account should be taken in their assignment of their qualifications and aptitudes'. Although no comprehensive survey of the situation regarding special youth schemes has been made, schemes involving compulsory participation appear to be now in operation only to a limited extent.

III. The Problems of Forced Labour for Political Purposes

224. Another aspect of the questions dealt with in the 1957 Convention (No. 105) relates to forced labour *for political purposes*. The difficulties encountered in this field arise mainly from the imposition of penal labour on persons sentenced as a result of certain acts or activities, such as expression of opinions, etc. In a number of countries, the legislation contains penal provisions of a wide scope which might permit the imposition of sanctions involving an obligation to work as a measure of political coercion or as a punishment for persons who hold or express certain views. Some of these provisions prohibit the expression of any opposition of a political or ideological character to the established system, while others relate to given ideological doctrines or tendencies. Problems may also arise from the large discretionary powers of preventive control, not subject to judicial appeal, which the legislation of certain countries has granted to the executive or various administrative authorities and by virtue of which individuals may find themselves exposed to the application of penal sanctions involving compulsory labour as a means of political coercion or as a punishment for expressing views. Extensive or unduly prolonged recourse to emergency powers or suspension of constitutional guarantees may result in a similar possibility. In all cases where limitations on freedom of expression and related rights are enforced by sanctions involving liability to penal labour, it becomes necessary to examine to what extent these limitations are legitimate safeguards in a democratic society or on the contrary must be considered an undue impairment of the rights and freedoms in question.[1]

1. See *Rep. Com. Exp*. 1968, pp. 238–240, paras. 140–146.

IV. The Problems of Forced Labour as a Means of Labour Discipline

225. Convention No. 105 prohibits forced or compulsory labour *as a means of labour discipline*. Provisions applicable to workers generally which permit this type of compulsory labour – that is to ensure the performance by a worker of his service under compulsion of law or as a punishment for breaches of labour discipline – are now found in some countries only, but there is still a rather great number of provisions on labour discipline in the public service and as regards seafarers. In this field it is necessary to take account of the need to protect the general public interest, but only to the extent that there may exist an effective danger, not mere inconvenience, and provided the workers concerned remain free to terminate their employment by reasonable notice.

226. While Convention No. 105 prohibits forced labour 'as a punishment for having participated in *strikes*', the reports of the Conference Committee which considered the draft Convention indicated agreement that 'in certain circumstances penalties could be imposed for participation in illegal strikes and that these penalties might include normal prison labour'.[1] It therefore appeared to the supervisory bodies[2] not incompatible with the Convention to impose penalties for participation in strikes in essential services, provided that compensatory guarantees in the form of appropriate alternative procedures for the settlement of disputes are granted. Procedural requirements – such as previous notice – may also be imposed, or the right to resort to strike action may be suspended during conciliation and arbitration proceedings. The procedures should, however, be adequate, impartial and speedy. Such temporary restrictions must be distinguished from systems of compulsory arbitration. Where the penalties take the form of civil sanctions (such as damages or dismissal), the Convention can have no application.

1. See *Rec. Proc. Conf.*, 40 1957, p. 709, para. 14.
2. *Rep. Com. Exp.* 1968, pp. 217–218, paras. 94–99.

227. Convention No. 105 also prohibits forced or compulsory labour 'as a means of racial, social, national or religious discrimination'. Such instances are now few, as there is a growing body of constitutional and legislative guarantees of equality of citizens. There are still, however, some cases of punishment involving an obligation to perform labour for non-observance of laws affecting certain persons defined in terms of their race or social group.

228. In a general way, resort to forced or compulsory labour for political or social purposes can be the reflexion of problems which present themselves in countries which undergo rapid change and development. More generally certain limitations may be imposed on the rights of individual in the wider interest of society. However, within these limits, the individual must be protected against any compulsion in his work and any coercion through forced or compulsory labour in industrial relations and in the exercise of his rights as a citizen. 'The concept of freedom here involved is not a negative one, but presupposes the development of opportunities for all to participate fully and responsibly in the economic, social and political life of their community.'[1]

1. See *Rep. Com. Exp.* 1968, p. 240, para. 146.

§5. Other International Standards

229. The Universal Declaration of Human Rights, which, as the International Covenant on Civil and Political Rights was also to do, established that 'No one shall be held in slavery or servitude' (Art. 4), also affirmed that 'everyone has the right . . . to free choice of employment' (Art. 23). The *International Covenant on Economic, Social and Cultural Rights* also provided for the recognition, as part of the right to work, of 'the right of everyone to the opportunity to gain his living by work which he freely chooses or accepts' and prescribed that the State Parties to the Convention 'will take appropriate steps to safeguard this right' (Art. 6, para. 1). The *International Covenant on Civil and Political Rights* refers to forced labour in greater detail. After laying down (Art. 8, para. 3)

a. that 'No one shall be required to perform forced or compulsory labour', it gives certain definitions of forced labour in the following terms:
b. Para. 3(a) shall not be held to preclude, in countries where imprisonment with hard labour may be imposed as a punishment for a crime, the perfor-

mance of hard labour in pursuance of a sentence to such punishment by a competent court;

c. For the purpose of this paragraph, the term 'forced or compulsory labour' shall not include:
   i) Any work or service, not referred to in sub-paragraph b), required of a person who is under detention in consequence of a lawful order of a court, or of a person during conditional release from such detention;
   ii) Any service of a military character and, in countries where conscientious objection is recognized, any national service required by law of conscientious objectors;
   iii) Any service exacted in cases of emergency or calamity threatening the life or well-being of the community;
   iv) Any work or service which forms part of normal civil obligations.'

230. The above provisions which they follow closely the wording of the European Convention on Human Rights and, to a certain extent, that of the 1930 Convention give a wider latitude than the ILO standards.[1]

1. See *Comparative Analysis of the International Covenants on Human Rights and International Labour Conventions and Recommendations*, ILO, *O.B.*, vol. LII, 1969, No. 2, pp. 181–216.

231. At the regional level, the 1950 European Convention on Human Rights also prohibits forced labour (Art. 4, paras. 2 and 3) in terms similar, to a large extent, to those which were to be used later in the International Covenant on Civil and Political Rights.[1] As these provisions are, to a certain extent, less precise than the 1930 ILO Convention, the European Commission of Human Rights has decided some cases submitted to it, in a less strict manner than if they had had to be considered in the light of the ILO standards.

1. Article 4, paras. 2 and 3 of the European Convention reads as follows:
'2. No one shall be required to perform forced or compulsory labour.
3. For the purpose of this Article, the term "forced or compulsory labour" shall not include: a. any work required to be done in the ordinary course of detention imposed according to the provisions of Article 5 of this Convention (relating to the right to liberty and security of the person) or during conditional release from such detention; b. any service of a military character or, in case of conscientious objectors in countries where they are recognized, service exacted instead of compulsory military service; c. any service exacted in case of an emergency or calamity threatening the life or well-being of the community; d. any work or service which forms part of normal civic obligations.'

232. The *American Convention on Human Rights*, signed in November 1969, contains provisions which follow closely those of the European Convention, with some differences, the most important of which is that it contains an additional guarantee using the wording of ILO 1930 Forced Labour Convention (No. 29), to the effect that any work or service exacted from a person as a consequence of a conviction in a court of law must be carried out under the supervision and control of a public authority and that the said person shall not be hired or put at the disposal of private individuals, companies or associations.

233. As regards the *European Social Charter*, Article 1, para. 2 states that the Contracting Parties undertake 'to protect effectively the right of the worker to earn his living in an occupation freely entered upon'.

Chapter III. Discrimination in Employment

§1. General Outline

234. The freedom of choice of employment, which the forced labour Conventions aim at ensuring, would often be meaningless if individuals were subjected to discrimination which would limit their opportunities for finding employment or which would put them at a disadvantage in respect of conditions of employment. Discrimination in itself has a humiliating character, and is incompatible with human dignity. At the national level discrimination increases the tensions between various groups of which it already is an indication. Internationally, the bad relations between populations of different racial or ethnic origin or of different religious or cultural or linguistic traditions are among the most serious threats to world peace. In this field ILO standards have a double aim: to eliminate inequality of treatment and to promote equality of opportunity.

235. At the level of its constitutional instruments, the ILO established the principle of non-discrimination in the Declaration of Philadelphia, adopted in 1944 and incorporated in its Constitution. As said above,[1] this Declaration affirms in this connection that 'all human beings, irrespective of race, creed or sex, have the right to pursue both their material well-being and their spiritual development in conditions of freedom and dignity, of economic security and equal opportunity'. We shall see soon[2] that direct legal consequences followed from this provision as regards the action of the ILO in the field of apartheid.

1. See above No. 5.
2. See below Nos. 259–261.

236. At the level of the standards contained in its Conventions, the question of discrimination was initially considered in a somewhat fragmentary way and from different points of view until it was dealt with as an overall problem. Thus the first Conventions in this field aimed at protecting special groups of workers against particularly serious types of discrimination: this was the case for women, foreigners, migrant workers, rural workers, workers in non-metropolitan territories, indigenous and tribal populations, plantations workers, etc. In other cases international standards protected all workers against certain forms of discrimination e.g. in the fields of employment service, and more generally employment, abolition of forced labour, vocational training, remuneration, social security, dismissal etc. The standards adopted in these different fields are explained in the relevant chapters of this study. In some instruments with a wider scope, the protection of various categories of workers is ensured by the generality of the terms used. As was said about the 1948 Freedom of Association Convention, a provision relating to workers and employers 'without distinction whatsoever' clearly aimed at prohibiting any possible discrimination in this field. It has been also said that the 1957 Abolition of Forced Labour Convention prohibits the resort to forced labour 'as means of racial, social, national or religious discrimination'.

237. The principle of non-discrimination was expressed in a more general way in a 1947 Convention (No. 82) which related to social policy in non-metropolitan territories and which provided (Art. 18) for the abolition of 'all discrimination among workers on grounds of race, colour, sex, belief, tribal association or trade union affiliation', and this in a wide range of fields and in particular in respect of labour legislation, admission to employment, vocational training, conditions of work, collective bargaining and wage rates. This Convention was revised in 1962 with a view to making the continued application and ratification of the new instrument (Convention No. 117) possible for independent States.[1]

1. As regards these Conventions, see below Nos. 409–412.

238. Following a resolution of the Economic and Social Council of the United Nations[1] in order to complete these various instruments by means of a set of comprehensive standards, the ILO adopted in 1958 a Convention and a Recommendation concerning Discrimination in Employment and Occupation (No. 111). These two instruments are the basic instruments in this field.[2]

1. Resolution 545 C(XVIII) of 29 July 1954 inviting the ILO to undertake the study of discrimination measures in the field of employment and occupation.
2. For the various instruments adopted by the ILO in this field, see *Discrimination in Employment and Occupation: Standards and Policy Statements Adopted under the Auspices of the ILO*, ILO, 1967.

239. The policy of *apartheid* of the Government of South Africa also gave rise to very acute problems.

240. Finally, as discrimination in employment and occupation are a particular aspect of the more general phenomenon of discrimination, mention should also be made in this context of the instruments adopted in this connection by the United Nations and by UNESCO, as well as at the European level.

§2. The Discrimination (Employment and Occupation) Convention and Recommendation, 1958 (No. 111)[1]

241. The Discrimination (Employment and Occupation) Convention, 1958 (No. 111) has been ratified by 96 States.

1. See in this connection the general surveys prepared in 1963 and in 1971 by the Committee of Experts for the Application of Conventions and Recommendations. See also *Fighting Discrimination in Employment and Occupation (A Workers' Education Manual)*, ILO, 1968. As regards national legislation and procedures in this field, see *Equality in respect of Employment under Legislation and other National Standards,* ILO, 1967, and *Special national procedures concerning non-discrimination in employment – A practical guide*, ILO, 1975.

I. Definition of the Term 'Discrimination'

242. The Convention defines the term 'discrimination' as including 'any distinction, exclusion or preference made on the basis of race, colour, sex, religion, political opinion, national extraction or social origin, which has the effect of nullifying or impairing equality of opportunity or treatment in employment or occupation'.

243. The term 'race' cannot be given a very precise scientific definition, the essential point being the way in which the persons concerned consider their differences, and the attitudes resulting therefrom in their relations with one another. Discrimination on account of race or colour stems, as a rule, from prejudice, but it is often also the result of differences in the degree of social and economic advancement and may be complicated by conflicts of economic and sometimes political interests.

244. Discrimination on grounds of *sex* seems to be the most frequent obstacle met by countries in connection with the ratification of the Convention. The difficulties relate both to access by women to employment and to conditions of employment, and in particular to equal remuneration.[1]

1. See in this connection below, Nos. 455 ss.

245. The term 'national extraction' does not refer to the position of persons of foreign nationality as such, which is dealt with by other standards,[1] but to distinctions made in a country between nationals of that country on the ground of foreign ancestry or foreign birth.[2] Consequently it includes discrimination against persons who have acquired the nationality of the country concerned through naturalization, or are descended from foreign immigrants, or belong to groups of different national extraction living together in the same State.

1. See below Nos. 537 ss.
2. See *Rec. Proc. Conf.*, 42, 1958, p. 710; and *Memorandum* of the ILO in reply to a request from the Government of Tunisia, *O.B.* vol. XLII, 1959, No. 7, pp. 395–397; *Rep. Com. Exp.* 1963, pp. 183–184, paras. 27–28.

246. The problem of discrimination on the basis of 'social origin' arises in an extreme form where society is divided into classes or 'castes', the members of which cannot have access to certain categories of employment. In societies in which such rigid classifications have disappeared, prejudice or privilege based on social origin may arise if steps are not taken to offer to certain classes of society the same opportunities for training and opportunities to move up the occupational ladder as are available to others. Social origin may also be considered as presumptive evidence of certain political opinions which work either to the advantage or disadvantage of the persons concerned.

247. While referring specifically to the various grounds for which it prohibits discrimination, the Convention adds that the term 'discrimination' also includes 'such other distinction, exclusion or preference which has the effect of nullifying or impairing equality of opportunity or treatment in employment or occupation as may be determined by the Member concerned after consultation with representative employers' and workers' organizations, where such exist, and with other appropriate bodies'. The other grounds of discrimination to which attention has been given in certain countries include language, age, disablement and membership or non-membership of a trade union. Other ILO instruments also refer to additional grounds of discrimination, such as marital status.[1] This is the case in the Termination of Employment Recommendation, 1963 (No. 119) which provides that marital status should not constitute a valid reason for termination of employment, as sometimes happens in the case of married women.

1. This is the case for the Termination of Employment Recommendation, 1963 (No. 119), which provides that marital status, *inter alia*, should not constitute valid reason for termination of employment.

248. It should also be noted that the discriminatory situations to which the Convention refers are those which have their origin, not only in law, but also – as this happens very frequently – in practice. Moreover, the Convention does not cover only the provisions or practices whose stated aim is to establish or maintain discrimination, but also those cases where discriminatory situations have been the objective consequences of provisions intended to be applicable to all. This results from the generality of the terms of the Convention, which relates the term of discrimination to distinctions, exclusions or preferences which have the effect of nullifying or impairing equality of opportunity or treatment.

II. Measures which are not Deemed to be Discrimination

249. There are certain distinctions, exclusions or preferences which are not deemed to be discrimination. The Convention refers to those which are based on the inherent requirements of a particular job, those which relate to activities prejudicial to the security of the State and those which constitute special measures of protection or assistance.

250. The Convention states, in the first place (Art. 1, para. 2) that 'any distinction, exclusion or preference in respect of a particular job based on the inherent requirements thereof shall not be deemed to be discrimination'. In this connection distinctions based on sex for certain jobs requiring a high degree of physical effort were considered as coming under this heading (as well as under that of special measures of protection). However, it would be incompatible with the Convention to exclude women from certain responsible positions, for example in the civil service, or to take into account political opinions for appointments in the civil service, apart from certain senior administrative posts involving special responsibility in the implementation of government policy. As regards national extraction, certain temporary restrictions concerning access by recently naturalized persons to certain official posts are found in the legislation of certain countries and it was felt that 'the desire for assurance as to the durability and finality of the person's attachment to his new nationality' could be taken into account in this connection.[1]

1. See *Rep. Com. Exp.* 1963, pp. 191–192, paras. 41–43.

251. A second category of measures which the Convention (Art. 4) does not deem to be discrimination are those 'affecting an individual who is justifiably suspected of, or engaged in activities prejudicial to the security of the State, provided that the individual concerned shall have the right to appeal to a competent body established in accordance with national practice'. The purpose of this provision is to safeguard the security of the State, while affording certain guarantees to the persons concerned. Its first requirement is that there should be individual activities (or a strong presumption of such activities) which are prejudicial to the security of the State. Measures taken merely as a result of membership of a particular group or community would therefore have a discriminatory character. Secondly, there should be a right of appeal, and this presupposes that there should be a 'body' to which appeals can be made, which should be independent from administrative or governmental authority, hierarchically above the authority which took the measure, offering guarantees of independence and impartiality, in a position to ascertain the reasons underlying the measure taken and giving the appellant facilities for fully presenting his case.[1]

1. See *Rep. Com. Exp.* 1963, pp. 193–194, paras. 47–49.

252. A third category of measures which are not deemed to be discrimination are 'special measures of protection or assistance provided for in other Conventions or Recommendations adopted by the International Labour Conference' (Art. 5). This provision mainly relates to the standards concerning the employment of women or indigenous populations. It is also provided that any Member State may, after consultation with representative employers' and workers' organizations, 'determine that other special measures designed to meet the particular requirements of persons who, for reasons such as sex, age, disablement, family responsibilities or social or cultural status, are generally recognized to require special protection or assistance, shall not be deemed to be discrimination'. In relation to measures of this kind the question has arisen as to whether distinctions or preferences resulting from arrangements made in countries comprising heterogeneous population groups may be considered to be part of a policy promoting equality of opportunity and treatment. There are, for example, measures which provide that a certain number of posts should be filled by members of special categories of the population, previously placed on footing of inferiority, in order to further their employment prospects and social advancement. It was felt that arrangements of this kind may be considered as not constituting discrimination if their effect is to secure an equilibrium between the different communities and ensure protection of minorities, or to compensate for discrimination against the economically less advanced population group. The compatibility of such measures with the Convention depends greatly on the factual situation which would justify them and from their application in practice.[1]

1. See *Rep. Com. Exp.* 1963, pp. 189–191, para. 39.

III. Individuals and Fields Covered

253. The Discrimination Convention and Recommendation refer to employment and occupation in a general way, and they contain no provision limiting their scope, as regards either individuals or occupations. They cover all human beings and all sectors of activity, public service or private employment, independent workers as well as wage-earners or salaried employees. The two instruments provide expressly that 'the terms "employment" and "occupation" include access to vocational training, access to employment and to particular occupations, and terms and conditions of employment'. According to the more specific provisions of the Recommendation (para. 2b) all persons should enjoy equality of opportunity and treatment in respect of the following fields:

i) access to vocational guidance and placement services;
ii) access to training and employment of their own choice on the basis of individual suitability for such training or employment;
iii) advancement in accordance with their individual character, experience, ability and diligence;
iv) security of tenure of employment;
v) remuneration for work of equal value;
vi) conditions of work including hours of work, rest periods, annual holidays with pay, occupational safety and occupational health measures, as well as social security measured and welfare facilities and benefits provided in connection with employment.

It is added in the Recommendation (para. 1f) that 'employers' and workers' organizations should not practise or countenance discrimination in respect of admission, retention of membership or participation in their affairs'.

IV. Action Designed to Eliminate Discrimination

254. The Convention and the Recommendation describe in general terms the action designed to eliminate discrimination and emphasize more the objectives to be attained than the means to be used to that effect. The first undertaking of States Parties to the Convention (Art. 2) is to declare a national policy designed to promote equality of opportunity and treatment in respect of employment and occupation. Secondly, the obligation of States Parties is to pursue such policy. However, the Convention provides that the implementation of this policy must be made 'by methods appropriate to national conditions and practice'. It does not therefore require that a given method be resorted to or that all discrimination be immediately eliminated. The objective of the national policy should certainly be to eliminate all the types of discrimination referred to by the Convention, but the latter leaves it to the discretion of States to adopt the methods and the timing of its application. The method will largely depend on the nature and extent of the problem in each country, as well as on its legal system and its practice. It will also often happen that the process of elimination of discriminatory practices cannot but be gradual.

255. The Convention lists, however (Art. 3) a number of measures to be taken by States in carrying out a national policy against discrimination. It provides that each State bound by the Convention 'undertakes, by methods appropriate to national conditions and practice –

a. to seek the co-operation of employers' and workers' organizations and other appropriate bodies in promoting the acceptance and observance of this policy;
b. to enact such legislation and to promote such educational programmes as may be calculated to secure the acceptance and observance of the policy;
c. to repeal any statutory provisions and modify any administrative instructions or practices which are inconsistent with the policy;
d. to pursue the policy in respect of employment under the direct control of a national authority;
e. to ensure observance of the policy in the activities of vocational guidance, vocational training and placement services under the direction of a national authority.'

256. Various other measures are also listed in the Recommendation, such as promoting, where practicable and necessary, the observance of the principles of non-discrimination, in respect of employment and vocational guidance, etc. other than those under the direct control of a national authority, by various methods such as encouraging State, provincial or local government departments or agencies and industries and undertakings operating under public ownership or control to ensure the application of the principles, making eligibility for contracts involving the expenditure of public funds dependent on observance of the principles and eligibility for grants to training establishments and for a licence to operate a private employment agency or a private vocational guidance office dependent on observance of the principles. The Recommendation also contemplates the establishment of appropriate agencies for the purpose of promoting application of the policy and in particular to take measures to foster public understanding and acceptance of the principles of non-discrimination and to examine and investigate complaints. It advocates continuing co-operation of the competent authorities with appropriate bodies to consider what further measures may be necessary, as well as with the authorities responsible for action against discrimination in other fields.

257. In considering the various measures which are advocated by the Convention and the Recommendation and their respective roles, account should be taken of the situations which these measures should remedy and the double objective which is aimed at: the elimination of inequality of treatment and the promotion of equality of opportunity. In this connection, discrimination no longer results generally from legislation (apart from some exceptional cases) but from factual situations and from the attitudes of mind and behaviour of individuals or groups, due to prejudice or interest. The fight against such a social phenomenon should therefore not be limited to legislative action, but should also comprise practical measures and in particular educational programmes. Moreover, inequality of opportunity and of treatment often results from inequality in the economic condition of various ethnic groups or simply from differences in individual situations due to education and training received, sex or the milieu in which people are living. Thus action in favour of real equality of opportunity calls for extensive measures in the field of education, and of vocational training, of placement services and of social promotion. These measures should be part in the wider framework of long-term policies of sustained and balanced economic growth which could guarantee to the whole community opportunities for technical training and employment.

258. In these circumstances, taking account of the nature of the problems to be solved as well as of the provisions of the Convention, the adoption of legislative steps cannot be considered as being necessary and sufficient in all the fields covered by the Convention. However, among the various methods which can be followed by means of a national policy of equality of opportunity and of treatment, legal standards have an important role to play. First, because in any event the Convention contains the obligation to repeal any legislative provision which might be incompatible with a non-discriminatory policy. Secondly, because official legal standards may be very influential in rallying public support to a national policy of equality in the field of employment. However, the scope and the precise legal effects of national standards in this matter, as well as the fields which such standards should cover could well vary considerably in relation to each national situation and each legal system.

§3. The Action in the Field of 'Apartheid'

259. Apartheid, which is practised in the Republic of South Africa differs basically from the situation in other countries where a certain measure of discrimination still persists. In South Africa, racial segregation constitutes the deliberate policy of the government and its effects in the field of employment are particularly severe. The effect of the South African legislation is to deprive African workers of opportunities for training, employment and promotion to a large number of jobs, by the application of a system of barriers based on race, to subject these workers to lower wages and conditions of work, to deprive the greater part of African workers of any job security, and reduce their status to that of migrant workers, to exclude African workers from the normal system of collective bargaining, to refuse to recognize officially trade unions of African workers and to prohibit these workers from going on strike, subject to heavy penalties.

260. For these reasons the International Labour Conference adopted unanimously, in 1964, a 'Declaration concerning the policy of *apartheid* in labour matters in the Republic of South Africa'. This Declaration is based on the principle, contained in the Declaration of Philadelphia, according to which 'all human beings, irrespective of race, creed or sex, have the right to pursue both their material well-being and their spiritual development in conditions of freedom and dignity, of economic security and equal opportunity'. It was also based on the fact that, by virtue of the Constitution of the ILO, which the Republic of South Africa had undertaken 'to perform and carry out', the Organization was created for the promotion of the objects set forth, in particular, in the Declaration of Philadelphia. On this basis, the International Labour Conference, 'acting as spokesman of the social conscience of mankind', condemned the policy of *apartheid* and called upon the government of South Africa to renounce it by repealing the various provisions by which it was created. At the same time, the ILO established a detailed programme for the elimination of *apartheid* in labour matters, which contains specific recommendations on the changes which should take place in three broad areas, namely equality of opportunity in respect of admission to employment and training, freedom from forced labour and freedom of association and the right to organize.

261. The Conference also requested the Director-General of the ILO to follow the situation in South Africa and to submit to it every year a special report concerning the application of the Declaration. While the government of South Africa withdrew from the ILO shortly afterwards, special reports on its policy of apartheid continue to be submitted each year to the International Labour Conference. These reports analyse the events which have taken place in this field both in South Africa (and they concentrate every year on one or more aspects of the labour situation in South Africa) and at the international level. They tend to show the way to a change of policy and they indicate, in this connection, the positive methods which should be taken in the field of labour in order to ensure the transition from a society established on the principle of separation of races to a society based on equality of opportunity and of treatment.[1] Studies were also made of the problems of discrimination in labour matters in Namibia and in Southern Rhodesia.[2] In June 1978, the Conference held a special sitting on *apartheid*[3] and its President concluded by expressing the wish that a Committee or Special Tripartite Group be set up to promote efficient compliance with action against apartheid in labour matters.

1. For the 'Declaration concerning the policy of *apartheid* of the Republic of South Africa', the 'ILO Programme for the Elimination of *Apartheid* in Labour Matters in the Republic of South Africa' and the two special reports submitted to the Conference in 1965 and 1966, see *'Apartheid' in Labour Matters*, Geneva, 1966. The subsequent reports, from 1967 to 1978, are available as special reports submitted to the corresponding sessions of the Conference. A booklet on *The ILO and Apartheid* was published in 1969 and more recent editions have been published since.
2. See *Labour and Discrimination in Namibia*, ILO, Geneva, 1977, and *Labour Conditions and Discrimination in Southern Rhodesia (Zimbabwe)*, ILO, Geneva, 1978.
3. See Provisional Rec. Proc. Conf. 1978, Nos. 19 and 20, pages 19/1 to 20/21.

§4. Other International Standards

262. The 1948 *Universal Declaration on Human Rights* provided in Article 2 that everyone is entitled to all the rights and freedoms which are set forth in the Declaration 'without distinction of any kind, such as race, colour, sex, language, religion, political or other opinions, national or social origin, property, birth or other status'. A provision drafted in analogous terms but formulated as an undertaking of States Parties is contained in the *International Covenant on Economic, Social and Cultural Rights* (Art. 2, para. 2). As both the Declaration and the Covenant also deal with the free choice of employment[1] and other rights in the labour field, the principle of non-discrimination should apply to all these rights. This principle is specifically reaffirmed in some other provisions of the Covenant, as in the field of remuneration (Art. 7a). The *Covenant on Civil and Political Rights* also contains a general provision (Art. 2, para. 1) similar to that of the Covenant on Economic, Social and Cultural Rights.

1. See above No. 229.

263. As regards more particularly racial discrimination, the General Assembly of the United Nations adopted first, in November 1963, a *Declaration on the Elimination of All Forms of Racial Discrimination* and later, in December 1965, an *International Convention* on that subject. The Convention entered into force in January 1969 and has been ratified by 100 States. After having recalled in its Preamble that the States Parties bear in mind, in particular, the ILO Convention and Recommendation concerning discrimination in respect of employment and occupation, the UN Convention, which adopts certain of the definitions of these standards, provides (Art. 5) that 'States Parties undertake to prohibit and to eliminate racial discrimination in all its forms and to guarantee the right of everyone, without distinction as to race, colour, or national or ethnic origin, to equality before the law in the enjoyment' of a certain number of rights. Among these rights the Convention refers to economic, social and cultural rights, and in particular to the rights to work, to free choice of employment, to just and favourable conditions of work, to protection against unemployment, to equal pay for equal work, to just and favourable remuneration, the right to form and join trade unions, the right to housing, the right to public health, medical care, social security and social services and the right to education and training.

264. In the field of *education*, the General Conference of UNESCO adopted in December 1966 a *Convention and a Recommendation against Discrimination in Education*. The Convention entered into force in May 1962.

265. At the regional level, the instruments are less numerous and less precise. Thus, it has been considered that discrimination in employment is implicitly prohibited by a provision (Art. 1, para. 2) of the *European Social Charter* relating to 'the right of the worker to earn his living in an occupation freely entered upon'.[1] The *European Convention on Human Rights* provides more specifically (Art. 14) that the enjoyment of the rights and freedoms set forth in this Convention – and which, as stated above, include the prohibition of forced labour and the right to form and join trade unions – 'shall be secured without discrimination on any ground such as sex, race, colour, language, religion, political or other opinion, national or social origin, association with a national minority, property, birth or other status'.

1. The question of equal remuneration between men and women, which will be dealt with later (Nos. 455 ss.), is covered by a special provision of the Charter.

Chapter IV. Employment

§1. General Outline

266. While, for the individuals concerned, employment is the basic condition for all other labour rights, the level of employment in a country is, more generally, a basic element for the development, the prosperity and the stability of the nation. Moreover, problems of employment and of population can have international repercussions. Problems of employment vary considerably from one region to another and between developed and developing countries. In Europe, the memories of the big economic depression of the thirties had dimmed, at least until a few years ago, but they inspired, after the Second World War, policies aiming at ensuring full employment. In the developed countries, most of which had practically reached full employment, the problem, until recently, was mainly to ensure the expansion of the economy while maintaining stability of prices and the highest possible level of employment. Under certain conditions, these three objectives did not seem to be incompatible. They were even interrelated and could reinforce one another through an active employment policy. However, the recession of the most recent period gave an acute character to the problem of employment, even in developed countries, while outside Europe unemployment and underemployment continued to prevail in large parts of Africa, Asia and the Americas. The adoption of international labour standards cannot, of course, bring by itself a solution to the problem. Employment raises broad questions of economic financial and monetary policy which go well beyond labour problems in the strict sense[1] and it finally calls for action of a practical character. International standards can, however, establish principles which might promote systematic and coordinated national and international action.

1. The relationship between economic and social matters has been often discussed since the establishment of the ILO. In the thirties, at the time of the massive unemployment caused by the economic crisis, the International Labour Conference adopted, in 1932, a resolution recommending the launching of big international and national works, the settlement of the general problems of currency and training and the examination of the problems of production and international trade. In 1944, the Declaration of Philadelphia underlined the link between the social objectives of the ILO and international and national policies of an economic and financial character and affirmed that these policies should be judged from the point of view of their repercussion on the achievement of fundamental social objectives.

267. In this connection, ILO standards have, since the establishment of the organization, followed an evolution and a development corresponding to the change in the situation and conditions since 1919. Initially, the questions which, in the field of employment, were given more attention were the immediate problems of unemployment, and later of placement. The Preamble of the ILO Constitution listed 'the prevention of unemployment' among the main objectives of the organization. Unemployment was the subject, in 1919, of the second Convention adopted by the ILO. Moreover the special problems of the unemployment of young persons, as well as the organization of public works, first as a means of action against unemployment, and later on from a more general point of view, were the subject of various Recommendations. As far as placement is concerned, it was regulated, in the first instance, for seamen, by a Convention of 1920. At a later stage, the fee-charging employment agencies were dealt with by a Convention (No. 34) of 1933 which was to be revised in 1949. Vocational education, vocational training and apprenticeship have also been the subject of various Recommendations, most of which were adopted shortly before the Second World War. The question of migrant workers was also dealt with at that period, in instruments which related both to questions of employment and to equality of treatment, and which were revised at a later stage.[1] Useful as these may have been, the standards thus adopted in that first period were mainly centered, in the field of employment, on immediate problems and they had a rather fragmentary character.

1. See below Nos. 539 ss.

268. In this field as in others, the 1944 Declaration of Philadelphia gave to the ILO a source of inspiration and the basis of a comprehensive programme for the years to come. The Declaration of Philadelphia put special emphasis on full employment but it also underlined the importance of economic growth. It stressed the need for coordinated international action bearing on the various economic factors which can influence employment and development. It referred to the employment of workers in the occupations in which they can have the satisfaction of giving the fullest measure of their skill and attainments and make their greatest contribution to the common well-being. It stressed, more generally, the need for a 'fuller and broader utilization of the world's productive resources' and for effective international and national action, including measures to expand production and consumption, to avoid severe economic fluctuations, to promote the economic and social advancement of the less developed regions of the world, etc.

269. During the years which followed, the ILO developed both its standard-setting and its practical activities in the field of employment. As compared with those adopted during the preceding period, the new standards have a more systematic character and provide an overall view of the question. Thus a 1948 Convention and Recommendation dealt in detail with the organization of the public employment service. The following year, these standards were supplemented by the revision of the 1933 Fee-charging Employment Agencies Convention. In the field of vocational training, standards more adapted to present conditions were adopted in 1962 and they were followed, in 1975, by two instruments, wider in conception on vocational guidance and vocational training in the development of human resources. However, it is mainly in the field of employment policy that the standard-setting activity of the ILO has been of the greatest importance: by the breadth of their conception, the Convention and Recommendation adopted on this subject in 1964 have become fundamental instruments in this field.

270. As regards the practical activities of the ILO, the majority of such activities relate to questions concerning employment. In 1969, the ILO launched a World Employment Programme which aimed at giving active encouragement to the adoption of national development policies which treat employment as one of their priority objectives. In June 1976, the ILO convened a Tripartite World Conference on Employment, Income Distribution and Social Progress, and the International Division of Labour. The question of the follow-up of that Conference has been placed on the agenda of the 1979 General Conference (for a general discussion on basic needs).

§2. Employment Policy

271. The first suggestions for an active employment policy can be found in a 1937 Recommendation on public works. A more comprehensive approach to the organization of employment, introducing the concepts of full employment and of a systematic use of human and material resources, was attained in Recommendations Nos. 71, 72 and 73 of 1944 and they helped to determine the description of the functions of the employment service as spelled out in the 1948 Convention and Recommendation.[1] The latest stage of the standard-setting activities of the ILO in the field of employment was the adoption in 1964, of the Employment Policy Convention and Recommendation,[2] which placed the problem in a wider context, were based on the concept of economic growth and duly took account of the human factor in the development of the economy. During the same period, the OECD Council adopted a recommendation on manpower policy as a means for the promotion of economic growth.

1. See below No. 290.
2. About these instruments, see the general Survey of the Committee of Experts (Report III, Part 4B) in 1972.

272. The Employment Policy Convention, 1964 (No. 122), provides, for each State which ratifies it, the obligation to declare and pursue, as a major goal, an active policy designed to promote full, productive, and freely chosen employment. This policy should aim at ensuring that there is work available for all who are available for and seeking work; that work should be as productive as possible, and that there should be freedom of choice of employment and the fullest possible opportunity for each person to qualify for, and to use his skills and endowments in, a job for which he is well suited, irrespective of race, colour, sex, religion, political opinion, national extraction or social origin. The employment policy should take due account of the stage and level of economic development and be pursued by methods appropriate to national conditions and practices. The measures to be adopted for attaining the objectives specified by the Convention should be decided on and kept under review within the framework of a co-ordinated economic and social policy, and steps should be taken as may be needed, including, when appropriate, the establishment of programmes. Representatives of employers and workers should be consulted concerning employment policies, with a view to taking fully into account their experience and views and securing their full co-operation in formulating and enlisting support for such policies.

273. While the guidelines contained in the Convention are in rather general terms, they are supplemented by the much more detailed and precise provisions which are contained in the Employment Policy Recommendation (No. 122). This Recommendation defines, in the first instance, the objectives of employment policy, and then deals with its general principles as well as with the general (long-term and short-term) and selective measures of such policy. It also considers the employment problems associated with economic underdevelopment and more particularly investment and income policy, promotion of industrial and of rural employment and population growth. The Recommendation also refers to action by employers and workers and their organizations and to international action to promote employment objectives. Finally an annex to the Recommendation contains very detailed suggestions concerning methods of application.

274. The Employment Policy Convention and Recommendation are considered as being among the fundamental instruments of the ILO. They are also those which are the most directly connected with its practical activities, and in particular its World Employment Programme,[1] launched in 1969. Some governments consider that they cannot ratify the Convention because they think it is impossible to realize its objective in due course. In fact the Convention does not require States to undertake to achieve full employment within a given time limit but rather to pursue a policy designed to promote it. Other problems relate to the inadequacy of the administrative structure of certain countries. Generally speaking, the present number of ratifications of the Convention (63) is very satisfactory and its implementation is followed closely by the supervisory bodies of the ILO. In the years which followed the adoption of the Convention, the size of the employment problem became more and more apparent, with an estimated 300 million unemployed and underemployed in the Third World and the prospect of having to create 1000 million new jobs in the next 25 years. In addition, the concern for the problems of unemployment and underemployment extended to the problem of poverty, which touches a great number of workers who are employed but do not have a sufficient income. In 1976, therefore, the ILO convened a Tripartite World Conference on Employment, Income Distribution and Social Progress and the International Division of Labour,[2] which adopted a detailed Declaration of Principles which constitute the guidelines for a Programme of Action in this field. It is stated in the Declaration that a priority objective of national development plans and policies should be the promotion of employment and the satisfaction of the basic needs of each country's population. The Conference saw increased productive employment as a vital factor in the basic needs strategy designed to provide a national minimum level for such essentials as food, shelter, clothing and community services. It spelled out the implications of such a policy in the field of international co-operation. The programme of action also focused on three aspects of the effort to promote employment: international action to limit the harmful effects of migration on people and their countries; the development of technologies which are best suited to the resources and future development potential of developing countries; and determined efforts to achieve full employment in developed countries. It was not possible to reach consensus on the role of multinational enterprises in developing countries.[3] In June 1979 the International Labour Conference will have on its agenda the question of the follow-up of the World Employment Conference (Basic Needs) for a general discussion resulting possibly in the adoption of standards.

1. The World Employment Programme was one of the main contributions of the ILO to the Second United Nations Development Decade. In the framework of this programme employment strategy missions were sent, as from 1970, to Columbia, Sri Lanka, Iran, Kenya, Philippines, Dominican Republic and Sudan and recommendations in the field of employment policy were prepared for the governments concerned. Other studies and reports were prepared for various other governments and regional employment teams have been active in many countries of Latin America, Africa and Asia.
2. See *Employment, Growth and Basic Needs. A world problem*. ILO 1976. Report of the Director-General of the ILO, on the basis of which the work of that Conference was based.
3. As regards multinational enterprises, see below No. 415.

275. In the field of standards, the 1976 World Employment Conference stated that Member States should ratify the Employment Policy Convention (No. 122) – but also that the question of its revision should be considered – that States should also implement and safeguard fair labour standards, such as the right to organize and to engage in collective bargaining, as laid down in Conventions Nos. 87, 98 and 135 and implement active labour market policies of the type set forth in the Human Resources Development Convention, 1975 (No. 142) and Recommendation (No. 150).

§3. Unemployment

I. The Unemployment Convention, 1919 (No. 2)

276. Unemployment was dealt with in one of the first Conventions of the ILO, Convention No. 2 of 1919, which has been ratified by 50 States. The Convention provides for the establishment, in ratifying countries, of a system of free public employment agencies, under the control of a central authority. Committees including representatives of employers and workers should be appointed to advise on the carrying on of these agencies. Where both public and private free employment agencies exist, steps should be taken to coordinate their operations. The Convention also referred to systems of insurance against unemployment. The principles contained in the Convention were naturally essential for any action against unemployment, but they called for still more precise standards. As will be said below, various instruments deal in detail with the organization of an employment service[1] and with unemployment insurance.[2] In order to fight against unemployment, Recommendations were also adopted in two more specific fields: the unemployment of young persons and the organization of public works.

1. See below No. 290.
2. See below Nos. 418 ss.

II. The Unemployment of Young Persons

277. With a view to supplementing a 1934 convention and recommendation on unemployment insurance and assistance, a Recommendation (No. 45) on unemployment among young persons was adopted the following year. In the Preamble, this instrument emphasized that involuntary idleness may undermine the characters and diminish the occupational skill of young persons and menace the future development of nations. Taking into account the experience already gained in many countries, the Recommendation advocated a series of concrete measures dealing with the school-learning age, the age for admission to employment, general and vocational education, recreational and social services for the young unemployed and action by trade organizations and private organizations. It also suggested the establishment of special employment centres for young unemployed persons, attendance at which should be strictly voluntary and which should offer various guarantees. Other suggestions related to the organization of public works for unemployed young persons, placing services and the development of opportunities for normal employment and the compilation of special statistics showing the extent of unemployment among persons below the age of 25. The question of special youth employment and training schemes for development purposes has been already dealt with above.[1]

1. See Nos. 222–223 above.

III. The Organization of Public Works

278. One of the traditional means of combating unemployment has always been public works, and the Conference has suggested, as from 1919, in the Unemployment Recommendation (No. 1), that States reserve public works as far as practicable for periods of unemployment. In 1937 the Public Works (International Co-operation) Recommendation (No. 50) was the first to launch the idea of an international plan of public works, while the Public Works (National Planning) Recommendation (No. 51) advocated a number of measures aiming at a suitable timing of public works in such a way as to reduce industrial fluctuations and unemployment. After the Second World War, these standards were supplemented by the Public Works (National Planning) Recommendation, 1944 (No. 73) which, apart from the concern for a proper timing of public works, sprang from needs arising out of the war.

§4. Placement

279. Already dealt with in principle in Convention No. 2 of 1919, which had provided for the establishment of a system of public employment agencies, and in Convention No. 9 of 1920 for seafarers, the question of placement was afterwards approached under its two complementary aspects: that of the abolition – or regulation – of fee-charging employment agencies and that of the organization of a public employment service.

I. The Abolition or Regulation of Fee-Charging Employment Agencies

280. While Recommendation No. 1 of 1919 suggested the prohibition of the establishment of fee-charging employment agencies and, for agencies already existing, a system of government licences and their abolition as soon as possible, it was a Convention No. 34 of 1933 which dealt with these agencies in a more general way. As it was ratified only by a limited number of countries (no more than ten), it was revised in 1949 to make it more flexible. The new Convention relating to Fee-Charging Employment Agencies (No. 96) of 1949, gives to States which ratify it the choice between two alternatives: either the progressive abolition of fee-charging employment agencies conducted with a view to profit and the regulation of other agencies, or the regulation of fee-charging employment agencies in general.

A. The Progressive Abolition of Fee-Charging Employment Agencies Conducted with a View to Profit and the Regulation of the Other Employment Agencies

281. For governments which accept the first alternative, the Convention provides that fee-charging employment agencies conducted with a view to profit should be abolished within a limited period of time determined by the competent authority. This abolition should not take place until a public employment service is established. Different periods may be prescribed for the abolition of agencies catering for different classes of persons. During the period preceding abolition, these agencies shall be subject to supervision and shall only charge fees and expenses approved by the competent authority, which shall consult the employers' and workers' organizations concerned.

282. Exceptions to the abolition of these employment agencies may be allowed by the authorities in exceptional cases in respect of categories of persons, exactly defined by national legislation, for whom appropriate placing arrangements cannot conveniently be made within the framework of the public employment service, but only after consultation of the organization of employers and workers concerned. The agencies for which such an exception is allowed shall be subject to the supervision of the competent authority. They shall be required to be in possession of a yearly licence renewable at the discretion of that authority. They shall only charge fees and expenses on a scale approved by that authority. They shall place or recruit workers abroad only if permitted to do so and under conditions determined by the legislation. The reports on the application of the Convention[1] should include information concerning the exceptions allowed, the number of agencies concerned and the scope of their activities, the reason for the exceptions and the arrangements for supervision of the activities of those agencies.

1. See below Nos. 591–592.

283. Fee-charging employment agencies not conducted with a view to profit shall be required to have an authorization and shall be subject to the supervision of the authorities. Charges and recruitment abroad are submitted to conditions similar to those mentioned above.

284. As regards non-fee-charging agencies, the competent authority should satisfy itself that they carry on their operations gratuitously.

285. Penalties, including the withdrawal of the licence or authorization should be prescribed in case of violation of the provisions of the convention or of the legislation giving effect to them.

B. The Regulation of Fee-Charging Employment Agencies

286. The second alternative given to ratifying States is to accept, instead of the abolition, the regulation of Fee-Charging agencies. In this case, their obligations in respect of fee-charging employment agencies conducted with a view to profit are analogous to those provided for, under the first alternative, in respect of the agencies conducted with a view to profit for which exceptions are allowed. As regards the other categories of agencies, and the questions of penalties and of information to be supplied in annual reports, the rules are similar in both cases.

C. Ratification and Problems of Application of Convention No. 96

287. Convention No. 96 has been ratified by 36 States, the great majority of which have accepted the first alternative offered by the Convention, i.e. the progressive abolition of fee-charging agencies conducted with a view to profit and the regulation of the other agencies. The application of the Convention has given rise to certain problems as regards the placement of performers and domestic servants.

D. The Problem of Temporary Work Agencies

288. In recent years, with the development of temporary work agencies, the question has arisen as to whether these agencies are covered by the Convention.[1] The question was put to the ILO in 1965 by the Government of Sweden and the reply[2] was that these agencies are covered by the definition of fee-charging employment agencies conducted with a view to profit given by the Convention (any agency which acts as an intermediary for the purpose of procuring employment for a worker or supplying a worker for an employer). The opinion of the ILO was that the Convention is applicable even to cases in which a contractual relationship is established between the worker and an agency and not between the worker and the person or undertaking at whose disposal he is placed by that agency, as the essential test is the actual nature of the transaction rather than its legal form. Account was also taken, in this connection, of a number of elements: the temporary work agency assumes no responsibility for the work performed; the temporary worker is paid only when he is placed at the disposal of a third party; it is the third party who decides what work is to be carried out and supervises its execution, and the temporary worker is under his authority; in many cases he becomes an integral part of the personnel of the undertaking making use of his services. This being so, while the agencies concerned should be considered as covered by the Convention, it may well be that the public employment service would be reluctant to assume the special type of duty which the temporary employment agencies undertake for their clients. Governments may therefore feel that they could resort, in respect of these agencies, to the exceptions allowed by the Convention for the 'categories of persons for whom appropriate placing arrangements cannot conveniently be made within the framework of the public employment service'. Governments should then consult the employers' and workers' organizations and observe, *mutatis mutandis*, the measures of supervision and the limitations provided for in such cases by the Convention.

1. See Valticos, 'Temporary Work Agencies and International Labour Standards', I.L.R. January 1973, pp. 43–56; *Travail temporaire dans la société moderne*, Actes de la Conférence internationale de l'Institut international du travail temporaire, Bruxelles, 1976.
2. See O.B. July 1966, pp. 390–396.

II. The Employment Service

289. The abolition of fee-charging employment agencies conducted with a view to profit can naturally be envisaged – and this is recognized by convention No. 96 – only to the extent to which there exists a public employment service, which should be able to perform the functions which were filled by these agencies. The obligation to establish a system of public employment agencies was provided for in general terms by Convention No. 2 as early as in 1919. Some years later, in 1933, with a view to supplementing Convention No. 34, which envisaged the abolition of fee-charging employment agencies, a

Recommendation (No. 42) advocated various measures, such as having specialized offices for particular occupations, aimed at solving the difficulties which would arise if these public employment offices were not in a position to take the place completely of the fee-charging agencies which would be abolished. It was, however, only in 1948 that the Employment Service Convention (No. 88) introduced precise standards on the organization of a public employment service.

290. Convention No. 88 of 1948 provides that ratifying States shall maintain or ensure the maintenance of a free public employment service, the essential duty of which shall be to ensure the best possible organization of the employment market as an integral part of the national programme for the achievement and maintenance of full employment and the development and use of productive resources. It contains detailed provisions relating to the organization of the service and its co-operation with other bodies with a view to ensuring effective recruitment and placement. It provides for the co-operation of representatives of employers and workers through advisory committees and other arrangements. It defines the functions of the employment service and the measures which should be taken by it and refers to the needs of particular categories of applicants. The Convention also contains provisions on the status and the conditions of service of the staff of the employment service. A Recommendation (No. 83) was adopted at the same time as the Convention and contains a number of supplementary provisions.

291. The convention has been ratified by 66 States. In 1971 it was denounced by Italy (because employers and workers were not participating in equal numbers in the employment committees) and by the United Kingdom (because the Government was considering introducing a system of charges to employers for services in connection with professional and executive vacancies). The Government of the United Kingdom stated however that in all other respects it would consider itself still bound by the Convention and would, on a voluntary basis, supply reports on its application.

292. The difficulties encountered in the ratification and the application of the Convention sometimes relate to the actual establishment of an employment service which, in certain countries, faces budgetary difficulties and personnel problems. In other cases, the obstacles are due to the organization, the competence and the working of the existing service, as they are not in full conformity with the standards of the Convention. However, the Convention has influenced the establishment and the organization of numerous national employment services and many governments continue to take it into account in the progressive development of these services.

§5. Apprenticeship, Vocational Guidance and Training

293. The Preamble of the ILO Constitution already referred in 1919, to 'the organization of vocational and technical education' among the improvements to be made in conditions of work. In 1921 a Recommendation (No. 15) was adopted as regards the development of technical agricultural education and, in 1937, together with various instruments concerning the building industry, a Recommendation (No. 56) referred to vocational education in that industry. The problem as a whole was however first dealt with in detail in two Recommendations of 1939 concerning Vocational Training (No. 57) and Apprenticeship (No. 60). After the Second World War, while further Recommendations dealt with vocational training of special categories of workers, as in the case of seafarers (No. 77 of 1946), fishermen (No. 126 of 1966), and in agriculture (No. 101 of 1956) a recommendation of a general character (No. 87) on vocational guidance was adopted in 1949 and it was followed, in 1950, by a Recommendation (No. 88) on vocational training of adults, including disabled persons. In 1962, the question of vocational training was dealt with in a more up-to-date Recommendation (No. 117) of a wider scope, which replaced the previous Recommendations on the subject. Finally, in 1975, two more broadly conceived instruments were adopted: the Convention (No. 142) and Recommendation (No. 150) concerning vocational guidance and vocational training in the development of human resources. The latter instrument, which is very detailed, supersedes Recommendations Nos. 87 of 1949, 101 of 1956 and 117 of 1962. Apart from these various instruments, which deal mainly with vocational training, many Conventions and Recommendations relating to other questions (social policy, plantations, indigenous and tribal populations) also include provisions on vocational training.

§6. Other International Standards

294. The Universal Declaration of Human Rights affirms (Art. 23 para 1) that 'everyone has the right to work, to free choice of employment . . . and to protection against unemployment'. In the *International Covenant on Economic, Social and Cultural Rights* (Art. 6), it is also provided that the States Parties 'recognize the right to work, which includes the right of everyone to the opportunity to gain his living by work which he freely chooses or accepts, and will take appropriate steps to safeguard this right', and that the steps to be taken by a State Party 'to achieve the full realization of this right shall include technical and vocational guidance and training programmes, policies and techniques to achieve steady economic, social and cultural development and full and productive employment under conditions safeguarding fundamental political and economic freedoms to the individual'.

295. At the European level, the *European Social Charter* contains certain provisions in the field of employment. It provides in particular that Contracting Parties undertake 'to accept as one of their primary aims and responsibilities the achievement and maintenance of as high and stable a level of employment as possible, with a view to the attainment of full employment' (Art. 1, para 1). The reference to full employment was included in this provision following a suggestion of the workers' members at the Tripartite Conference and in view of the fact that such an objective had also been mentioned in the Employment Service Convention, 1948 (No. 88) of the ILO. There was unanimous agreement on the inclusion of such a reference. Under the European Social Charter also States Parties undertake 'to establish or maintain free employment services for all workers (Art. 1, para 3)' and 'to provide or promote appropriate vocational guidance, training and rehabilitation'. In other provisions it deals with the right to vocational training (Art. 10) and the right of physically or mentally disabled persons to vocational training, rehabilitation and social resettlement (Art. 15.) On the whole, these various provisions follow to a large extent, although in general terms, the corresponding standards of the ILO and in their final wording account was taken of suggestions put forward at the Tripartite Conference.

296. As for the *European Communities*, they have devoted an important part of their activities to problems of employment, and this will be shown in the study relating to these Communities.

297. Finally, as indicated above,[1] bilateral agreements of varying scope are often concluded on the immigration of foreigners, circulation of persons, employment or manpower, and they contain mainly provisions on the recruitment and immigration of workers, on equality of treatment and sometimes on facilities to bring families together and on vocational training. Provisions on the training of executives are sometimes included in agreements on cultural, scientific and technical co-operation.

1. See above Nos. 143–150.

Chapter V. Wages

§1. General Outline

298. While wages are one of the main elements of conditions of employment and constitute an important question of labour law, it is clearly difficult to regulate the subject internationally in any precise way. There have naturally been various provisions of a general character about wages in international instruments. Thus, in 1919, the preamble of the ILO Constitution refused to 'the provision of an adequate living wage' and Art. 41 of the original text (Article 427 of the Treaty of Versailles) included, among the General Principles of the Organization, 'the payment to the employed of a wage adequate to maintain a reasonable standard of life as this is understood in their time and country'. In 1944, the Declaration of Philadelphia reaffirmed the need for 'a minimum living wage to all employees and in need of such protection'. Other international instruments, and in particular the Universal Declaration of Human Rights, also refer to the principle of 'just and favourable remuneration', as this will be seen later.[1] However, to reach concrete results, international action has of course to go beyond general principles. On the other hand, there is a field in which it would be hardly possible to envisage precise international regulations: this is the actual amount of the wages, as this depends closely on the economic, social and political conditions of each country. Nevertheless, there are other – and important – aspects of wages on which it appeared possible, and even essential, to establish more precise international standards.

1. See below No. 323.

299. Thus, standards were first set for the cases of exceptionally low wages. As from 1926, several instruments were adopted to provide for minimum-wage fixing machinery for such cases, and more recent instruments of wider scope complemented them in 1970. Another problem has been that of protecting wages in general against various types of abuse. This was the subject of 1949 instruments on protection of wages, which can be related to instruments adopted the same year on labour clauses in public contracts. The question of wages naturally also raises the well-known principle of equal pay. In this connection, the general problem of discrimination in employment has been discussed above[1] and the more specific question of equal remuneration between men and women will be dealt with below.[2] Some other special aspects of remuneration (such as in the case of holidays with pay and of overtime) will also be mentioned in a different chapter.[3]

1. See Nos. 234–265.
2. See Nos. 455 ff.
3. See, for overtime, No. 335 below.

§2. Minimum-Wage Fixing

I. Introduction

300. Following an inquiry made by the ILO as from 1921, the International Labour Conference adopted in 1928 a Convention (No. 26) and a Recommendation (No. 30) concerning minimum wage-fixing machinery. These two instruments did not cover agriculture, for which a special Convention and Recommendation were adopted in 1951. The 1928 and 1951 Conventions do not lay down any rule as to the level of the wages; they only provide for the establishment of minimum wage-fixing machinery. However the Recommendations which supplement them list certain criteria for the determination of these wages. More recently, the question of the revision of the 1928 instruments arose because of the fact that they were concerned only with machinery for minimum wage-fixing without requesting the actual determination of such wages. The Conference adopted, therefore, in 1970, a Convention (No. 131), supplemented by a Recommendation on minimum wage-fixing, specially as regards developing countries.

301. Apart from these instruments of general application, provisions on minimum wage-fixing can be found in instruments concerning special categories of workers, such as seafarers (who have been, as will be seen later,[1] the only category for which the amount of a minimum wage has been specified in an ILO Convention) and workers in non-metropolitan territories and in plantations. Resolutions relating to minimum wages have also been adopted by the International Labour Conference (in particular in 1945, 1948 and 1949) and by various Regional Conferences of the ILO. The question has also been discussed at meetings of industrial committees and analogous bodies.

1. See below No. 508.

II. The 1928 Minimum Wage-Fixing Machinery Convention (No. 26) and Recommendation (No. 30)

302. The Minimum Wage-Fixing Machinery Convention, 1928 (No. 26) provides that ratifying States undertake to create or maintain machinery whereby minimum rates of wages can be fixed for workers employed in certain of the trades (the term includes manufacture and commerce) or parts of trades (and in particular in home working trades) in which no arrangements exist for the effective regulation of wages by collective agreement or otherwise and wages are exceptionally low. The intention was to provide for the obligation to create, but not necessarily to operate wage-fixing machinery, and this opinion was based on the view that 'if the machinery existed, its application would necessarily follow in those cases in which the need for it was felt'.[1] Before the machinery is applied in a trade or part of trade, representatives of the employers and workers concerned should be consulted. Employers and workers concerned should also be associated in the operation of the machinery in equal numbers and on equal terms. The minimum rates fixed should be binding on the employers and workers concerned. They should not be subject to abatement by individual nor (except by authorization of the competent authority) by collective agreement. The Convention also provides for the establishment of a national system of supervision and sanctions, to ensure that persons concerned are informed of the minimum rates of wages in force and that wages are not paid at less than these rates. A worker who has been paid wages at less than the rates in question shall be entitled to recover, by legal proceedings, the amount by which he has been underpaid, subject to certain limitation of time. Information on the practical application of the Convention should be communicated to the ILO at periodic intervals.

1. See *Intern. Lab. Code*, note 95 under Art. 225, p. 171.

303. The supplementary Recommendation (No. 30) spelt out certain general principles on the matter. In particular, it advocated that investigations be conducted by the minimum wage-fixing machinery in the trade or part of trade concerned. It also called attention to the principle that men and women should receive equal remuneration for work of equal value. The Recommendation also indicated various means designed to secure greater authority for the rates that may be fixed (in particular by the direct and joint participation of the employers and workers concerned in the deliberations and decisions and by the participation of one or more independent persons selected, as far as possible in agreement with or after consultation with the employers' and workers' representatives). It was also stated that, for the purpose of determining the minimum rates, the wage-fixing body should take account of the necessity of enabling the workers concerned to maintain a suitable standard of living and of having regard to the rates of wages paid for similar work. Provision should also be made for the review of the rates fixed. The Recommendation also referred to arrangements for informing the employers and workers of the rates in force, official supervision of the rates actually paid, penalties as well as preventive measures.

304. Convention No. 26 has been ratified by more than ninety States. The reasons for which a number of States have not yet ratified it[1] often relate to the fact that its ratification is not considered to be useful in view of the existing national situation or system in the field of wages. Reference has been made, in this connection, to the existence of a highly developed system of collective bargaining and the scope of collective agreements which can be extended to all employers and workers. In other cases, the ratification is prevented by more substantial reasons, such as the difficulty of obtaining agreement on the rates of minimum wages or problems in relation with the consultation of employers and workers. In some cases, the obstacles to ratification are attributed to the federal structure of the country or to the fact that direct intervention of the government in wage-fixing would be considered to be incompatible with the economic system of the country.

1. See in this connection *Rep. Com. Exp*. 1969, pp. 225–226.

III. The 1951 Minimum Wage-Fixing Machinery (Agriculture) Convention (No. 99) and Recommendation (No. 89)

305. Convention No. 99, which was adopted in 1959 follows the provisions of Convention No. 26. It applies to agricultural undertakings and related occupations, but allows governments to exclude certain categories of persons. It authorizes the partial payment of minimum wages in kind under certain conditions. States are free to decide the nature and form of the minimum wage-fixing machinery, after consultation of representative organizations of employers and workers. Employers and workers concerned shall take part in the operation of the machinery on a basis of complete equality. Minimum rates of wages fixed shall be binding, but the competent authority may permit exceptions in individual cases, to prevent curtailment of the opportunities of employment of physically or mentally handicapped workers. The Convention contains provisions similar to those of Convention No. 26 as regards publicity, supervision and penalties and the right of workers to recover the amounts by which they have been underpaid.

306. A special feature of Recommendation No. 89, which supplements the Convention, is that, after stating that, in the determination of minimum wages, account should be taken of the necessity of enabling the workers concerned to maintain a suitable standard of living, it listed a certain number of factors in this connection: the cost of living, fair and reasonable value of services rendered, wages paid for similar or comparable work under collective bargaining agreements in agriculture, and the general level of wages for work of a comparable skill in other industries in the area where the workers are sufficiently organized. The Recommendation also follows the main provisions of that of 1928, which have been described above.[1] It adds that a sufficient number of qualified inspectors, with powers analogous to those provided by the Labour Inspection Convention, 1947 (No. 81),[2] should be employed. It also suggests, in order to facilitate supervision, that employers might be required to issue workers pay books or similar documents containing the necessary information.

1. See above No. 303.
2. See below No. 556.

307. Convention No. 99 has been less widely ratified than Convention No. 26 (46 ratifications). The reasons for which certain countries have not ratified it are similar to those which prevented them from ratifying Convention No. 26.[1] In other cases, non-ratification is due to the fact that there is no supervision or appropriate system of labour inspection covering wages in agriculture. Sometimes reference has been made to the relative inexistence of agriculture.

1. See above No. 304. See also *Rep. Com. Exp*. 1969, pp. 228–229.

IV. The 1970 Minimum Wage-Fixing Convention (No. 131) and Recommendation (No. 135)

308. As stated above, it was found, more recently, that the standards set in 1928 were no longer sufficient and the International Labour Conference adopted, in 1970, a Convention (No. 131) supplemented by a Recommendation (No. 135) on minimum wage-fixing, with special reference to developing countries. These instruments stressed that the 1926 and 1951 Conventions had played a valuable part in protecting disadvantaged groups of wage earners, but that the time had come to adopt a further instrument complementing these conventions and providing protection for wage-earners against unduly low wages, which, while of general application, would pay special regard to the needs of developing countries.

309. The States which ratify the Convention (now 23) undertake to establish a system of minimum wages which covers all groups of wage earners whose terms of employment are such that coverage would be appropriate. These groups would be determined by the competent authorities in each country, in agreement or after full consultation with the representative organizations of employers and workers. States should list in their first reports on the application of the Convention the groups which may not have been covered and the reasons, and state in subsequent reports the position in respect of these groups.

310. It is provided that minimum wages shall have the force of law and shall not be subject to abatement, and that failure to apply them shall make the person concerned liable to penal or other sanctions. The elements in the determination of the level of minimum wages shall, as far as possible include: a. the needs of the workers and their families, taking into account the general level of wages in the country, the cost of living, social security benefits, and the relative living standards of other social groups, and b. economic factors, including the requirements of economic development, levels of productivity and the desirability of obtaining and maintaining a high level of employment. Machinery for fixing minimum wages for the groups protected and adjusting them from time to time should be created or maintained. It should be adapted to national conditions and requirements. The Convention also provides for full consultation of representative organizations of employers and workers concerned and for direct participation, in the operation of the machinery, of representatives of these organizations and of persons with recognized competence. Finally, the Convention refers to measures of inspection and other necessary measures to ensure the effective application of all provisions relating to minimum wages.

311. The 1970 Recommendation deals with the purpose of minimum wage-fixing, the criteria for determining the level of the minimum wages, the coverage of the system, the machinery itself, the adjustment of minimum wages and enforcement.

V. The Social Policy Conventions

312. Two Conventions dealing with social policy, the one adopted in 1947 (No. 82) and relating to non-metropolitan territories and the second, adopted in 1962 (No. 117) and dealing more generally with the Basic Aims and Standards of Social Policy,[1] contain provisions relating to minimum wage-fixing machinery, based on the principles defined in the existing instruments on minimum wage-fixing. However the Social Policy Conventions also stress that 'the improvement of standards of living shall be regarded as the principal objective in the planning of economic development'.[2] They provide, from that point of view, for measures to secure for independent producers and wage-earners conditions which will give them scope to improve living standards by their own efforts and will ensure the maintenance of minimum standards of living.

1. On these Conventions, see below Nos. 409–412.
2. Art. 6 of Convention No. 82 and Art. 2 of Convention No. 117.

VI. Provisions Concerning Special Categories of Workers (Seafarers and Plantations Workers)

313. As stated above, the Wages, Hours of Work on Board Ship and Manning Convention, which has been revised several times, and lastly in 1958, is the only ILO instrument which fixes a specific amount as a minimum wage. Higher amounts have been fixed, first in the complementary Recommendation (No. 109) of 1958, later in a resolution adopted by the Maritime Conference in 1970, and more recently by the Joint Maritime Commission in 1976. The amounts are determined in pounds sterling and US dollars, but the salary can be paid in the equivalent in another currency. It was felt possible to determine a minimum wage in the maritime field because of the international character of this industry, but the attempt has not been successful. The Convention has not obtained the number of ratifications necessary for its entry into force.[1]

1. See also below No. 508.

314. Finally, the 1958 Plantations Convention, contains provisions about minimum wage-fixing which are analogous to those included in the 1947 Social Policy (Non-Metropolitan Territories) Convention (No. 82) and based on the Minimum Wage-Fixing Conventions.

§3. Protection of Wages

315. Following studies conducted by the ILO on the truck system and similar practices, certain provisions on protection of wages were included, in 1939 and in 1947 in Conventions concerning contracts of employment of indigenous workers and social policy in non-metropolitan territories. The matter afterwards became the subject of two instruments of more general application: the 1949 Protection of Wages Convention (No. 95) and Recommendation (No. 85). The purpose of these instruments was to protect the workers against practices which might place them under the excessive dependence of the persons who employ them and also to ensure the prompt and full payment of wages.

316. After defining the term 'wages', and the persons to whom it applies, the Convention allows the exclusion of certain persons who are not employed in manual labour or are employed in domestic service. As regards substance, the Convention set a number of standards relating to the form in which the wages should be paid, the conditions to which partial payment in kind should be subject, and the freedom of the worker to dispose of his wages, it prohibits coercion to make use of the works stores operating in the undertaking. When access to other stores is not possible, the goods in stores operating in the undertaking should be sold at fair and reasonable prices; when run by the employer, the stores should not be operated for the purpose of securing a profit. The Convention also includes provisions on limitations to deductions from wages, protection against attachment or assignment to the extent necessary for the maintenance of the worker and his family, the treatment of workers as privileged creditors in the event of bankruptcy or judicial liquidation of an undertaking, the regular payment of wages, the day and place of payment, information of workers, penalties and other measures to ensure the application of the Convention.

317. The Recommendation adopted at the same time as the Convention contains a number of complementary provisions as regards deduction from wages, periodicity of wage payments, notification to workers of wage conditions, wages statements and payroll records, and association of workers in the administration of works stores.

318. The difficulties which have prevented a number of governments from ratifying the Convention[1] sometimes lie in the compulsory character of most of its provisions, while in the countries concerned the principle of freedom of negotiation, in particular in the field of wages, is generally accepted. In other countries, the main difficulty is found to be the scope of the Convention, which is wider than that of national legislation. Some countries have stated that particular provisions of the Convention, such as that on works stores, were not given effect to in their legislation. The federal structure of certain States has also raised problems in two countries.

1. See *Rep. Com. Exp.* 1969, pp. 230–232.

§4. Labour Clauses in Public Contracts

319. The main reason which led to the adoption of standards concerning labour clauses in public contracts is that, as public contracts are as a rule awarded to the undertakings which offer the most favourable terms, the parties tendering for the public contract might be tempted, in order to obtain the contract, to reduce the labour costs by paying lower wages and affording less satisfactory conditions of work than those practiced in similar industries. More generally, the adoption of good labour standards by the public authorities may have a positive influence on the standards followed in the occupations and industries concerned.

320. The International Labour Conference therefore adopted in 1949 a Convention (No. 94) and a Recommendation (No. 84) on Labour Clauses in Public Contracts. The Convention applies to all contracts which are passed by a public authority (the central authority of a Member State), involve the expenditure of public funds and the employment of workers by the other party, and are for the construction, etc., of public works, the manufacture, etc., of materials, supplies or equipment or the performance of supply of services. Exclusions are authorized for contracts involving the expenditure of an amount not exceeding a certain limit, subject to consultation with the organization of employers and workers concerned. The contracts to which the Convention applies should include clauses ensuring to the workers concerned wages (including allowances), hours of work and other conditions of labour which are not less favourable than those established for work of the same character by collective agreement, arbitration award or national laws or regulations. The Convention also deals with measures to ensure fair and reasonable conditions of health, safety and welfare for the workers concerned. It contains provisions relating to the publicity of the instruments giving effect to the Convention, a system of inspection, to sanctions (such as the withholding of contracts) and measures for enabling the workers concerned to obtain the wages to which they are entitled (in particular by the withholding of payments under the contract).

321. The complementary Recommendation advocates that similar clauses be used in cases when private employers are granted subsidies or are licensed to operate a public utility. It also describes the questions which should be dealt with – either directly or by reference to appropriate provisions contained in laws, collective agreements, etc. – in the labour clauses of the public contracts.

322. The ratification and application of the Convention have met with certain difficulties. Thus the view was held by certain governments that it was not necessary to include in public contracts the labour clauses specified in the Convention since the social legislation of these countries was applicable to all workers, and consequently also to those employed by parties to public contracts. On this Convention, the Committee of Experts on the Application of Conventions has observed that the fact that the labour legislation of a country is applicable to all workers does not exempt the States bound by the Convention from the obligation to include labour clauses in public contracts, as the provisions contained in national legislation often set only minimum standards which can be exceeded by collective agreements. Following this clarification, a number of governments took the necessary measures for the inclusion of labour clauses in public contracts.

§5. Other International Standards

323. The *Universal Declaration of Human Rights* affirms that 'everyone who works has the right to just and favourable remuneration ensuring for himself and his family an existence worthy of human dignity . . .' (Art. 23, para. 3). Similarly, the *International Covenant on Economic, Social and Cultural Rights* refers to 'remuneration which provides all workers, as a minimum, with: 1. Fair wages and equal remuneration for work of equal value without distinction of any kind . . .; 2. A decent living for themselves and their families . . .' (Art. 7(a)).

324. As for the *European Social Charter*, it includes, in accordance with a recommendation made by the Tripartite Conference following a suggestion from the workers, the undertaking of Contracting Parties 'to recognize the right of workers to a remuneration such as will give them and their families a decent standard of living' (Art. 4, para. 1). The Charter also deals with deductions from wages and provides that such deductions should be permitted only under conditions and to the extent prescribed by national laws or regulations or fixed by collective agreements or arbitration awards' (Art. 4, para. 5).

325. Finally, as already stated,[1] bilateral treaties frequently include clauses providing that the wages of migrant workers who are nationals of one contracting State should not be lower than those of the corresponding nationals of the country of immigration.

1. See above Nos. 143 ss.

Chapter VI. General Conditions of Work

§1. Hours of Work

I. General Outline

326. The reduction of hours of work and in particular the eight-hour day had been since the middle of the 19th century one of the most constant demands of the labour movement and it proved to be the most prized of their achievements. In the early days of industrialization it was not uncommon that working hours amounted to 14 or 16 per day, but they were progressively reduced to 12, 11 then 10 per day and the latter figure was of fairly general application in Europe at the beginning of the First World War. During and at the end of the war, the pressure brought by organizations of workers accelerated the progress towards the eight hour day. It was introduced progressively in various countries of Europe and in the United States, either by law or by collective agreements.

327. It is therefore not surprising that, at the establishment of the ILO, the eight-hour day was placed among its chief objectives. The Preamble of Part XIII of the Treaty of Versailles referred to 'the establishment of a maximum working day and week' among the measures urgently required to improve the conditions of labour; similarly, the General Principles which Article 427 of the Treaty considered as being of special and urgent importance included 'the adoption of an eight-hour day or a forty-eight hour week' as the standard to be aimed at where it has not been attained.

328. The question of the application of the principle of the eight-hour day or of the 48 hour week was therefore the first to be placed on the agenda of the first session of the International Labour Conference, which met in Washington in October 1919. The Hours of Work (Industry), 1919 which sanctioned this principle and put it in concrete form was the first Convention to be adopted by the Conference, with an almost unanimous vote (83 votes to two, with one abstention).

329. However, in the years which followed, the ratification of the Convention came up against great difficulties and gave rise to heated discussions.[1] The economic problems of the post-war period, the exaggerated fears as regards the effect which the eight-hour day might have on production,[2] the obsession with international competition and some legal problems on the scope of the Convention hindered the great industrial European States from ratifying. Although legislation and practice in Europe, Australia, and many countries in Latin America had introduced the eight-hour day and the 48-hour week, many States hesitated to commit themselves, by ratifying the Convention, for a period of ten years. The discussions and the uncertainty went on for several years with ups and downs. The Ministers of labour of the industrial countries of Western Europe met twice, in particular in London in 1926, to discuss the problem and at one stage the obstacles seemed to have been overcome. In 1924 and 1929, Germany and Great Britain appeared to be on the point of ratifying but new difficulties arose at the last moment. Finally, of the countries which participated in the London Conference, only Belgium ratified unconditionally, while France, through fear of competition, ratified in 1927, subject to the condition of the ratification of the Convention by Germany and Great Britain, despite the fact that the 1919 Convention had, as a rule, been largely drafted on the basis of French legislation. Austria and Italy also ratified conditionally. In 1931 Albert Thomas, in describing the vicissitudes of the Convention, wondered what was 'the magic spell' which still held the Governments back.[3]

1. See Scelle, *op. cit.*, pp. 258–268; Schaper, *Albert Thomas*, Assen (Netherlands), 1959, pp. 251–255.
2. See the experience of Belgium where, in spite of the introduction of the eight-hour day in 1924, economic activity continued to make progress (Troclet and Vogel-Polsky 'The influence of international labour conventions on Belgian Labour Legislation', *I.L.R.* November 1968, p. 403.)
3. *Rec. Proc. Conf.* 15, 1931, p. 7.

330. It was felt at that time that the fact that the Convention was not ratified by the major industrial countries had been a serious setback for the ILO. This is largely true, but nevertheless the Convention exercised a considerable influence. Its very existence contributed to the consolidation of the eight-hour day standard and put a check on attempts to bring it into question after the First World War. The Convention also exercised a positive influence in many countries[1] which, on ratifying it, introduced its provisions into their legislation, which became the first national measures to limit the duration of work of adults. The influence of the Convention was also felt in countries which did not ratify it.[2]

1. This was the case in countries like Belgium, Chile, Greece, Romania (see *The International Labour Organization – The first decade*, London, 1931, pp. 300 ss.) and also India (V. K. R. Menon, 'The influence of International Labour Conventions on Indian Labour Legislation', *I.L.R.* June 1956, pp. 551 ss.)
2. See *The International Labour Organization, op. loc. cit.*

331. A new attempt was made by the ILO in the field of hours of work when it adopted, in 1930, a Convention providing for the same standard of an eight-hour day and 48-hour week, but in commerce and offices. Similar conventions for other occupations (mines in 1931 and road transport in 1939) followed, but the demand for a 40-hour week had already appeared and was making progress. In fact, the new methods of production, then the crisis in the thirties brought about a new reduction of hours of work in many of the major industries in the United States and the introduction of the five-day week of 40 or 45 hours. Envisaged by a resolution adopted by the Conference in 1932 as a means to combat economic depression and unemployment, the reduction of the working week to 40 hours became a new objective for international regulation. A first attempt was made in 1934 to have adopted two Conventions on that basis (the one for industry and the other for commerce and offices) but it was not successful, as the draft instruments did not obtain the necessary majority. A different formula was then tried, that of a Convention affirming merely the principle of 40 hours, with the understanding that distinct instruments would deal with its application in various sectors of the economy. This was Convention No. 47 of 1937. In fact in the course of the following years some special Conventions were adopted for certain sectors, but it did not prove possible to do so for a sizeable number of other activities. In 1939, the examination of draft Conventions the aim of which was to generalize the reduction of the working week to 40 hours was postponed *sine die* because of the international situation.

332. After the Second World War and the first period of reconstruction, the question of the reduction of the hours of work was raised once more, and once more the attempt was not successful. A first draft Recommendation, in 1961, did not obtain the necessary majority, but the Conference adopted, the following year, a Recommendation (No. 116) providing for the progressive reduction of hours of work to the 'social standard' of 40 hours. It will also be seen[1] that, in the maritime field, a Convention on hours of work on board ships – already mentioned as it also dealt with wages – adopted in 1936 and repeatedly revised since has not yet come into force.

1. See below No. 508.

333. In all, 14 Conventions and 10 Recommendations have been adopted on hours of work, apart from the instruments on connected questions, such as weekly rest, and from provisions on hours of work included in Conventions on other aspects of conditions of work. The standard-setting activity of the ILO in this field has been one of those where the greatest difficulties have been encountered. Convention No. 1 on the eight-hour day and 48-hour week has now been ratified by more than 40 countries, but it is not ratified or in force as regards some great industrial countries where this standard has been exceeded in certain respects. The facts that certain provisions of the Convention may be too strict or that, in some countries, hours of work are settled by collective agreements may explain the position, but only to a certain extent. In any event, the general influence of the various standards on hours of work cannot be denied.

II. The Standard of the Eight-Hour Day and the 48-Hour Week

A. The Hours of Work (Industry) Convention, 1919 (No. 1)

334. Convention No. 1 applies to persons employed in public or private industrial undertakings and it defines of these undertakings. It provides that the working hours shall not exceed eight in the day and 48 in the week.

335. The Convention authorizes various exceptions. It excludes persons holding positions of supervision or management, and persons employed in a confidential capacity. When the hours of work on one or more days of the week are less than eight, the limit may be exceeded on the remaining days, but not by more than an hour. It is also permissible to exceed the eight-hour limit in the case of shift work, but the average number of hours over a period of three weeks should not exceed the general standard of the Convention. Exceptions are also permitted in cases of accident, actual or threatened, of urgent work to be done to machinery or plant, or of *force majeure*, but only so far as may be necessary to avert serious interference with the ordinary working of the undertaking. In the case of necessarily continuous processes, the convention authorizes an average of 56 hours in the week. In exceptional cases where the standard of the eight-hour day and 48-hour week cannot be applied, the daily limit of work can be calculated over a longer period, with the agreement of the occupational organizations concerned. Finally the Convention authorizes a number of permanent and temporary exceptions. Regulations should be made, after consultation with the organizations concerned, to fix the maximum of additional hours authorized. The rate of pay for overtime shall not be less than one and one-quarter times the regular rate. The Convention – like a limited number of other Conventions – authorizes the suspension of its application in the event of war or other emergency endangering the national safety.

336. The Convention also provides that employers should notify workers of the hours of work and rest intervals and should keep a record of additional hours worked. It specifies that it should be made an offence against the law to employ a person outside the hours provided in the Convention.

B. The Hours of Work (Commerce and Offices) Convention, 1930 (No. 30)

337. Convention No. 30, which has been ratified by some 30 States, sets the same standard as Convention No. 1, but it is applicable to persons employed in commercial undertakings, including postal, telegraph and telephone services, and in establishments and administrative services in which the persons employed are mainly engaged in office work. It applies to both public and private establishments.

338. The Convention allows certain exceptions. It also authorizes the maximum hours of work in the week to be so arranged that hours of work in any day do not exceed ten hours. It permits, under certain conditions, an increase of the hours of work in the day for the purpose of making up hours of work which have been lost in case of local holidays, accidents of force majeure. It authorizes, in exceptional cases, the distribution of hours of work over a period longer than the week, provided that the average hours of work do not exceed 48 hours in the week and that hours of work in any day do not exceed ten hours. It also provides, as does Convention No. 1, for various permanent or temporary exceptions, and has analogous provisions as regards overtime.

339. Provisions similar to those of Convention No. 1 also deal with consultation of employers and workers' organizations and measures of information and enforcement (with an additional provision about inspection).

C. The Special Conventions

340. On the basis of the general standard set in the two Conventions described above,[1] two further conventions were adopted for special sectors of activity. The one relates to *coal mines*. Although work in mines is covered by Convention No. 1, a special Convention, adopted in 1931 (No. 31) and revised in 1935 (No. 46) limited the working time spent in underground hard coal mines to seven hours and 45 minutes in the day as a rule and required also that weekly rest be observed. The entry into force of the Convention was made subject to special conditions, and the ratifications necessary to this effect have not been obtained.

1. The general standard was also reaffirmed in the Reduction of Hours of Work Recommendation, 1962 (No. 116) which, while providing for the reduction of hours of work to forty per week, advocated that, when the duration of the normal working week exceeds 48 hours, immediate steps should be taken to bring it down to this level, without any reduction of the wages of the workers.

341. Another special Convention, adopted in 1939, relates to hours of work and rest periods in *road transport* (Convention No. 67). This instrument also was based on the 48-hour week, but because of the detailed and somewhat rigid character of its provisions it was ratified by four countries only. The International Labour Conference held a first discussion, in June 1978, on the possibility of adopting new instruments in this field and decided that this item shall be included in the agenda of its 1979 session with a view to the adoption of a Convention and a Recommendation.

III. The Standard of the Forty-Hour Week

A. The Forty-Hour Week Convention, 1935 (No. 47)

342. Adopted in 1935, the Forty-Hour Week Convention (No. 47) entered into force only in 1947 and has not yet obtained more than six ratifications. States which ratify it are not required to do more than declare their approval of the principle of the 40-hour week, applied in such a manner that the standard of living is not reduced in consequence, and of the taking or facilitating of appropriate measures to secure this end. States bound by the Convention also undertake to apply this principle to classes of employment in accordance with the detailed provisions to be prescribed by any separate Conventions which it may ratify.

B. The Special Conventions

343. As provided for by the 1935 Convention, the ILO started to prepare special Conventions with a view to regulating the application of the 40-hour principle in different sectors. Already in 1934, a Convention (No. 43) had set, for automatic sheet-glass works, a working week of 42 hours, and had provided that the length of a spell of work could not exceed eight hours. The same standard was set, the following year, by a Convention (No. 49) concerning glass-bottle works. In 1936 and 1937, in two Conventions (Nos. 51 and 61), relating respectively to public works and to the textile industry, the standard was reduced to an average 40-hour week, with a number of exceptions. The general structure of these Conventions followed to a certain extent that of Conventions Nos. 1 and 30. These various Conventions were ratified by a very limited number of countries, while the attempts to lay down similar Conventions in certain other fields were not successful.

C. The Reduction of Hours of Work Recommendation, 1962 (No. 116)

344. This Recommendation provides that each State should formulate and pursue a national policy designed to promote by methods appropriate to national conditions and practice and to conditions in each industry the adoption of the principle of the progressive reduction of normal hours of work with a view to attaining the social standard of the forty-hour week. It also provides that immediate steps should be taken to bring down to 48 the duration of the normal working week where it exceeds this level. The Recommendation mentions the various elements which should be taken into account in connection with the reduction of hours of work (e.g. the level of economic development and various economic factors such as the risk of creating inflationary pressures, the progress achieved or possible in raising productivity by the application of modern technology, automation and management technique, the need in developing countries for improving the standard of living of their people, etc.). The Recommendation also describes the stages by which the principle of the progressive reduction of hours of work may be applied and the priorities to follow. It specifies the methods of application of the measures advocated, as regards the definition of hours of work, their determination, the exceptions authorized, overtime consultation of employers and workers and supervision.

IV. Difficulties of Ratification and Application of the Standards on Hours of Work

345. The obstacles to ratification and the difficulties of application of the standards on hours of work related to different questions. In certain cases they are due to the general economic conditions of the countries concerned, while in other cases they relate to the implementation of various provisions of the instruments concerned. In particular, difficulties have appeared as regards the methods of application (in countries like the United Kingdom where hours of work are mainly regulated by collective agreements), the scope of national legislation (which is sometimes more limited than that of the Conventions) or the distribution of hours of work which, in many countries, is made over a longer period than is provided for in the Conventions. The most frequent difficulties relate to the exceptions which may be authorized. Problems are also encountered as regards the limitation and remuneration of overtime and the supervision of the application of the provisions on overtime. Finally, in certain countries, the difficulties arise from the federal structure of the State.

V. Other International Standards

346. The *Universal Declaration of Human Rights* (Art. 24) and, more recently the *International Covenant on Economic, Social and Cultural Rights* (Art. 7, para. d) provide for the 'reasonable limitation of working hours', but without specifying any given duration.

347. Similarly, under the *European Social Charter* (Art. 2, para. 1) the Contracting Parties undertake 'to provide for reasonable daily and weekly working hours, the working week to be progressively reduced to the extent that the increase of productivity and other relevant factors permit'. At the Tripartite Conference of 1958, the workers' members proposed that the hours of work should be specified and that the objective should be set at the 40-hour week. This request was not accepted by the majority of the Tripartite Conference, nor subsequently by the Governmental Social Committee of the Council of Europe, notwithstanding the Consultative Assembly's opinion in favour of a reference to the 40-hour week. The Social Charter also refers (Art. 4, para. 2) to 'the right of workers to increased rates of remuneration for overtime work, subject to exceptions in particular cases'.

§2. Weekly Rest

I. General Outline

348. Weekly rest was one of the first questions dealt with by the ILO. It was mentioned in the general principles contained in Article 427 of the Treaty of Versailles and as soon as 1921 the International Labour Conference adopted a Convention concerning weekly rest in industry and a Recommendation concerning weekly rest in commerce and offices. On this latter question the adoption of a Convention was interrupted by the outbreak of the Second World War and this was finally only brought about in 1957. Weekly rest is also dealt with in Conventions relating to seafarers[1] and plantation workers.[2]

1. See below No. 508 about the Wages, Hours of Work and Manning (Sea) Convention (Revised), 1958 (No. 109) which also provides for reduced hours of work on the weekly day of rest when the vessel is in port.

2. The Plantations Convention, 1958 (No. 110) includes the main provisions of Convention No. 14.

II. Weekly Rest in Industry

349. The Weekly Rest (Industry) Convention, 1921 (No. 14) which has been ratified by some 90 States defines its scope on terms anologous to those of the Hours of Work (Industry) Convention, 1919 (No. 1). It provides that the whole of the staff employed in any industrial undertaking, public or private, shall enjoy, in every period of seven days, a period of rest comprising at least twenty four consecutive hours. Wherever possible, this period of rest should be granted simultaneously to the whole of the staff of each undertaking and should coincide with the days already established by the traditions or customs of the country or district. The Convention authorizes a number of exceptions for which, as far as possible, compensatory periods of rest should be provided. As in the case of the Hours of Work (Industry) Convention, 1919 (No. 1), it provides that the employers should take certain measures to inform the staff of the days and hours of rest. The main difficulties in the application of the Convention have related to its scope.

III. Weekly Rest in Commerce and Offices

350. The Weekly Rest (Commerce and Offices) Convention, 1957 (No. 106) applies to trading establishments as well as to establishments, institutions and administrative services, whether public or private, in which the persons employed are mainly engaged in office work, including offices of persons engaged in the liberal professions. It also covers the services of a certain number of other establishments. Finally it may equally be applicable to persons employed in certain kinds of establishments (such as those providing personal services, post and tele-communications services, newspaper undertakings and theatres, etc.) to the extent that the States which ratify the Convention specify in a declaration accompanying or following the ratification. The Convention authorizes a number of exceptions, special schemes and temporary exemptions.

351. As in the case of industry, the Convention sets the standard of a weekly rest period of not less than 24 hours in the course of each period of seven days. It includes similar provisions as regards the simultaneous character of the rest and its coincidence with the day established by the traditions or customs of the country or district. A Recommendation (No. 103) which was adopted at the same time as the Convention advocates that the period of rest be at least of 36 hours, if possible consecutive. It also recommends various improvements as regards a number of provisions of the Convention. The Convention specifies that the application of the standards on weekly rest should not result in any reduction of the income of the persons covered. Appropriate measures of supervision and inspection, and if appropriate of sanctions, are also provided for by the Convention.

352. The Convention has been ratified by 46 States. The main difficulties in the way of its ratification relate to its scope, the conditions to which exceptions to weekly rest are subject and the supervision of the effective application of the relevent provisions.

IV. Other International Standards

353. As in the case of hours of work, the *Universal Declaration of Human Rights* states in general terms (Art. 24) that 'everyone has the right to rest and leisure', and the *Covenant on Economic, Social and Cultural Rights* also refers (Art. 7 al d) to rest and leisure without being more specific.

354. The *European Social Charter* (art. 2 para 5) contains the undertaking of contracting parties 'to ensure a weekly rest period which shall, as far as possible, coincide with the day recognized by tradition or custom in the country or region concerned as a day of rest'. A proposal to provide that the weekly rest be of an uninterrupted duration of at least 36 hours was submitted by the Consultative Assembly, but was not accepted by the Governmental Social Committee.

§3. Paid Leave

I. General Outline

355. As it happened at the national level, the right of workers to annual holidays with pay was recognized at the international level much more recently than was the case for the reduction of the hours of work and for weekly rest. Until 1936, there were relatively few countries whose legislation provided for annual holidays with pay applicable to the whole of workers, while in countries where the question was regulated by collective agreements, it was not a common practice to grant holidays on such a general basis. The evolution gained in impetus as from 1936 with the adoption, on the one hand, of ILO Convention No. 52 and, on the other hand, of the French Act of 20 June 1936. Convention No. 52 was itself the result of prolonged efforts. The question had been already raised at the first session of the International Labour Conference in 1919 and it was placed four times on its agenda before being adopted, in 1936.

356. At the time of its adoption, Convention No. 52 had been considered as an advanced standard. Since, however, in view of the extension which holidays with pay have taken and the continuing increase of their duration (as there are now few countries where the legal holiday is of less than two weeks), the need was felt after some time of setting a higher standard. This was achieved first by a recommendation (No. 98) adopted in 1954, which provided that the duration of the holiday should be at least two weeks per year. At the same period, a Convention and a Recommendation on Holidays with Pay in Agriculture were adopted in 1952 and provisions on this subject were included in the Plantations Convention, 1958. Special conventions also dealt with the question of holidays with pay as regards seafarers.[1] The first of these instruments were adopted in 1946 and 1969 and they fixed the duration of the holidays at not less than 18 working days in the case of masters, officers or operators and not less than 12 working days in the case of the other members of the crew.

1. See below No. 509.

357. However the basic instrument still was the 1936 Convention and the standard which it had set became more and more outdated. It was revised in 1970, by Convention No. 132 which provided for a three-week annual paid holiday. More recently, in 1976, thè maritime session of the International Labour Conference revised the 1949 maritime convention in the light of the general Convention of 1970. Meantime, in 1974, the new notion of paid educational leave was introduced by a Convention and a Recommendation.

II. The 1936 Holidays with Pay Convention and Recommendation

358. The Holidays with Pay Convention, 1936 (No. 52), which has been ratified by some 50 States is applicable to a large variety of undertakings and establishments, public or private, which it lists, and which are engaged in industrial or commercial activities. It authorizes a very limited number of exceptions. It provides that the persons protected shall be entitled after one year of continuous service to an annual holiday of at least six working days. The holiday should be of at least twelve days for persons under 16, including apprentices. Public and customary holidays and interruption of attendance at work due to sickness should not be included in the annual holiday with pay. During his holiday, the worker should receive either his usual remuneration, including the cash equivalent of his remuneration in kind, or the remuneration determined by collective agreement.

359. The convention specifies that any agreement to relinquish the right to an annual holiday or to forgo such a holiday shall be void. It does not contain any provision on the possible postponement or accumulation of the holiday. It was felt[1] that as regards any part of the holiday which exceeds the minimum duration prescribed by the Convention, a postponement would not be incompatible with it, nor with the interests of both employers and workers, and that exceptions could also be acceptable in cases where a worker has been unable to take his holidays for a valid reason beyond his control. It is however essential to maintain the principle that, in the course of the year, the worker must be granted at least part of his leave in order to enjoy a minimum amount of rest and leisure.

1. *Rep. Com. Exp.* 1964, pp. 271–273, paras. 177–181.

360. The Convention also provides that if a person engages in paid employment during the course of his holiday, he may be deprived of his right to payment in respect of that period. If a worker was dismissed for a reason imputable to the employer before he has taken a holiday due to him, he should receive, in respect of every day of holiday due, the remuneration provided by the Convention. Finally, the employers should keep a record of leaves and States should establish a system of sanctions.

361. Among the various obstacles to ratification and application of the Convention, reference can be made to its scope, to the fact that in certain countries the question is regulated principally by way of collective agreements, and to certain special provisions of the Convention, such as that according to which public holidays and days of sickness should not be included in the annual holiday. Difficulties are also found in a number of countries as regards the prohibition of agreements to relinquish the right to a holiday, or the silence of the Convention as regards the possibility to divide the holiday or postpone it to another year.

III. The 1954 Holidays with Pay Recommendation

362. The Holidays with Pay Recommendation, 1954 (No. 98), which applies to all employed persons, with the exception of seafarers and agricultural workers, set the standard of two working weeks for twelve months of service (proportionally to the length of service performed with one or more employers during the year). It provided for a longer period for young workers under 18. The Convention referred to the remuneration which should be granted during the holiday and included, more generally, various provisions on the conditions under which the holiday should be taken, and which are often left to be determined by the appropriate machinery in each country. It provided that the standards which it set may be given effect by means of public or voluntary action, through legislation, statutory wage fixing machinery, collective agreements or arbitration awards, or in any other manner consistent with national practice. It added, however, that the adoption of any of these procedures should not prejudice the particular concern of governments to call into action all appropriate constitutional or legal machinery when voluntary action, action by employers' and workers' organizations or collective agreements do not give speedy and satisfactory results.

IV. The 1952 Standards on Holidays with Pay in Agriculture

363. The standards concerning holidays with pay in agriculture are contained in a Convention (No. 101) and a Recommendation (No. 93) adopted in 1952. The Convention itself, which has been ratified by some 40 States, does not specify the precise duration of the holiday. It provides that workers employed in agricultural undertakings and related occupations should be granted an annual holiday with pay after a period of continuous service with the same employer, and that the minimum duration of the annual holiday with pay shall be determined by national laws or regulations, collective agreement, or arbitration award, or by special bodies, etc. The Recommendation refers to a minimum length of one working week for a period of one year's continuous service. The Convention includes a series of provisions which are analogous to those of Conventions No. 52, but leave a greater freedom to governments in some respects. On certain of these points, the Recommendation contains more detailed provisions and gives some general guidelines.

364. As regards plantation workers, the 1958 Convention (No. 110) reproduced most of the provisions of the 1952 Holidays with Pay in Agriculture Convention (No. 101).

V. The 1970 Revised Convention on Holidays with Pay

365. As the need was more and more felt to adapt earlier standards, and in particular the 1936 Convention (No. 52) to more recent trends, a revised Convention on annual holidays with pay was adopted in 1970. The new Convention (No. 132), which has been ratified by 13 States, specifies in the first instance that its provisions, in so far as they are not otherwise made effective by means of collective agreements, arbitration awards, court decisions, statutory wage fixing machinery or in such other manner consistent with national practice, shall be given effect by national laws or regulations. It applies to all employed persons, with the exception of seafarers. Limited categories of persons can be excluded under certain conditions. Ratifying States may accept the obligations of the Convention separately in respect of employed persons in economic sectors other than agriculture and in agriculture.

366. The Convention provides that each ratifying State shall specify the length of the holiday in a declaration appended to its ratification, and that the holiday shall not be less than three working weeks for one year of service. A longer period may be notified by a further declaration. When the length of service in a year is less than twelve months, a holiday with pay proportional to the length of service should be granted, but a minimum period of no more than six months may be required for entitlement to holiday. Absence from work for reasons beyond the control of the person concerned, as illness, injury or maternity shall be counted as part of the period of service. On the other hand, public and customary holidays shall not be counted as part of the holiday and, under conditions to be determined at the national level, periods of incapacity for work resulting from sickness or injury may not be counted as part of the holiday. The Convention also deals with the remuneration of the worker during the holiday.

367. As regards the division of the annual holiday into parts, it may be authorized by the national authorities but, unless otherwise provided in an agreement applicable to the employer and the employed person concerned, one of the parts should consist of at least two uninterrupted working weeks. The uninterrupted part should be granted and taken no later than one year, and the remainder no later than 18 months, from the end of the year in respect of which the holiday entitlement has arisen. Any part of the holiday which exceeds a stated minimum may be postponed beyond that period with the consent of the employed person concerned. In principle, the time at which the holiday is to be taken shall be determined by the employer after consultation with the employed person concerned or his representatives, account being taken of the work requirements and the opportunities for rest and relaxation available to the employed person. Upon termination of employment, an employed person who has completed a minimum period of service of six months should receive a holiday with pay proportional to the length of his service, or compensation, or the equivalent holiday credit.

368. The Convention includes the provisions of earlier instruments according to which agreement to relinquish the right to holiday or to forgo it shall be null and void or prohibited. It authorizes national authorities to adopt special rules in respect of cases in which the employed person engages, during the holiday, in a gainful activity conflicting with the purpose of the holiday. Finally the Convention refers to measures to ensure the proper application and enforcement of the provisions concerning holidays with pay, by means of inspection or otherwise.

VI. Paid Educational Leave

369. In 1974, the Conference adopted a Convention (No. 140) and a Recommendation (No. 148) concerning paid educational leave. The Convention, which has been ratified by 13 States, provides that ratifying States should formulate and apply a policy designed to promote, by methods appropriate to national conditions and by stages as necessary, the granting of paid educational leave for the purpose of training at any level, general, social and civic education and trade union education. It specifies the objectives of such a policy, in particular the acquisition, improvement and adaptation of occupational and functional skills, the promotion of employment and job security in conditions of scientific and technological development and economic and structural change; competent and active participation of workers and their representatives in the life of the undertaking and of the community; human, social and cultural advancement of workers; and generally the promotion of appropriate continuing education and training and helping workers to adjust to contemporary requirements. This policy should take account of the stage of development and the needs of the country and be coordinated with general policies concerning employment, education, training and policies concerning hours of work. The leave might be granted by legislation, collective agreements, arbitration awards and any other means consistent with national practice. The public authorities, employers' and workers' organizations and education and training institutions should be associated with the formulation and application of the policy. The financing should be on a regular and adequate basis and in accordance with national practice. The leave should not be denied to workers on the grounds of race, colour, sex, religion, political opinion, national extraction or social origin. Periods of paid educational leave should be assimilated to periods of effective service for the purpose of establishing claims to social benefits and other rights deriving from the employment relation. These essential provisions are supplemented by the Recommendation, which deals, in particular, with the formulation of policy and methods of application, with measures for promotion of paid educational leave, with financing and with conditions for granting of paid educational leave.

VII. Public Holidays

370. There are no ILO standards relating to public holidays as such. It is only provided that public and customary holidays should not be included in the annual holiday with pay.

VIII. Other International Standards

371. The *Universal Declaration of Human Rights* (Art. 24) and the *Covenant on Economic, Social and Cultural Rights* (Art. 7, para. d) recognized in general terms the right of everyone to 'periodic holidays with pay' but did not specify the duration of such holidays. The latter provision also provided for 'remuneration for public holidays'.

372. The *European Social Charter* (Art. 2, para. 3) provided for 'a minimum of two weeks annual holiday with pay' and added (Art. 2, para. 4) that workers engaged in dangerous or unhealthy occupations should be entitled to additional paid holidays or reduced working hours. It also provided that the duration of the annual holiday with pay should not be less than three weeks for persons under 18 (Art. 2, para. 7). The Worker members of the Tripartite Conference, and subsequently the Consultative Assembly proposed that the minimum duration of the holiday with pay be fixed at three weeks in general and at four weeks for persons under 18 years, but these proposals were not accepted. The Charter also includes an undertaking of the Contracting Parties 'to provide for public holidays with pay' (Art. 2, para. 2).

§4. Industrial Hygiene and Safety

I. General Outline

373. The questions of industrial hygiene and safety were, even before the establishment of the ILO, among the first to be dealt with at the international level, as it has also been the case at the national level. There were two reasons for that: firstly, these questions affect directly the health and even the life of workers, and secondly, some of the measures which are necessary for the protection of workers call more particularly for a concerted international action for reasons of a technological or simply economic and commercial nature. The Preamble of the ILO Constitution already referred to 'the protection of the worker against sickness, disease and injury arising out of his employment'. A large part of ILO standards, i.e. more than 50 Conventions and 50 Recommendations relate, directly or indirectly, to hygiene and safety.[1] The present section will refer only to those standards which concern principally this question. The matter is however also dealt with in instruments concerning social security (e.g. as regards medical care) and the work of women or young persons (e.g. as regards medical examination).[2]

1. See in this connection Robert and Parmeggiani, 'Fifty Years of International Collaboration in Occupational Safety and Health', *I.L.R.*, January 1969.
2. Thus, reference can be made to the Conditions of Employment of Young Persons (Underground Work) Recommendation, 1965 (No. 125) which contains precise provisions on questions of heatlh, safety and welfare.

374. The standards adopted in the field of hygiene and safety related, in most cases, to specific risks or hazards or to problems of safety and hygiene concerning special branches of activity. Other instruments dealt with the more general questions of the methods and institutions for the prevention of industrial accidents and the protection of workers' health (more particularly the occupational health services). While these various standards aimed mainly at preventive action, others related to the definition of occupational diseases which would give rise to compensation and are therefore of interest also from the point of view of social security. Apart from the various Conventions and Recommendations adopted in this field, numerous model codes and codes of practice, as well as the important studies published by the ILO[1] contribute to the information of the public authorities and of professional circles.

1. E.g. the *Encyclopedia of Occupational Safety and Health*, 5th impression, 1976 and the publications of the *International Occupational Safety and Health Information Centre*, which was created by the ILO in 1959.

II. Standards Relating to Specific Risks

A. White Phosphorus

375. As it has already been said,[1] a Convention on the Prohibition of the Use of White Phosphorus in the Manufacture of Matches had been adopted as early as in 1906, before the establishment of the ILO. In 1919, at its first session, the International Labour Conference requested all member States, by a special recommendation (No. 6), to adhere to the 1906 Convention if they had not done so. The Convention has been ratified by some 50 States.

1. See above No. 2.

B. White Lead

376. In the same year of its establishment, the ILO was faced with an occupational disease which had been more harmful than white phosphorus: that was lead poisoning, which was caused by lead compounds, and in particular white lead. A Recommendation (No. 4) concerning the protection of the health of women and of young persons under 18 years against lead poisoning was adopted in 1919. The more general question of the use of white lead in the painting of the buildings was raised at the same time. The studies made by the ILO showed the very serious risks due to lead compounds, and in particular white lead, and the question was brought before the International Labour Conference in 1921 for the adoption of a Convention. However, while the gravity of risks due to lead compounds was generally admitted, views differed as regards the measures which should be taken. There were objections to the prohibition of the use of white lead, especially because of the interests of the manufacturers of white lead. Finally, the Conference decided, after a long debate, in favour of the prohibition, on the basis of a formula of compromise. The White Lead (Painting) Convention, 1921 (No. 13) was thus adopted almost unanimously. This Convention prohibits the use of white lead and sulphate of lead and all products containing these pigments, but only in the internal painting in buildings. It authorizes a number of exceptions. On the other hand, it provides for various measures of hygiene. Fifty-two States have ratified the Convention, but many industrial States have not yet done so. Nevertheless, lead is now less prevalent, and this may be due to the influence which the Convention has had, even in countries which did not ratify it.

C. Anthrax

377. At the same session of 1919, the Conference also adopted a Recommendation (No. 3) concerning the Prevention of Anthrax and in particular the disinfection of wool. However, more concrete results could not be achieved.

D. The Hazards of Poisoning Arising from Benzene

378. At a more recent date, i.e. in 1971, the Conference adopted a Convention (No. 136), which has been ratified by more than 20 States since, and a Recommendation (No. 144) concerning the hazards of poisoning due to benzene. This Convention applies to all activities involving exposure of workers to the aromatic hydro-carbon benzene C_6H_6 and to products the benzene content of which exceed 1 per cent by volume. It provides that whenever harmless or less harmful substitute products are available, they should be used instead of benzene, subject to certain exceptions. The use of benzene and of products containing benzene should be prohibited in certain work processes. Occupational hygiene and technical measures should be taken to ensure effective protection of workers exposed to benzene, and in particular to prevent the escape of benzene vapour into the air of places of employment. The Convention describes certain of these measures. Moreover, pregnant women and nursing mothers, as well as young persons under 18 years, should not be employed in work processes involving exposure to benzene. As for the Recommendation, it contains additional provisions in this field, in particular about the restrictions to the use of benzene, occupational prevention, hygiene in work, medical prevention and workers education.

E. Occupational Cancer

379. In 1974, the Conference adopted a Convention (No. 139) – ratified by 14 States until now – and a Recommendation (No. 147) concerning occupational cancer. Under the Convention, ratifying States should periodically determine the carcinogenic substances and agents to which occupational exposure shall be prohibited or controlled. They should make every effort, *inter alia*, to have carcinogenic substances and agents replaced, to prescribe the measures to be taken to protect workers against the relevant risks, to supply all available information to workers concerned, and to ensure that they are provided with medical examinations, tests or investigations as are necessary. The Recommendation includes detailed provisions, in particular on preventive measures, on supervision of health of workers, on information and education, and on measures of application.

F. Radiation Protection

380. At a relatively recent date, international standards were adopted for the protection of workers against ionizing radiations. The effect of X-rays and radioactive substances had already been studied by the ILO as from 1930 and the pathological manifestations due to such rays and substances had been included in the list of occupational diseases of the 1934 Convention (No. 42). In 1949, the ILO entrusted a group of experts to supplement the *Model Code of Safety Regulations for Industrial Establishments* (for the guidance of governments and industry) by a chapter concerning dangerous radiations. The *Model Code of Safety Regulations (Ionising Radiations)* which was prepared then was later updated in 1957, 1959 and 1965. Meanwhile, as from 1955, when, in connection with the first UN International Conference on the peaceful uses of atomic energy, the ILO submitted a substantial study concerning the protection of workers against radiation, the preparatory work for the adoption of a Convention in this field was undertaken. It was completed with the adoption, in 1960, of the Convention (No. 115) – ratified by 35 States – and the Recommendation (No. 114) on the protection against radiations. These instruments apply to all activities involving exposure of workers to ionizing radiations in the course of their work and they put an emphasis on the necessary preventive measures, both medical and technical. The standards included in the Convention and the Recommendation, as well as in the Model Code, were themselves clarified by a series of illustrated practical guides which supplied useful details of application. The technological changes which have taken place more recently will probably call for a revision of this Convention.

G. The Guarding of Machinery

381. For a number of years, the ILO had been trying to find a solution to the serious risks caused by inadequately guarded machinery. The adoption of international standards was made difficult by the great variety of machinery and of the ways to use them, and also at the level of international trade, by the differences between the prescriptions of the various countries. Initially, only a Recommendation (No. 32) could be adopted, in 1929. Finally, in 1963, the International Labour Conference succeeded in adopting a Convention (No. 119), now ratified by 35 States and a Recommendation (No. 118) on the guarding of machinery. The Convention applies to all power-driven machinery, new or second-hand. It provides that the *sale* or *hire* of machinery of which the dangerous parts are without appropriate guards should be prohibited. As regards the *use* of machinery, the prohibition is extended to its point of operation. The Convention also defines the obligations of employers to inform workers of the dangers arising in the use of machinery. As regards sale and hire of machinery, the obligation to ensure compliance rests on the vendor, the person letting out on hire or transferring the machinery, or the exhibitor, and, where appropriate, on their agents. As regards use, the responsibility rests on the employer. The Recommendation clarifies certain provisions of the Convention, and it extends its scope to the manufacture and the exhibition of machinery.

H. Maximum Weight

382. In spite of technical progress, manual work remains the lot of the greater part of mankind and it is still usual, even in developed countries. To face such a frequent cause of accidents, the International Labour Conference adopted, in 1967, a Convention (No. 127) – now ratified by 20 States – and a Recommendation (No. 128) on maximum weight. The Convention establishes the general principle that no worker shall be required or permitted to engage in the manual transport of a load which, by reason of its weight, is likely to jeopardize his health or safety. It provides in particular that States shall take appropriate steps to ensure that workers assigned to manual transport of loads, other than light loads, receive adequate training or instruction in working techniques. Suitable technical devices should also be used, as much as possible. The assignment of women and young workers to manual transport of loads other than light loads should be limited and, where they are engaged in the manual transport of loads, the maximum weight of such loads should be substantially less than that permitted for adult male workers. As for the

Recommendation, it deals more particularly with various measures of training, of safety and of hygiene which should be taken in this field, and with technical devices to be used. It also provides that the maximum permissible weight for adult male workers should not be more than 55 kilos, that it should be substantially less for women workers and for young workers, and that the minimum age for assignment to regular manual transport of loads should be 18 years.

I. Working Environment: Atmospheric Pollution, Noise and Vibrations

383. The problem of the working environment was the main theme of the discussion at the International Labour Conference in June 1972. The Conference had before it a report of the Director-General of the ILO on *Technology for Freedom (Man in his Environment)* and it adopted a Resolution concerning the contribution of the ILO to the protection and enhancement of the environment related to work. More recently, in 1977, the Conference adopted a Convention (No. 148) and a Recommendation (No. 156) concerning the Working Environment (Air Pollution, Noise and Vibration). The Convention, which applies to all branches of economic activity contains a number of general provisions on the measures to be taken in this field, and then it deals more specifically with preventive and protective measures. The Recommendation contains more detailed provisions, as regards these preventitive measures, and it also deals with the supervision of the health of the workers, training, information and research.

III. Standards Concerning Special Branches of Activity

A. Industrial Establishments

384. In the field of industrial establishments in general, the ILO adopted, in 1929 a Recommendation (No. 31), dealing with the prevention of industrial accidents. At a later stage, a *Model Code of Safety Regulations for Industrial Establishments for the Guidance of Governments and Industry* was approved by a tripartite technical Conference, and was since supplemented and revised many times. The standards contained in this Model Code, as in the case of similar other such Codes, or Codes of practice, do not involve commitments for States, but this text has nevertheless exercised a considerable influence on the establishment of national safety regulations.

B. Building and Construction

385. Very detailed standards were also adopted as regards the industry of building and construction. This was done in the Safety Provisions (Building) Convention, 1937 (No. 62) which has been ratified by 27 States and which was supplemented by four Recommendations (Nos. 53 to 56) in the same year.

C. Bakeries

386. Reasons of health are behind the prohibition of night work in bakeries, which was provided by a Convention (No. 20) adopted in 1925 and ratified by 16 States up to now. In this connection, the Convention prohibits the work both of employers and of workers taking part in the making of bread and other flour confectionery, and this type of prohibition had – as said above[1] – raised the question of the competence of the ILO to decide about a standard on such a question, but the Permanent Court of International Justice pronounced itself in the affirmative. One of the reasons for which this Convention has obtained a limited number of ratifications only is to be found in the system of work by shifts, which functions in the great modern bakeries.

1. See above No. 58.

D. Work in Offices and Commerce

387. Standards on questions of hygiene as regards work in offices and commerce were laid down in a Convention on Hygiene (Commerce and Offices), 1964 (No. 120), which has been ratified by some 40 States and supplemented the same year by a Recommendation (No. 120).

E. Dock Work

388. Standards concerning dock work were contained in the Marking of Weight (Packages Transported by Vessels) Convention, 1929 (No. 27) – ratified by 55 States – and mainly in the Protection Against Accidents (Dockers) Convention (Revised), 1932 (No. 32) – ratified by some 40 States – in which very detailed provisions deal with the measures of safety which should be taken on shore and on board ships to protect against accidents the workers engaged in loading and unloading. Moreover a code of practice on safety and health in dock work was established in 1956 and the 4th edition appeared in 1971. The Convention was supplemented by a Recommendation (No. 40) adopted the same year, in which States concerned were asked to confer with a view to securing reasonable uniformity in the application of the Convention, including more particularly the mutual recognition of the arrangements made for testing, examining and annealing and of relevant certificates and records. More recently, the changes in technical processes rendered necessary the revision of Convention (No. 32) and a first discussion in this connection took place in 1978. Following this discussion, the International Labour Conference decided that this item shall be included in the agenda of its 1979 Session with a view to the adoption of a Convention and a Recommendation. The more general problem of the social repercussions of new methods of cargo handling in docks is referred to later.[1]

1. See below No. 413.

F. Maritime Work

389. Many Conventions and Recommendations concerning seafarers and fishermen relate to hygiene and safety. They will be mentioned in greater detail in the chapter relating to that category of worker.[1]

1. See below No. 510.

G. Other Activities

390. Among other activities about which provisions relating to hygiene and safety were adopted, reference can be made to the Plantations Convention, 1958 (No. 110) which provides (Art. 89–91) that medical services should be available for plantation workers and their families. Model Codes, guides or codes of practice have also been established as regards activities such as work in mines, agriculture and forestry.

IV. Standards Concerning Methods and Institutions for the Prevention of Industrial Accidents and the Protection of Workers' Health

A. The Prevention of Industrial Accidents

391. In 1923 already, the labour inspection Recommendation (No. 20) provided that labour inspectors should be entrusted with various tasks aiming at the prevention of industrial accidents. A few years later, in 1929, the question of the prevention of industrial accidents as such was dealt with in a special Recommendation (No. 31). This instrument advocated the adoption of a series of measures based on the experience which, at that time, had been gained in different countries. These measures included inquiry into the causes and circumstances of accidents, the collection and collation of statistics relating to industrial accidents, the development of labour inspection, the adoption of concrete measures, described in detail and aiming at the improvement of safety, the co-operation of employers and workers, the establishment of exhibitions, the publication of monographs, the inclusion in the curricula of the schools of appropriate lessons, the adoption of legislative instruments, the co-operation of insurance institutions and companies in the work of accident prevention.

B. The Protection of Workers' Health

392. After the Second World War, the Protection of Workers' Health Recommendation, 1953 (No. 97) provided for a number of detailed measures of protection against the risks to the health of workers in places of employment, medical examination of workers employed in occupations involving special risks to their health, the notification of occupational diseases, first aid and emergency treatment. At the same time, the International Labour Conference adopted a special resolution in which it asked States to encourage measures for the training of physicians qualified in occupational health and to study the organization of industrial medical services.

C. The Occupational Health Services

393. After having taken shape during the First World War, as a result of the initiative of Albert Thomas, then Minister of Munitions of France, occupational health services developed by becoming more and more integrated within the industrial establishment for which they were responsible, in order to be in a position to fulfil the very wide mission with which they are now entrusted. In 1959, the International Labour Conference, on the basis of the work of a group of experts from different countries, adopted a Recommendation (No. 112) on occupational health services in places of employment, which defined these services and provided in some detail what should be their organization and functions which should be essentially preventive. It also contained provisions on the personnel and equipment of these services. The Recommendation set the principle of full professional and moral independence of the physicians in occupational health services in relation with the employer and the workers. It also set the principle that these services should not involve the workers in any expense. This Recommendation has been the first international instrument dealing with the problem of the workers' health in its relation with the exercise of the medical profession and it has exercised a considerable influence.[1] While a number of countries have reservations because of the orientation of the Recommendation towards mainly preventive occupational medicine, this instrument appears to have retained its general usefulness, but the workers consider that a Convention should be envisaged on the subject.

1. The Committee of Experts on the Application of Conventions and Recommendations made, in 1970, a general survey of the effect given to this instrument.

V. Standards Defining the Occupational Diseases which Give Rise to Compensation

394. Naturally, it was not sufficient to provide for the prevention of occupational accidents and diseases. It was also necessary to establish standards relating to their compensation. While this question belongs to social security,[1] it may be useful to refer here to the main aspects of the system of compensation of occupational deseases organized by ILO standards. This system is based on a list of diseases which should be considered as being of occupational origin when they affect workers who are engaged in determined trades, industries or processes. The principle of the double list establishes a presumption for the occupational origin of the disease and exempts the worker from the burden of the proof, which would often have been difficult to produce so that compensation would be problematical. This overriding concern prevailed over objections based on the difficulties of a fully satisfactory definition of occupational diseases and of the inconveniences of too rigid a framework.

1. In this connection see briefly below No. 418.

395. The first Convention on workmen's compensation for occupational diseases was adopted in 1925 (Convention No. 18), and has been ratified by 59 States. It gave a list of only three diseases (poisoning by lead, poisoning by mercury and anthrax infection) but a Recommendation (No. 24) adopted the same year asked each country to adopt a simple procedure by which the list of diseases considered occupational in its national legislation may be revised. The 1925 Convention was revised in 1934 and the new Convention (No. 42), which has been ratified by some 50 States, includes a list of ten occupational diseases.[1] Following the introduction in this new list of silicosis, the importance of which had been underestimated previously, a series of measures were taken in many countries as regards this disease.

1. It added the following diseases to those mentioned in the 1925 list: silicosis, poisoning by phosphorus, arsenic, benzene or its homologues, the halogen derivatives of hydrocarbons of the aliphatic series, pathological manifestations due to radioactive substances and the primary epitheliomatous cancer of the skin.

396. The questions evolved, however, since 1934, and the Conference therefore adopted, thirty years later, a Convention (No. 121) concerning employment injury benefit. This Convention, which has been ratified by 17 States, also includes a list of occupational diseases, which was more detailed than that of 1934. However, in view of the diversity of the existing national systems of compensation of occupational diseases, the Convention gives ratifying States an option between three possibilities; either the establishment of a list of occupational diseases comprising at least those enumerated in the Convention, or the adoption of a general definition of occupational diseases which would be broad enough to cover at least those enumerated in the Convention, or a combination of the two formulae.

397. At the same time, the Conference adopted, in 1964, a Recommendation (No. 121) which advocated that where national legislation contained a list establishing a presumption of occupational origin in respect of certain diseases, proof should be permitted of the occupational origin of diseases not so listed and of diseases listed when they manifest themselves under conditions different from those establishing a presumption of thier occupational origin.

398. Among the various systems which are now recognized in the different countries, the system of the double list, on which the 1925 and 1934 Conventions were based, certainly is the one which offers the greater guarantees to workers, because of the presumption which it involves. However, it results may sometimes be unjust, as it could exclude the compensation of diseases which in fact might be of an occupational origin. On the other hand, the opposite system, described as being of global coverage, ensures, in principle, the compensation of any occupational disease, but it requires that the worker concerned brings the evidence, or at least that there exists in each concrete case a sufficient degree of presumption, that the disease really is of an occupational origin. Finally, the system will depend to a great extent on the value of the medical diagnosis. For these reasons, the mixed system, which has been introduced by certain countries, appears to be able to remedy both the exceedingly absolute and restrictive character of the lists and the uncertainties of the global coverage.

VI. Future Prospects

399. However long it may appear to be, the above enumeration of the existing instruments relating to industrial safety and hygiene should not give the impression that the standard-setting activities of the ILO in this field, important as they may be, can be considered as achieved. Certain of the existing standards should be reviewed in the light of technological change. Others are not contained in Conventions, i.e. in instruments which can, as a result of their ratification, give rise to legal obligations. Moreover, among existing Conventions, while some deal with specific aspects of safety in industry and while the influence exercised by the Model Code of Safety in industrial establishments should not be underestimated, there is no Convention dealing in a general way with safety and hygiene in industry. Finally, while certain hazards which were important in the past have been covered by various standards and have more generally been successfully dealt with (as in the case of anthrax infection, lead poisoning and, to a certain extent, silicosis), other hazards remain serious, new occupational diseases appear and the prevention of industrial accidents still constitutes a matter of major concern. Technical progress reduces certain hazards but also gives rise to new ones. Thus further instruments are being contemplated about new harmful substances in the working environment such as asbestos, pesticides and herbicides in agriculture, as well as the adoption of an over-all standard on measures aiming at reducing industrial accidents and occupational diseases. It has been decided that the question of 'safety and health and the working environment' will be placed on the agenda of the 1980 Session of the International Labour Conference.

VII. Other International Standards

400. At the universal level, the *International Covenant on Economic, Social and Cultural Rights* provides in general terms that the just and favourable conditions of work which everyone should enjoy should ensure in particular 'safe and healthy working conditions' (Art. 7, para. b). At the European level, the *European Social Charter* contains a provision (Art. 3) relating to safe and healthy working conditions. Following a suggestion of the workers at the 1958 Tripartite Conference, this provision specifies that Contracting Parties undertake

'1. to issue safety and health regulations;
2. to provide for the enforcement of such regulations by measures of supervision;
3. to consult, as appropriate, employers' and workers' organizations on measures intended to improve industrial safety and health.'

§5. Welfare Facilities, Housing and Spare Time

I. Welfare Facilities for Workers

401. Adopted in 1956, a Recommendation (No. 102) on Welfare Facilities, which applies to manual and non-manual workers employed in public or private undertakings (excluding workers in agriculture and sea transport) has set the principles and defined the standards concerning welfare facilities relating to feeding (canteens, buffets and trolleys, messrooms and other suitable rooms, mobile canteens, other facilities etc.), to rest in the undertakings (seats and rest rooms), to recreation, to management and financing of feeding and recreation facilities, and finally to transport facilities to and from work.

402. Considering the problem from a more general point of view, the European Social Charter included a provision (Art. 14) on 'the right to benefit from social welfare services', in which it is specified that States undertake 'to promote or provide services which, by using methods of social work, would contribute to the welfare and development of both individuals and groups in the community, and to their adjustment to the social environment' and 'to encourage the participation of individuals and volunteers or other organizations in the establishment and maintenance of such services'.

II. Housing

403. Already in 1921, the question of housing for workers had been dealt with in a Recommendation (No. 16) drafted in general terms and relating to living-in conditions of agricultural workers. The provision of adequate housing appeared in the programme assigned to the ILO by the 1944 Declaration of Philadelphia. The Universal Declaration of Human Rights, which was adopted by the United Nations four years later, referred to housing among the elements which should constitute a satisfactory standard of living (Art. 25, para. 1) On the basis of the common interest which the two organizations thus had in the matter, it was recognized by them in 1949 that the United Nations have a general responsibility in the field of housing and of urban and rural development and the ILO have a special interest as regards housing of workers.

404. In these circumstances, a Recommendation (No. 115) on workers' housing was adopted in 1961.[1] This Recommendation first defines the objectives of national housing policy and the responsibility of public authorities.

Then it deals with housing provided by employers, the question of financing, housing standards, measures to promote efficiency in the building industry, house building and employment stabilization and finally town, country and regional planning. The Recommendation also contains detailed suggestions concerning methods of application of the principles which it has set, as well as some connected questions, such as rent policy.

1. Before the adoption of this over-all Recommendation, other instruments referred to housing for special categories of workers. Apart from the 1921 Recommendation on agricultural workers, Conventions were adopted more recently on accommodation of crews for seamen and fishermen (see No. 510 below) and provisions about housing are also contained in the 1958 Plantations Recommendation (No. 110).

405. Among the other international standards in the field of housing, reference can be made, following the terms of the Universal Declaration of Human Rights, which has already been mentioned above, to a provision of the International Covenant on Economic, Social and Cultural Rights (Art. 11, para. 1) in which reference is made to 'adequate housing' among the elements which constitute to an 'adequate standard of living'.

406. More recently, in the framework of the right of migrant workers and their families to protection and assistance, the European Social Charter (Art. 19, para. 4-c), using to a large extent the same wording as a provision of the ILO Migrant Workers (Revised) Convention, 1949 (No. 97), provided that migrant workers who are lawfully within the territory of a Contracting Party are entitled to treatment not less favourable than that of their own nationals in respect of remuneration and other employment and working conditions, membership of trade unions and enjoyment of the benefits of collective bargaining and accommodation.

III. Workers' Spare Time

407. A few years after it adopted, in 1919, the Convention on the eight-hour day, the International Labour Conference considered the problem of the utilization by the workers of the spare time which would thus become available. A detailed Recommendation (No. 21) was adopted in 1924 on that question. This instrument advocates in the first instance the preservation of spare time by the conclusion of collective agreements which would ensure a normal standard of living to workers in exchange for their legal hours of work and which would determine the measures to prevent workers from having recourse to additional paid work. It also recommended that the working day be so arranged as to make the periods of spare time as continuous as possible. It also dealt with questions of social hygiene, of housing policy and of institutions for the utilization of spare time. It stressed, in particular the need to take into account the desires, the tastes and the special requirements of the workers concerned, while recommending to take certain types of initiatives, which it described. It also underlined the principle of free use of institutions and it emphasized the necessity of safeguarding the individual freedom of the workers against any system or scheme which has any tendency towards compelling the workers directly or indirectly to use any particular institution. It was also reminded in the preamble of the Recommendation that, etymologically 'leisure' means to do as one pleases. Such insistence was particularly appropriate at a period at which organized spare time was going to be greatly developed in countries with authoritarian regimes. Finally, without envisaging any systematic organization of spare time, the Conference recommended measures of co-ordination and of propaganda in that field.

408. More recently, leisure was mentioned in general terms in the Universal Declaration (Art. 24) and in the International Covenant on Economic, Social and Cultural Rights (Art. 7, para. d).

Chapter VII. Social Policy

§1. General Principles of Social Policy

409. While, generally, each International Labour Convention and Recommendation deals with a well defined subject, it seemed useful to adopt certain instruments relating to social policy as a whole, in order to encourage governments to pursue a systematic and co-ordinated action in this field. This was first the case in 1947, when the ILO Conference adopted the Social Policy (Non-Metropolitan Territories) Convention (No. 82). The Convention was ratified by four States responsible for such territories and remains applicable to twenty-four territories with or without modifications. Later, the Convention was revised when many countries to which it was applicable became independent. A new Convention (No. 117) was adopted in 1962, mainly to allow independent States to continue to apply it or to ratify it. The revised instrument contains the main provisions of the 1947 Convention but omits those which related to the situation of non-metropolitan territories. In this wider conception, the title of the Convention in its revised form is 'Convention concerning basic aims and standards of social policy'.

410. The general principle laid down in the Convention is that all policies shall be directed to the well-being and development of the population and to the promotion of its desire for social progress. It also adds that all policies of more general application shall be formulated with due regard to their effect upon the well-being of the population. Then, the Convention sets certain standards of which governments should take account to reach these objectives. Thus, the improvement of standards of living should be regarded as the principal objective in the planning of economic development. A series of measures are advocated in order to harmonize economic development with a healthy evolution of the communities concerned,[1] to promote the productive capacity and improve the standards of living of agricultural producers,[2] and to secure for independent producers and wage earners conditions which will give them scope to improve living standards by their own efforts.

1. Study of the causes and effects of migratory movements and appropriate action where necessary, promotion of town and village planning, prevention and elimination of congestion in urban areas, improvement of living conditions in rural areas and establishment of suitable industries.
2. Elimination of the causes of chronic indebtedness, control of the alienation of agricultural land to non-agriculturalists, control of the ownership and use of land and resources to ensure that they are used in the best interests of the inhabitants of the country, supervision of tenancy arrangements and of working conditions with a view to securing for tenants and labourers the highest practicable standards of living, reduction of production and distribution costs, in particular by forming, encouraging and assisting producers' and consumers' cooperatives. On the latter point a recommendation adopted in 1966 (No. 127) dealt with the role of co-operatives in the economic and social development of developing countries.

411. The Convention also includes special provisions concerning migrant workers, remuneration of workers and related questions of protection of wages. It provides that it shall be an aim of policy to abolish all discrimination among workers on grounds of race, colour, sex, belief, tribal association or trade union affiliation in respect of the various fields of employment and conditions of work. It finally provides for the progressive development of broad systems of education, vocational training and apprenticeship and requires that the school-leaving age and the minimum age for and conditions of employment be prescribed by national laws or regulations.

412. Convention No. 117 has been ratified by 27 countries, mainly developing ones. A number of governments felt unable to proceed with its ratification, for very different reasons.[1] Some developed countries referred to the origin of the Convention and considered that it is mainly directed to developing countries or to countries which became independent at a recent date. In other cases, on the contrary, difficulties were encountered by developing countries which, while giving their support to the principles on which the Convention was based, considered that existing economic and social conditions prevented them from giving full effect to the provisions of the Convention. However the flexibility of the terms of the Convention has often been underlined and its ratification made good progress over the years.

1. See the general survey made by the Committee of Experts in 1969.

§2. Social Repercussions of Technical Progress

413. Some particular aspects of social policy have also been examined at more recent dates. This was the case in 1972 and in 1973, when the International Labour Conference dealt with two questions arising out of technical progress. One of them related to the social repercussions of the new methods of cargo handling in docks, about which the Conference adopted, in 1973, a Convention (No. 137) ratified by 11 States until now, and supplemented by a Recommendation (No. 145).

414. As regards the labour and social implications of automation and other technological developments, the Conference adopted, in 1972, a Resolution stating the principles and programmes which should guide governments, employers and workers and their organizations, in particular as regards labour-management relations, full employment (by pointing out that in situations of widespread unemployment, the employment effects of using advanced technology must be considered together with its role in economic development), preventing or minimizing job loss, assistance to workers who lose their employment, preparation for new occupational requirements, health and safety and some other conditions of work (in particular from the point of view of reduction of hours of work). The Resolution invited the ILO to carry out a number of studies on specific social problems of technological development and requested that the question of the social effects of technological change be put on the agenda of future sessions of the International Labour Conference, with a view to the adoption of international instruments.

§3. Multinational Enterprises and Social Policy

415. The problem of multinational enterprises and social policy has been examined by the ILO for a number of years and a number of studies[1] and meetings were devoted to it. In this connection, among the questions which were considered was that of the usefulness and feasibility of international principles and guidelines on social policy for multinational enterprises.[2] In November 1977, the ILO Governing Body approved an 'ILO Tripartite Declaration of Principles concerning Multinational Enterprises and Social Policy' which had been prepared by a Tripartite Advisory Meeting. This Declaration deals with general policies, employment (employment promotion, equality of opportunity and treatment, security of employment), training, conditions of work and life (wages, benefits and conditions of work, safety and health) and industrial relations (freedom of association and the right to organize, collective bargaining, consultation, examination of grievances, settlement of industrial disputes).

1. *Multinational Enterprises and Social Policy*, ILO, Geneva 1973.
2. See *International principles and guidelines on social policy for multinational enterprises: their usefulness and feasibility*, Geneva, ILO, 1976.

Chapter VIII. Social Security

416. As social security is not covered by the present Encyclopedia, we shall not deal here in any detail with the various ILO and other international instruments which have been adopted in this field. For the sake of completeness, we shall only give a very brief outline of the general trend of the various international standards which relate to social security.[1]

1. For a more detailed account of the international standards on social security see our book on *Droit international du travail,* Paris, 1970 (pages 386–426) and the more recent edition in Spanish *'Derecho internacional del trabajo'*, Madrid, 1977 (pages 356–385).

417. The Preamble of the ILO Constitution requested the Organization already when it was established, in 1919, to improve conditions of work, in particular by 'the prevention of unemployment, ... the protection of the worker against sickness, disease and injury arising out of his employment, ... provision for old-age and injury'.

418. During an initial period, from 1919 to 1936, a series of distinct instruments mainly based on the notion of social insurance, were adopted to protect given categories of workers against a certain number of risks. The first of these standards dealt with the subject of unemployment (Convention No. 2) in 1919 and workmen's compensation (accidents and occupational diseases) (Conventions Nos. 17, 18 and 19) in 1925. Then, in 1927, the ILO launched the systematic adoption of separate Conventions providing for the establishment of social insurance schemes relating each to a specific contingency and a major economic sector, i.e. sickness, old-age, invalidity and survivors on the one hand in industry and on the other in agriculture. In 1934, the 1925 Convention on occupational diseases was revised, as indicated above,[1] and a Convention and a Recommendation (No. 44) were adopted to grant benefits or allowances to unemployed persons. The following year another Convention (No. 48) was adopted in an attempt to deal with the difficult question of the maintenance of Migrants' Pension Rights. During the same period, and more particularly in 1936, Conventions were adopted to provide for compensation in case of sickness or accidents occurring to seafarers.

1. See above No. 396.

419. During a second period, which started in 1944, the standards were based on the wider notion of social security, the aim of which was to provide a basic income for all those who need such protection, as well as full medical care. The new approach was based on the principles of universality and of unity of the function entrusted to social security. In 1944, it received an impetus, at the international level, from the Declaration of Philadelphia, which advocated 'the extension of social security measures to provide a basic income to all in need of such protection and comprehensive medical care' and from two Recommendations', the one of which (No. 67) related to income security and the other (No. 69) dealt with medical care.

420. In 1952, the ILO adopted the basic post-war Convention in the field of social security, i.e. Convention (No. 102) concerning social security (minimum standards), now ratified by 29 States. This instrument is based on the principle of a general standard of social security which could be reached by each State, without regard to its own situation and the stage of its economic and social development. The Convention provides for a general scheme of social security covering all the risks and benefits and being gradually extended to all the population. The Convention deals with the nine main branches of social security (medical care, sickness benefit, unemployment benefit, old-age benefit, employment injury benefit, family benefit, maternity benefit, invalidity benefit, survivors' benefit). A State should accept three at least of these branches to ratify this instrument. The Convention also authorizes certain exceptions for States 'whose economy and medical facilities are insufficiently developed'. The minimum standard provided by the Convention is defined in the first instance as regards the scope of the protection, which should cover either 50 per cent of all employees, or prescribed classes of economically active population, constituting not less than 20 per cent of all residents, or all residents whose means during the contingency do not exceed given limits. The Convention also establishes a minimum standard as regards the benefits, which must comprise benefits in kind (medical care, etc.), as well as benefits in cash consisting of periodic payments, for which it determines their minimum level by reference to the general level of wages in each country.

421. Following the adoption of Convention No. 102, the ILO undertook the establishment of a series of new instruments with a view to supplementing or revising the previous ones and sometimes to providing for a higher degree of protection than Convention No. 102. Thus, in 1962, the Conference adopted the Equality of Treatment (Social Security) Convention (No. 118), in 1964 the Employment Injury Benefits Convention (No. 121), in 1967 the Invalidity, Old-Age and Survivors' Benefits Convention (No. 128) and Recommendation (No. 131) and in 1969 the Medical Care and Sickness Benefits Convention (No. 130) and Recommendation (No. 134). The programme for the revision of existing social security standards includes those relating to unemployment benefits. Consideration is also being given to the possibility of a new instrument on family benefits and to the revision of the Maintenance of Migrants' Pension Rights, 1935 (No. 48). Apart from the establishment and revision of social security standards of general application, the ILO has pursued the adoption and revision of conventions containing social security standards relating to special categories of workers, such as seafarers, in particular.[1]

1. See below No. 512.

Chapter IX. Industrial Relations

§1. General Outline

422. The question of industrial relations is closely linked to that of freedom of association,[1] which constitutes a basic condition for healthy industrial relations, in the same way as industrial relations constitute the normal development of freedom of association. It is a matter of fact that, in many respects, industrial relations in the world are not yet fully satisfactory. This is clearly shown by the number and sometimes the gravity of industrial disputes which take place even in highly industrialized countries. In spite of this, great progress has been accomplished during the last decades and this is due to a large extent to the action of the ILO.[2] The tripartite structure of the ILO has, since the Organization was created stimulated the establishment of national systems of industrial relations based on the recognition by States of workers' representative organizations, on consultation and on social dialogue. At the level of ILO Constitutional principles, the 1944 Declaration of Philadelphia listed, among the main objectives of the Organization, 'the effective recognition of the right of collective bargaining, the co-operation of management and labour in the continuous improvement of productive efficiency, and the collaboration of workers and employers in the preparation and application of social and economic measures'.

1. See above No. 164 ss.
2. See G. Spyropoulos 'An Outline of Developments and Trends in Labour Relations', *I.L.R.*, March 1969.

423. As regards international standards in the technical meaning, the general principle of the right to collective bargaining was set in the Right to Organize and Collective Bargaining Convention, 1949 (No. 98), to which reference was made above,[1] in the framework of freedom of association. Following the adoption of that Convention, various aspects of industrial relations were dealt with in a number of Recommendations. These Recommendations related to collective agreements, voluntary conciliation and arbitration, co-operation at the level of the undertaking, consultation at the industrial and national levels, termination of employment, communications within the undertaking and the examination of grievances. Moreover it has been explained above[2] that a Convention and a Recommendation were adopted in 1971 in regard to the protection and the facilities to be afforded to workers' representatives in the undertaking. Reference was also made to the question of labour relations in the public service which was considered by the International Labour Conference in 1978.[3] Finally, standards relating to industrial relations were adopted in certain special fields, e.g. as regards Seamen's Articles of Agreement and the contracts of employment of indigenous workers.[4]

1. Nos. 189 ss.
2. Nos. 196 and f.
3. See above Nos. 202 and 535.
4. See below Nos. 506–507 and 525–526.

§2. Collective Agreements

424. The question of collective agreements was dealt with in a Recommendation (No. 91) adopted in 1971. In this field, as for the other aspects of industrial relations, the form of a Recommendation was considered to be more appropriate than that of a Convention, in view of the variety of national situations. The Recommendation first refers to the machinery of collective agreements and leaves it to the parties concerned or to national legislation to establish 'machinery appropriate to the conditions existing in each country'. It defines collective agreements as meaning 'all agreements in writing regarding working conditions and terms of employment concluded between an employer, a group of employers or one or more employers' organizations, on the one hand, and one or more representative workers' organizations or, in the absence of such organizations, the representatives of the workers duly elected and authorized by them in accordance with national laws and regulations'.

425. The Recommendation then deals with the effects of collective agreements. It sets the principle that they should bind the signatories and those on whose behalf the agreement is concluded and that if contracts of employment concluded between employers and workers who are bound by a collective agreement contain stipulations contrary to the agreement, such stipulations should be regarded as null and void, unless they are more favourable to the workers. The Recommendation also considers the possibility of extension of collective agreements to all the employers and workers included within the industrial and territorial scope of the agreement. It specifies certain conditions subject to which such extension could take place.

426. The last provisions of the Recommendation relate to the interpretation of collective agreements, to the supervision of their application and to various measures of publicity, such as the requirement for employers to bring to the notice of the workers concerned the texts of collective agreements applicable to their undertakings and the registration or deposit of collective agreements and subsequent changes. Finally, it is specified that national laws may make provision for a minimum period during which, in the absence of any stipulation to the contrary in the agreement, collective agreements shall be deemed to be binding unless revised or rescinded at an earlier date by the parties.

§3. Voluntary Conciliation and Arbitration

427. In 1951 also, the International Labour Conference adopted the Recommendation (No. 92) concerning Voluntary Conciliation and Arbitration. As regards voluntary conciliation, the Recommendation provides that a machinery should be made available to assist in the prevention and settlement of industrial disputes between employers and workers. Where voluntary conciliation machinery is constituted on a joint basis, it should include equal representation of employers and workers. The procedure should be free of charge and expeditious, and time limits should be fixed in advance and kept to a minimum. It should be possible to set the procedure in motion either on the initiative of any of the parties to the dispute or *ex officio* by the voluntary conciliation authority. If a dispute has been submitted to conciliation procedure with the consent of all the parties concerned, the latter should be encouraged to abstain from strikes and lockouts while conciliation is in progress. All agreements which the parties may reach should be drawn up in writing and be regarded as equivalent to agreements concluded in the usual way.

428. As regards voluntary arbitration, the Recommendation provides that, if a dispute has been submitted for final settlement to arbitration with the consent of all parties concerned, the latter should be encouraged to abstain from strikes and lockouts while the arbitration is in progress and to accept the arbitration award. Finally, it is specified that no provision in the Recommendation may be interpreted as limiting the right to strike. The provision was adopted 'to emphasize the purely optional character of the procedures referred to'[1] in the Recommendation.

1. Intern. Lab. Code, page 709, note 36 under art. 876M.

§4. Co-operation at the Level of the Undertaking

429. Standard-setting in the field of industrial relations was pursued in 1952 with the adoption of a Recommendation (No. 94) concerning Co-operation at the Level of the Undertaking.[1] The Recommendation is drafted in general terms and it provides, in the first place, that steps should be taken to promote consultation and co-operation between employers and workers at the level of the undertaking on matters of mutual concern not within the scope of collective bargaining machinery, or not normally dealt with by other machinery concerned with the determination of terms and conditions of employment. In accordance with national custom or practice, such consultation and co-operation should be facilitated by the encouragement of voluntary agreements between the parties or promoted by laws or regulations which would establish bodies for consultation and co-operation and determine their scope, functions, structure and methods of operation as may be appropriate in the various undertakings. Such consultation and co-operation might also be facilitated or promoted by a combination of these two methods.

1. See, more generally, de Givry, 'Developments in Labour-Management Relations in the Undertaking', *I.L.R.*, January 1969.

§5. Consultation at the Industrial and National Levels

430. A few years later, in 1960, a further Recommendation was adopted in order to supplement the previous one by providing for the consultation and co-operation which should be instituted between public authorities and employers' and workers' organizations – or between the latter – at the industrial and national levels.[1] The Recommendation provides that measures appropriate to national conditions should be taken to promote such effective consultation and co-operation. Consultation and co-operation of this kind should aim, in particular:

a. at joint consideration by employers' and workers' organizations of matters of mutual conern with a view to arriving, to the fullest possible extent, at agreed solutions;
b. at ensuring that the competent public authorities seek the views, advice and assistance of employers' and workers' organizations in respect of such matters as:
   (i) the preparation and implementation of laws and regulations affecting their interests;
   (ii) the establishment and functioning of national bodies, such as those responsible for organization of employment, vocational training and

retraining, labour protection, industrial health and safety, productivity, social security and welfare; and

(iii) the elaboration and implementation of plans of economic and social development.

More generally, such consultation and co-operation should have the objective of promoting mutual understanding and good relations between public authorities and employers' and workers' organizations, as well as between these organizations, with a view to developing the economy as a whole or individual branches of it, improving conditions of work and raising standards of living.

1. See in this connection the general survey prepared in 1976 by the Committee of Experts on the Application of Conventions and Recommendations.

431. The Recommendation specifies that measures to promote such consultation and co-operation should be applied without discrimination of any kind against these organizations or amongst them on grounds such as race, sex, religion, political opinion or national extraction of its members. The consultation and co-operation should not derogate from freedom of association or from the rights of employers' and workers' organizations, including their right of collective bargaining.

432. The Recommendation refers to various methods to provide for or facilitate consultation and co-operation, in accordance with national custom or practice, such as voluntary action on the part of the employers' and workers' organizations, promotional action on the part of the public authorities, laws or regulations, or a combination of any of these methods.

§6. Termination of Employment at the Initiative of the Employer

433. In 1963, the adoption of the Recommendation concerning Termination of Employment at the Initiative of the Employer (No. 119) contributed an important development from the point of view both of industrial relations and of security of employment. It has been one of the ILO instruments which, in a few years, had the greatest impact.[1] While leaving a large measure of freedom as regards its methods of application (national laws or regulations, collective agreements, work rules, arbitration awards, court decisions, etc.), the Recommendation, which has a wide scope,[2] establishes the general standard that termination of employment should not take place unless there is a valid reason connected with the capacity or conduct of the worker or based on the operational requirements of the undertaking, establishment or service. While leaving the definition or interpretation of such valid reason to the methods of implementation of each country, the Recommendation provides that the following should not constitute valid reasons for termination of employment:

a. union membership or participation in union activities outside working hours or, with the consent of the employer, within working hours;

b. seeking office as, or acting or having acted in the capacity of, a workers' representative;
c. the filling in good faith of a complaint or the participation in a proceeding against an employer involving alleged violation of laws or regulations; or
d. race, colour, sex, marital status, religion, political opinion, national extraction or social origin.

1. See in this connection the general survey established in 1974 by the Committee of Experts on the Application of Conventions and Recommendations. See also Yemin, 'Job Security: Influence of ILO Standards and Recent Trends', *I.L.R.*, January-February 1976. This Recommendation has, in a few years, influenced the legislation of some 20 countries.
2. The Recommendation applies to all branches of economic activity and all categories of workers but allows for certain exceptions, such as workers engaged for a specified period of time, etc.

434. As a general rule, a worker who feels that his employment has been unjustifiably terminated should be entitled to appeal against that termination to a body established under a collective agreement or to a neutral body such as a court or an arbitrator. That body should be empowered to examine the reasons given for the termination of employment – but this does not imply that it should be empowered to intervene in the determination of the size of the work force of the undertaking – and to order that the worker concerned, unless reinstated with payment of any unpaid wages, should be paid adequate compensation.

435. A worker whose employment is to be terminated should be entitled to a reasonable period of notice or compensation. During the period of notice, he should be entitled to a reasonable amount of time off without loss in pay in order to seek other employment. The worker whose employment has been terminated should be entitled to receive a certificate from the employer specifying the dates of his engagement and termination and the type of work on which he was employed. Nothing unfavourable to the worker should be inserted in such certificate. The Recommendation also provides for some form of income protection for the workers concerned (such as unemployment insurance, severance allowance, etc.). In case of dismissal for serious misconduct, a period of notice or compensation need not be required and the severance allowance may be withheld. Dismissal for serious misconduct should take place only in cases where the employer cannot in good faith be expected to take any other course, and the worker should be given the opportunity to state his case promptly, with the assistance where appropriate of a person representing him, before a decision to dismiss him for serious misconduct becomes finally effective.

436. The Recommendation also includes supplementary provisions concerning reduction of the work force. These provisions relate, in particular, to the adoption of measures to avert or minimize as far as possible reactions of the work force without prejudice to the efficient operation of the undertaking, to consultation with workers' representatives when a reduction of the work force is contemplated and to notification to the public authorities if a proposed reduction of the work force is on such a scale as to have a significant bearing on the manpower situation of a given area or branch of economic activity. The Recommendation also refers to the criteria according to which the selection of the workers to be affected by a reduction of the work force should be made. It lists certain of these criteria, such as the need for the efficient operation of the undertaking, the ability, experience, skill and occupational qualifications of individual workers, length of service, age and family situation. It is also provided that workers whose employment has been terminated owing to a reduction of the work force should be given priority of re-engagement, to the extent possible by the employer, and the rate of their wages should not then be adversely affected as a result of the interruption of their employment.

437. In the field of termination of employment, the European Social Charter contains a provision (Art. 4, para. 4) which was included following a suggestion made by the Tripartite Conference and which relates to the 'right of all workers to a reasonable period of notice for termination of employment'. The Appendix to the Charter adds, as it had also been agreed by the Tripartite Conference, that this provision does not prohibit 'immediate dismissal for any serious offence'.

§7. Communications and Examination of Grievances in the Undertaking

438. The question of co-operation at the level of the undertaking, which was initiated in 1952 by Recommendation No. 94, was pursued in 1967 by two Recommendations relating to particular aspects of this matter. The first of these instruments (Recommendation No. 129) deals with communications between management and workers within the undertaking. It recommends that employers and their organizations as well as workers and their organizations should, in their common interest, recognize the importance of a climate of mutual understanding and confidence within undertakings that is favourable both to the efficiency of the undertaking and to the aspirations of the workers. It advocates various measures to promote this climate, in particular the adoption by management of an effective policy of communication with the workers and their representatives. Such a policy should ensure that information is given and that consultation takes place between the parties before decisions on matters of major interest are taken by management, in so far as disclosure of the information will not cause damage to either party. After having specified that the communication methods should in no way derogate from freedom of association, the Recommendation describes the various elements for a communications policy.

439. The second Recommendation (No. 130) relates to the examination of grievances within the undertaking with a view to their settlement. It provides that any worker who, acting individually or jointly with other workers, considers that he has grounds for a grievance should have the right to submit such grievance without suffering any prejudice as a result and to have such grievance examined pursuant to an appropriate procedure. The Recommendation, which does not deal with collective claims aimed at the modification of terms and conditions of employment, specifies the grounds for the grievances to which it relates. It advocates the association of workers' organizations or of the representatives or workers in the undertaking, with equal rights and responsibilities, with the employers or their organizations, in the establishment and the implementation of grievance procedures within the undertaking. With a view to minimizing the number of grievances, it calls attention to the establishment and proper functioning of a sound personnel policy, which should take into account and respect the rights and interests of the workers. The grievance procedures should not result in limiting the right of workers to apply directly to the competent labour authority or to a labour court or other judicial authority. The Recommendation also contains a number of suggestions about the grievance procedures within the undertaking and the procedures which might be followed for the adjustment of unsettled grievances.

Chapter X. Work of Women

440. In the field of work of women, international action has been guided by two main considerations. The first has been the desire to protect women against excessively arduous conditions of work, in particular in the case of maternity. This concern for protection against abuse, which was manifested in the XIXth century was at the origin of one of the two Bern Conventions of 1906. In 1919 it found its expression in the Preamble of the Constitution of the ILO. A parallel concern aimed at ensuring equality of rights and of treatment between women and men. The question has already been mentioned in connection with discrimination in employment.[1] The most well-known aspect of discrimination on the basis of sex is the question of equal remuneration which was already, in 1919, among the general principles of the ILO and which was dealt with, in 1951, in a Convention which had a big impact. In some cases, these two different considerations appeared to be in conflict and certain advocates of the principle of equality opposed protective measures which appeared to them to be such as to jeopardize the realization of this principle and to lead to or imply a certain degree of discrimination. In resolutions adopted in 1975, the International Labour Conference requested that the ILO study the need for new instruments concerning equal opportunity and equal treatment for women and men in occupation and employment with a view to supplementing the existing Conventions (Nos. 100 and 111) and that there should be a review and a revision, if necessary, of ILO standards relating to the employment of women, in order to determine whether their provisions are still adequate. The present chapter will deal in particular with international standards relating to maternity protection, night work of women, employment of women in unhealthy or dangerous occupations, equal remuneration and employment of women with family responsibilities.

1. See above No. 234 ff.

§1. Maternity Protection

441. Maternity protection was first dealt with in a Convention (No. 3) adopted by the ILO Conference at its first session, in 1919 and ratified by 28 States. This instrument was revised by Convention No. 103, adopted in 1952 and ratified by 17 States. While the former Convention applied to industry and commerce, the latter covers industry, non-industrial occupations, including domestic work and agricultural occupations. The two Conventions apply to workers of public or private undertakings, irrespective of age, nationality, race or creed, whether married or unmarried. Convention No. 103, the scope of which is wider, authorizes exceptions for family undertakings. It also allows for exceptions for certain categories of non-industrial occupations, for agricultural undertakings, other than plantations, for domestic work for wages in private households, for women wage earners working at home, and for transport by sea. The categories in respect of which a State has recourse to this possibility of exception have to be specified in a declaration accompanying the ratification, and the State concerned shall indicate in its annual reports on the application of the Convention the position of its law and practice in respect of the occupations or undertakings concerned and the extent to which effect has been given or is proposed to be given to the Convention in respect of such occupations or undertakings.

442. The Conventions provide that the period of maternity leave shall be at least twelve weeks. While Convention No. 3 required that six weeks should be taken before and six weeks after confinement, Convention No. 103 is more flexible and only provides that the 12 weeks shall include a period of compulsory leave after confinement, which shall in no case be less than six weeks. The leave before the presumed date of confinement shall be extended by any period between that presumed date and the actual date of confinement and the period of leave after confinement shall not be reduced on that account. The leave shall also be extended in case of illness arising out of pregnancy or confinement.

443. During her leave, the woman shall be entitled to receive cash and medical benefits. The rates of cash benefit should be sufficient for the full and healthy maintenance of herself and her child in accordance with a suitable standard of living. Medical benefits should include pre-natal, confinement and post-natal care as well as hospitalization care where necessary, freedom of choice of doctor and of hospital should be respected. The benefits should be provided either by means of compulsory social insurance or by means of public funds. Both Conventions – the latter more explicitly – exclude that the employer be individually liable for the cost of the benefits, in order to prevent the practice of discriminatory measures as regards employment of women and also to avoid any difficulties of obtaining payment. Convention No. 103 added that when cash benefits provided under compulsory social insurance are based on previous earnings, they should be at a rate of not less than two-thirds of the woman's previous earnings taken into account.

444. If the woman is nursing her child she should be entitled to interrupt her work for this purpose, and the interruptions for that purpose should be counted as working hours and remunerated accordingly. Convention No. 3 provided that the woman should be allowed half an hour twice a day for this purpose, but Convention No. 103 is drafted in more general terms and also permits that the matter be determined by collective agreements.

445. Finally, the Conventions prohibit that notice of dismissal be given to a woman during her absence from work on maternity leave or at such a time that the notice would expire during such absence.

446. At the same time as it adopted Convention No. 103, in 1952, the International Labour Conference adopted a Recommendation (No. 95) which advocated some more precise measures and set some higher standards, such as the extension of the leave to 14 weeks, in certain cases, and the fixing of cash benefits at a higher rate, equalling, when practicable, 100 per cent of the woman's previous earnings. The Recommendation also dealt with the medical benefits, with facilities for nursing mothers and infants, with protection of employment (in particular by suggesting that the period during which the woman is protected from dismissal should be extended to begin as from the date when the employer has been notified of her pregnancy and to continue until one month at least after the end of maternity leave) and with protection of the health of employed women during the maternity period.

447. The Conventions on maternity protection set standards which were well above the level of most national legislations. Their influence in various countries has been considerable. In spite of this, the rate of their ratification has been slow and the present figures still do not correspond to the importance of the matter. At the present time 36 States are bound by one or other of the two Conventions, or by both. As regards Convention No. 103, the main obstacles[1] relate to the wide scope of the Convention, to the required level of cash benefits and even to the duration of the leave which, in some countries, has not yet reached 12 weeks. Difficulties are also met, in a number of countries, in connection with some other provisions, such as the need to extend the leave in case of mistake in estimating the date of confinement or of illness arising out of pregnancy or confinement, the prohibition of making the employer liable for the cost of the benefits and the prohibition of dismissing the woman during her leave.

1. *Rep. Com. Exp*., 1969, pp. 248–250.

§2. Night Work

448. Night work of women was one of the first matters on which international standards were adopted. It was one of the two subjects of the 1906 Bern Convention. In 1914 the Bern Convention on Night Work of Women was in force for 13 countries. At the first session of the International Labour Conference, in 1919, the text of this Convention was reviewed and amplified by the ILO Night Work (Women) Convention (No. 4). At that stage there was a parallel trend in international standards relating to night work of woman and to night work of young persons. However, these two questions have developed in different directions. While the standards relating to night work of young persons were subsequently revised with a view to raising their level, the standards on night work of women faced some serious difficulties and had to be revised twice to be made more flexible.

449. The initial ILO Convention of 1919 provided that women without distinction of age shall not be employed during the night in any public or private industrial undertaking, and it defined the term 'night' as signifying a period of at least eleven consecutive hours, including the interval between ten o'clock in the evening and five o'clock in the morning. Exceptions were allowed for the undertakings in which only members of the same family are employed, for cases of *force majeure* and those where the work has to do with raw materials or materials in course of treatment which are subject to rapid deterioration. A certain flexibility was also permitted in undertakings which are influenced by the seasons and in all cases where exceptional circumstances demand it, as well as in countries where the climate renders work by day particularly trying to health. The Convention was ratified by close to 60 States, but the strict character of the prohibition of night work constituted an obstacle to a wider ratification and created difficulties in its application. As mentioned above,[1] the question was raised, in particular, as to whether the Convention applied to women who hold positions of supervision or management and are not ordinarily engaged in manual work. The advisory opinion given by the Permanent Court of International Justice in 1932 was in the affirmative.

1. No. 59.

450. Following this opinion and in the light of the difficulties which had been encountered, a revised Convention (No. 41) adopted in 1934. While maintaining the prohibition of work during the same period of night as well as the other provisions of the 1919 Convention, the revised instrument authorized a greater flexibility in the way of calculating the interval which should be included in that period. It also excluded from its scope – and this was the most important change – 'women holding responsible positions of management who are not ordinarily engaged in manual work'.

451. The new Convention was ratified by 37 States but the revision proved to be insufficient and the Convention had to be revised once more, in 1948, by Convention No. 89 which leaves greater freedom in the determination of the interval which should be included in the night period. According to the new Convention, the period of 11 consecutive hours should include an interval of at least seven consecutive hours falling between ten o'clock in the evening and seven o'clock in the morning, and different intervals may be prescribed for different areas, industries, undertakings, etc. but the competent authority should consult employers' and workers' organizations before prescribing an interval beginning after eleven o'clock in the evening. Moreover, the condition excludes from its scope women holding responsible positions of a managerial or technical character, as well as women employed in health and welfare services who are not ordinarily engaged in manual work. This Convention was ratified by 56 States.

452. The above Conventions on night work of women were widely ratified – 75 States being parties to at least one of them – and they still are considered in many countries as corresponding to a real need. However, doubts are expressed in an increasing number of quarters as to the suitability, in the light of the principle of equality, of maintaining the prohibition of night work of women, while similar rules do not apply to men. It was agreed that this prohibition might have adverse repercussions on the access of women to employment and on equal remuneration. As a result, seven countries, up to now, denounced one of these Conventions without ratifying a revised one.[1] The matter was also raised when the European Social Charter was being drafted, as will be seen below.[2] In 1971, the Swiss Government asked the ILO to initiate, once again, the procedure of revision of the Convention, which it considered as outdated. The International Labour Office prepared a report on the application of the Convention and consulted the governments about the desirability of the revision. The question was then discussed by the Governing Body of the ILO. It appeared that there are important differences of views between countries and between occupational organizations. The question is still being considered.

1. For the reasons given by one of these countries (the Netherlands) see *O.B.*, vol. LV, 1972, No. 1.
2. See below No. 466.

§3. The Employment of Women in Unhealthy or Dangerous Occupations

453. Various instruments aimed at protecting women against the risks which are inherent in employment in unhealthy or dangerous occupations. Thus the arduous character of underground work and the abuse in the employment of women in mines led to the adoption, in 1935, of a Convention (No. 45) prohibiting the employment of women on underground work in any mine, subject to certain exceptions. The Convention was ratified by 84 States, but, in this case also, there has been in certain countries, a move towards the employment of women in mines. For example, Sweden denounced the Convention in 1967, but made it clear[1] that its decision should in no way be interpreted as a negative evaluation of the importance of the Convention as an international instrument and that 'in countries where work in mines was carried out under other conditions, less satisfactory from the point of view of industrial hygiene than those prevailing in Swedish mines, the Convention was . . . of unquestionable importance in preventing the employment of women under unsatisfactory conditions and in work for which they were not physically equipped'.

1. See *O.B.*, vol. L, No. 3, July 1967, pp. 322–324.

454. Various other instruments, either relating more particularly to women, or of more general scope, contain provisions concerning the risks which certain occupations would involve for women. This is the case, in particular, as regards lead poisoning (Recommendation No. 4 of 1919), use of white lead (Convention No. 13 of 1921), ionizing radiations (Recommendation No. 114 of 1960) and maximum weight (Convention No. 127 of 1967).

§4. Equal Remuneration

455. 'The principle that men and women should receive equal remuneration for work of equal value' was mentioned, as from 1919, in the General Principles contained in the initial text of the ILO Constitution. When the Constitution was amended, in 1946, the principle was introduced in the Preamble of the new text of the Constitution. Various instruments adopted by the International Labour Conference or by the Regional Conferences referred expressly to equal remuneration. However, it was in 1951 that a Convention and a Recommendation dealing specifically with this question were adopted by the Conference.[1]

1. Two general surveys on these instruments were prepared by the Committee of Experts on the Application of Conventions and Recommendations in 1956 and 1975.

456. The Equal Remuneration Convention, 1951 (No. 100) lays down the general principle that each State which ratifies it shall promote and, in so far as consistent with the methods in operation in its country for determining rates of remuneration,[1] ensure the application to all workers of the principle of equal remuneration for men and women workers for work of equal value.

1. The term 'remuneration' includes the ordinary basic or minimum wage or salary and any additional emoluments whatsoever payable directly or indirectly, in cash or in kind, by the employer to the worker and arising out of the worker's employment.

457. The notion of 'work of equal value' which is used by the Convention has a wider meaning than that of 'equal work'. It aims, in particular, at avoiding indirect limitations in the implementation of the principle. However, its application may raise difficult questions of comparison of different types of work. For that reason the Convention and the Recommendation advocate systems of objective appraisal of the work to be performed. The main criterion is that the sex of the worker who is doing or might do a certain work is not taken into consideration in the determination of rates of remuneration. The term 'work of equal value' figured already, as said above, among the general principles enunciated in Part XIII of the Treaty of Versailles. Following ILO Convention No. 100, it was also used by the European Social Charter and by the 1966 International Covenant relating to economic, social and cultural rights, while the 1948 Universal Declaration on Human Rights referred to 'equal work'. The Rome Treaty which established the European Economic Community also referred, in its Article 119, to the more limited notion of 'equal work'. However the interpretation given to that notion by the organs of the EEC results in a situation very similar to that which is contemplated by Convention No. 100.

458. Convention No. 100 also provides that the principle of Equal Remuneration for Work of Equal Value may be applied by means of national laws or regulations, legally established or recognized machinery for wage determination, collective agreements or a combination of these means. It requests States to co-operate as appropriate with the employers' and workers' organizations concerned for the purpose of giving effect to its provisions.

459. Convention No. 100 is supplemented by a Recommendation (No. 90) of 1951, which gives more detailed guidance on the means of application of the principle of equal remuneration. It points out in greater detail the measures which could be taken in the fields in which the government exercises direct or indirect control and the manner by which the practical application of the principle of equal remuneration might be promoted (job analysis, vocational guidance, employment counselling, placement, welfare and social services, promoting public understanding, investigations, etc.).

460. The Equal Remuneration Convention, 1951 (No. 100) has been one of the ILO instruments which aroused most interest, even if its ratification and application have encountered serious obstacles.[1] The difficulty, to which reference is made the most frequently, is the fact that in certain States, the government does not interfere directly in the determination of wages in the private sector. But the Convention did take this fact into account and it imposes on governments the obligation to ensure equal remuneration only when this is compatible with the wage-fixing methods in the country. In some cases, the difficulty is in determining whether certain types of work are of equal value, in particular when the work is not performed by both men and women and when it is exclusively women who are employed in certain occupations. These difficulties are increased where there does not exist a system of objective appraisal of the work to be performed. More generally, reasons of an economic nature have been put forward both by certain industrialized countries where there is a high proportion of female workers and by developing countries. Problems arise also, in certain countries, in connection with the supervision of the application of the principle and in particular the question of guarantees and of sanctions. In some cases the difficulties are due to the federal structure of the country. In spite of these difficulties, the Convention has been ratified by 96 States and its implementation is making steady progress.

1. See *Rep. Com. Exp.* (Report III, Part 4B), paras. 163 and f., pp. 67 and f.

461. Reference has already[1] been made to the fact that equality of treatment in conditions of work, without distinction on the basis of sex, is one of the requirements of Convention No. 111 of 1958 which relates to discrimination in employment and occupation. Provisions on equal remuneration and on the decrease of differentials between rates of remuneration resulting from discrimination based, in particular, on sex are also contained in the two Social Policy Conventions (Art. 18 of Convention No. 82 of 1947 and Art. 14 of Convention No. 117 of 1962).

1. See above Nos. 242 and 244.

§5. Employment of Women with Family Responsibilities

462. In increasing numbers, women with family responsibilities work outside their homes and they face the difficult problem of reconciling their dual responsibilities at home and at work. The importance of the problem led to the adoption, in 1965, of a special Recommendation (No. 123) on this matter.[1] The general principle laid down in this Convention is that the competent authorities in each country should pursue a policy with a view to enabling women with family responsibilities who work outside their homes to exercise their right to do so without being subject to discrimination. Services should be developed to enable women to fulfil their various responsibilities harmoniously. Appropriate measures of public information and education should be taken, and child-care services and facilities should be provided. The Recommendation also advocates various measures to enable women to become integrated in the labour force (general education, vocational guidance, role of the employment service), as well as to re-enter the labour force (by the extension of maternity leave and by taking into consideration for re-employment those whose employment has been terminated following maternity). Finally various other steps are mentioned, such as the organization of public transport, the harmonization of working hours and hours of schools, child-care services or facilities, and provision at low cost of the facilities required to simplify and lighten household tasks. In a Resolution adopted by the International Labour Conference in 1975 it has been suggested that the question of a new instrument on *workers* with family responsibilities be submitted to the Conference. It has been decided that the question of 'equal opportunity and equal treatment for men and women workers: workers with family responsibilities' will be placed on the agenda of the 1980 Session of the Conference.

1. A general survey on this Recommendation was established in 1978 by the Committee of Experts on the Application of Conventions and Recommendations (Report III, Part 4B to the 64th Session of the ILC).

§6. Standards Relating to Particular Aspects of the Work of Women

463. Apart from the instrument described in the previous sections, which deal with the main questions of the protection of the work of women, certain more particular aspects of that work have been covered either in separate recommendations or in special provisions included in instruments of a more general scope. Some of these provisions aimed at protecting women against too arduous conditions of work. The objective of other provisions was to promote equality of treatment between women and men. As regards conditions of work, it has been recommended (Recommendation No. 116 of 1962) that in carrying out measures for reducing hours of work priority should be given to industries and occupations where the workers concerned consist mainly of women (as well as of young persons). As regards minimum wage, special regard might be had to trades or parts of trades in which women are ordinarily employed

(Recommendation No. 30 of 1928). In the field of employment, recourse to forced or compulsory labour was prohibited for women (Convention No. 29 of 1930). In connection with migration for employment, the protection of emigrant women and girls on board ship was the subject of a special Recommendation (No. 26 of 1926), while the general Convention on migrant workers (Convention No. 97 of 1949) included women's work among the matters in respect of which migrant workers should not be treated less favourably than national workers. Finally the Labour Inspection Convention, 1947 (No. 81) provides that women as well as men should be eligible for appointment to the inspection staff, and that, where necessary, special duties may be assigned to them.

§7. Other International Standards

464. The 1948 *Universal Declaration of Human Rights* stated, on the one hand, that 'Everyone without any discrimination, has the right to equal pay for equal work' (Art. 23, para. 2) and, on the other hand, that 'Motherhood and childhood are entitled to special care and assistance' (Art. 25, para. 2). The 1966 *International Covenant on Economic, Social and Cultural Rights* provided for 'fair wages and equal remuneration for work of equal value without distinction of any kind, in particular women being guaranteed conditions of work not inferior to those enjoyed by men, with equal pay for equal work' (Art. 7, sub-para. a (1)). The Covenant also provides that 'special protection should be accorded to mothers during a reasonable period before and after childbirth. During such period working mothers should be accorded paid leave or leave with adequate social security benefits' (Art. 10, para. 2). The following year, in November 1967, the General Assembly of the United Nations adopted a *Declaration on the Elimination of Discrimination against Women*, Art. 10 of which deals with equal rights in the field of economic and social life and in particular in labour matters.

465. *The European Social Charter*. At the European level, the European Social Charter contains a special provision (Art. 8) about the right of employed women to protection. The first paragraphs of this article relate to the protection of motherhood and provide, as ILO Conventions do, that women should be entitled to take leave before and after childbirth up to a total of at least 12 weeks. However the Charter differs from ILO standards when it lays down that such leave should be provided either by paid leave, by adequate social security benefits or by benefits from public funds, while ILO Conventions authorize only the latter two methods of financing and prohibit that the employer be made liable for the cost of these benefits, for the reasons given above.[1] The Consultative Assembly voted by a great majority in favour of an amendment adopting this provision to international labour standards by deleting the possibility of paid leave, but the Social Committee of the Council of Europe preferred to keep it in. The Social Charter also states, as the ILO Conventions do, that it should be unlawful for an employer to give a woman notice of dismissal during her absence on maternity leave or at such a date that the notice would expire during such absence. It also provides, as the ILO Conventions, that women workers should have sufficient time to nurse their infants.

1. See above No. 443.

466. As regards more generally employment of women, the Social Charter provides for regulation of the employment of women workers on night work in industrial employment and prohibits the employment of women workers in underground mining and, as appropriate, on all other work which is unsuitable for them by reason of its dangerous, unhealthy or arduous nature. This version follows a proposal by the Tripartite Conference based on a suggestion by the Workers' representative. It is in some way a compromise between two opposing views. It does not go so far as the corresponding international labour Conventions, which prohibit night work of women generally, with the exception of certain particular occupations, while the Social Charter provides merely for regulation of night work of women in industry. On the other hand, the Social Charter prohibits underground work as an ILO Convention does, and it also provides for the prohibition, as appropriate, of dangerous, unhealthy or arduous work. When the Charter was being prepared, certain Scandinavian delegations expressed their opposition to the principle of protection of women workers in general, except for expectant or nursing mothers, but a proposal which would have attenuated the terms prohibiting employment of women in mining and dangerous, unhealthy or arduous work was rejected by the Consultative Assembly. A proposal by the Consultative Assembly itself, to generalize regulation of employment of women to cover all night work was not followed by the Social Committee, which kept the original text relating only to industrial occupations.

Chapter XI. Work of Children and Young Persons

467. As it happened at the national level, the work of children has been, at the international level, one of the first fields in which regulations were adopted. Based on the notion of protection of the weakest, these regulations aimed at eliminating the very serious abuses to which child work had given rise at the beginning of the industrial era. This concern for the protection of children against conditions of work which had shocked public opinion had even, more widely, been at the origin of the whole concept of labour law, international as well as national. The fact that children of five or six years of age were employed in spinning mills had been one of the main reasons which prompted the first campaigns in favour of international action in the field of labour. This action developed considerably in the course of years. The need to protect children against entry into employment at too early an age and against excessively arduous conditions of work remained the basic concern, but the trend has also been to supplement and to extend progressively this protection, e.g. by raising the minimum age of admission to employment and by requiring a medical examination. At the same time a certain number of measures in the field of employment aimed at providing facilities for the training, the development and the employment of young persons.

468. At the national level, the first labour laws related to protection of children, as those adopted in England at the beginning of the XIXth century and the French law of 1841 which fixed at 8 years of age the minimum age of admission to industrial work (the age having been raised to 12 in 1874 and 13 in 1892). At the international level, the protection of children and young persons was considered, when the ILO was established, as one of its main tasks. As from 1919 it appeared both in the Preamble of its Constitution and in the general principles enunciated in it. The Conventions which were adopted since by the ILO aim, more particularly, at the protection of children and young persons from three points of view: minimum age for admission to employment, night work and medical examination. In addition, standards relating to unemployment of young persons, vocational guidance, apprenticeship and vocational training were laid down in recommendations.[1] Moreover, special provisions in favour of young persons were included in many Conventions of a more general scope. The question of the protection of children and young workers has also been dealt with in resolutions of the International Labour Conference.

1. See above Nos. 277 and 293.

§1. The Minimum Age for Admission to Employment

469. Since 1919, there have been ten consecutive Conventions dealing with minimum age for admission to employment, first in industry, then in other occupations. These Conventions laid down the general standard of 14 years of age, then raised it to 15, while providing for a higher age for particularly arduous types of work. The principle of fixing a minimum age was also included among the main elements of a social policy. In 1973, the existing standards were consolidated and a general convention was adopted in the field of minimum age.

I. The General Standard of 14 Years and its Variations

470. A Convention (No. 5) adopted by the International Labour Conference at its first session, in 1919, introduced the first international regulation of minimum age for admission to employment. This Convention, which has been ratified by more than 60 countries, prohibits that children under the age of 14 years be employed or work in any public or private industrial undertaking. The only exceptions which it authorizes are undertakings in which only members of the same family are employed and work done in technical schools, if it is approved and supervised by public authority. The Convention also laid down lower standards, as in the case of some other ILO instruments adopted at that time, for certain specified countries (in that case India and Japan). In order to facilitate the enforcement of the Convention, it was provided that employers in industrial undertakings should keep a register of all persons under the age of 16 years employed by them, and the dates of their birth.

471. In the course of the following two years, three other conventions were adopted in the field of minimum age. In 1920 a Convention (No. 7), ratified since by 48 States, laid down the age of 14 for admission to *maritime work*. This Convention contains provisions similar to those of the Convention relating to industry, from the point of view both of the exceptions which it authorized and of the mentions which should be made on a register of persons employed on board or in the articles of agreement. In 1921, again in the field of maritime work, a Convention (No. 15), ratified since by 63 States, provided for the age of 18 for the admission to work on board ships as trimmers or stokers.

472. In 1921 also, a Convention (No. 10) dealing with minimum age for admission to employment *in agriculture* was adopted and has been ratified by 47 States. The standard laid down in that instrument was much more flexible than the Conventions relating to industrial employment. It does not contain an absolute prohibition of the employment of children below a certain age. It only provides that children below the age of 14 may not be employed or work in public or private agricultural undertakings, save outside the hours fixed for school attendance and that the employment, if they are employed outside these hours, shall not be such as to prejudice their attendance at school. Moreover, for purposes of practical vocational instruction, the periods and hours of school attendance may be so arranged as to permit the employment of children on light agricultural work, in particular connected with the harvest, provided that such employment shall not reduce the total annual period of school attendance to less than 8 months. Finally the Convention authorizes an exception for work done in technical schools, if such work is approved and supervised by public authority.

473. Some ten years later the standard of 14 years and even of a higher age for children who are still required to attend primary school, was also laid down as regards *non-industrial employment* by Convention No. 33, which has been ratified by 25 States. That Convention allows for certain exceptions, in particular for children over 12 years of age who may, outside the hours fixed for school attendance, be employed on light work under certain conditions. On the other hand, a higher age should be fixed by national legislation for admission of young persons to any employment which is dangerous to life, health or morals, as well as to employment for purposes of itinerant trading in the streets and similar occupations. Finally, the Convention provided for various measures of inspection, supervision and sanctions. It was supplemented, the same year, by a Recommendation (No. 41) which deals with light work, employment in public entertainment, dangerous employment, prohibition of employment of children by certain persons and enforcement of the Convention.

II. The General Standard of 15 Years

474. A few years after the adoption of this first series of instruments, three conventions raised the general standard to 15 years for maritime employment, industry and non-industrial work. This was not only due to the concern for a greater protection of young persons, but also, during that period which just followed the great economic crisis of the thirties, to the desire to contribute in that way to a reduction of the number of unemployed persons. In this connection, even before the adoption of conventions based on the standard of 15 years, a 1935 Recommendation concerning unemployment among young persons advocated a number of measures against unemployment, and in particular the fixing of a minimum age of less than 15 years of age for leaving school and being admitted to employment.

475. The first convention which raised to 15 years the minimum age for admission to employment related to *maritime work*, as the 1920 Convention (No. 7) was revised in 1936 by Convention No. 58, now ratified by 48 States. This new instrument authorizes, however, the employment of children under 14 years on the basis of certificates showing that a school or other authority satisfied itself that this employment is in the interest of the child. For *industrial work*, the 1919 Convention (No. 5) was revised in 1937 by Convention No. 59, which also raised the minimum age to 15 years and has been ratified by 34 States. In its revised form, the Convention authorizes exceptions which generally are analogous to those of the earlier instrument, but in addition it provides that a higher age should be fixed for the occupations which are dangerous for the life, health or morals of the persons employed. Moreover, the obligation laid on the employer to keep a register of the young persons whom he employs was raised to persons under 18 years of age. Finally, for *non-industrial work*, the 1932 Convention (No. 33) was revised in 1937 by Convention No. 60, which also raised the minimum age to 15 years and has been ratified by 11 States only. Like the 1932 Convention, the revised instrument of 1937 authorized exceptions under certain conditions (light work – for which the minimum age was also raised from 12 to 13 or 14 years, according to the case – public entertainment, etc.), it requested that a higher age be fixed in certain cases (dangerous occupations, itinerant trading, etc.) and it provided for measures for inspection, supervision and sanctions. The age of 15 was also fixed later by a 1959 Convention (No. 112) which related to the admission to work of *fishermen*, and was ratified by 31 States.

III. Minimum Age for Certain Arduous Occupations

476. It was already stated that, for certain arduous occupations, international standards provide for an age of admission which is higher than the general standard. Thus, this age has been fixed at 18 years for trimmers and stokers on board sea-going vessels (Convention No. 15 of 1921) or fishing vessels (Convention No. 112 of 1959). Other conventions, as indicated above, provide that, as regards occupations dangerous for life, health or morals and for itinerant trading, national legislation should fix a minimum age which would be higher than the general age of 14 or 15. This was the case for Convention No. 33 of 1932, and Conventions Nos. 59 and 60 of 1937. More specifically as regards underground work in mines, there was first a Recommendation (No. 96) of 1953 and later a Convention (No. 123) of 1965 – now ratified by 38 States, which dealt with minimum age. Any State which ratifies this Convention is under an obligation to specify the minimum age of occupation to such work, and this age can never be lower than 16 years.

IV. The Principle of the Fixing of a Minimum Age as an Element of Social Policy

477. Apart from the conventions which lay down a specific minimum age for admission to employment, other instruments merely establish the principle of such a rule while leaving to national legislation the responsibility of actually determining the age in question. This was the case, in the first instance, of the Social Policy (Non-Metropolitan Territories) Convention, 1949 (No. 82) (Art. 18), then of the Social Policy (Basic Aims and Standards) Convention, 1962 (No. 117) (Art. 15). These instruments provide that national laws or regulations shall prescribe the school-leaving age and the minimum age for and conditions of employment. They also provide that the employment of persons below the school-leaving age during the hours when the schools are in session shall be prohibited in areas where educational facilities are provided on a scale adequate for the majority of the children of school age.

V. The Consolidated General Standard of 1973

478. While, over the years, ten conventions in succession were adopted in the field of minimum age for admission to employment, with a view to covering the various branches of activity and to providing a standard first of 14 and later of 15 years, it appeared that the time had arrived, in 1973, to consolidate these various instruments in a single convention. The new Convention (No. 138), which has been supplemented by a recommendation, has a general scope and it provides that States which ratify it undertake to pursue a national policy designed to ensure the effective abolition of child labour and to raise progressively the minimum age for admission to employment or work at a level consistent with the fullest physical and mental development of young persons. Ratifying States should specify a minimum age for admission to employment or work, which should not be less than the age of completion of compulsory schooling and, in any case, should not be less than 15 years – or 14 as an initial step for developing countries. A higher age (18 years) is laid down for any type of employment or work which might jeopardize the health, safety or morals of young persons. Certain limited categories of employment or work may be excluded from the application of the Convention. These categories may be wider for developing countries, but the Convention specifies the industries to which it should in any way be applicable. The Convention revises the earlier instruments dealing with minimum age. It has been ratified by 14 States up to now. The recommendation which supplements the Convention gives more detailed guidance as regards the national policy to be followed in this field, and more particularly as regards the minimum age itself (which States should have as an aim to raise progressively to 16 years, while steps should be taken urgently, where the minimum age is still below 15 years, to bring it to that level), dangerous employment or work, conditions of employment and measures of application.

VI. Problems of Ratification and of Application of Minimum Age Conventions

479. There is no doubt that the minimum age conventions have greatly contributed to reducing the abuses which existed in this field. At the present time 87 States are bound by one of the three main Conventions (Nos. 5, 59 and 138) which set at 14 or 15 the age of admission to industry. However, there still remain serious obstacles to their ratification and application in the world, particularly as regards the 15-year standard, and there are many countries the legislation of which does not reach the level of the international standard. The minimum age for admission to employment, which depends to a great extent on the state of economic development, greatly varies from one country to another. It is now fixed at 16 years in many countries and at 15 by a great number of national legislations, but the standard of 14 remains the most frequent and is laid down in the legislation of some 50 countries. Moreover, the practice often does not correspond to the legal minimum age, and the standard of living of families as well as the deficiencies of national supervision account for widespread abuses. The legal minimum age is even still at 12 or 13 years in some countries, where this is already a progress in relation with a not too distant past.[1] In a general way, in spite of the great progress which has taken place, child labour still is widely prevalent in many regions of the world, in particular in small undertakings and in agriculture. It often happens that national legislations on minimum age do not deal with all occupations but relate mainly to industry or provide different ages or authorize more or less important exceptions according to whether they concern industrial or non-industrial work.

1. It is in the field of minimum age that, in 1924, Albert Thomas approached the Persian Government – although Persia had not ratified the Convention concerned – about the employment of very young children in the carpet factories of Kerman. About this step, which was described as a humanitarian intervention, see Scelle pp. 111–112.

480. The minimum age for admission to employment is closely linked to the age for compulsory school attendance, as it is naturally desirable to avoid any gap between the end of the studies and the admission to work. Thus, difficulties such as the shortage of school masters or schools add to those relating to admission to employment itself. Conversely, international labour standards served as a stimulus to encourage States to extend compulsory school attendance and to develop technical education. In spite of certain delays, there is a steady trend in raising the two ages. ILO standards have contributed substantially to this trend, particularly as regards the 14-year standard.[1] In the case of the 15-year standard, progress is slower, but continuing. In the course of the last twenty years, a sizeable number of States were able to ratify the 1937 Convention which laid down that standard and to change their legislation to that effect.

1. See *Rep. Com. Exp.*, 1960, p. 120, para. 130.

§2. Night Work of Young Persons

481. Night work of young persons was dealt with in a Convention adopted in 1919 and revised in 1948. The Night Work of Young Persons (Industry) Convention, 1919 (No. 6), which has been ratified by 56 States, provided that young persons under eighteen years shall not be employed during the night in public or private industrial undertakings. It authorizes an exception for young persons over the age of sixteen in certain specified industries on work which has to be carried on continuously day and night. The term 'night' to which such prohibition applies signifies a period of at least eleven consecutive hours, including the interval between ten o'clock in the evening and five o'clock in the morning. Special provisions relate to mines, the baking industry and tropical countries. Exceptions are also authorized for persons between the ages of sixteen and eighteen in case of emergencies and when in case of serious emergency the public interest demands it.

482. The revision of this Convention took place in 1948, and the revised Convention (No. 90) has been ratified by some 40 States. In the new instrument the night period was extended from 11 to 12 hours and a greater flexibility was introduced as regards the interval which should be included in that period (i.e. for young persons under 16 years, the interval should be between 10 in the evening and 6 in the morning and for those between 16 and 18 years, it should be of at least seven consecutive hours falling between 10 in the evening and 7 in the morning). The revised Convention also authorized exceptions for purposes of apprenticeship or vocational training of young persons between 16 and 18 years. Finally, it provided that measures should be taken to ensure that national laws or regulations in this field are known to the persons concerned, that adequate penalties for any violation be prescribed, that a system of adequate inspection to ensure effective enforcement be maintained and that employers should be required to keep registers or official records showing all persons under 18 years employed by them.

483. While the two above-mentioned conventions relate to industry, the only standards applying to *agriculture* are contained in a Recommendation (No. 14) dating back to 1921. In this instrument it was provided that the employment of children under the age of 14 years in agricultural undertakings during the night should be regulated in such a way as to ensure them a period of rest of not less than ten consecutive hours, while, for young persons between the ages of 14 and 16, the period of rest at night should be of not less than nine consecutive hours.

484. As regards *non-industrial occupations*, a 1946 Convention (No. 79), ratified by 16 States, provides that children under 14 years of age admissible for full-time employment and children over fourteen years who are still subject to full-time compulsory school attendance shall not work at night during a period of at least 14 consecutive hours, including the interval between 8 in the evening and 8 in the morning. This period is fixed at 12 hours for children over 14 years who are no longer subject to full-time compulsory school attendance and young persons under 18 years.

485. These standards were supplemented by a Recommendation (No. 80) adopted the same year which contains more detailed provisions on matters such as the scope of regulations, employment in public entertainment and methods of supervision.

486. On the whole, the conventions dealing with night work of young persons exercised a considerable influence over national legislations.[1] Seventy-three States are now bound by one or other of the two conventions relating to Industry (Nos. 6 and 90). However, there are still obstacles to their ratification, as the legislation of many countries has not yet reached the level prescribed as regards the total duration of night rest, in particular as regards the 12 hours provided by the 1948 revised convention. Nevertheless, the more flexible terms of the latter convention in relation with the interval which should be included in the night rest have to a certain extent facilitated its ratification and application.

1. See *Rep. Com. Exp.*, 1960, page 120, para. 130.

§3. Medical Examination

487. While, in the maritime field, a Convention (No. 16) was adopted as early as in 1921 – and has been ratified since by more than 60 States – to provide that the employment of children and young persons under 18 years of age on any vessel shall be conditional to medical examination and that this examination shall be repeated at intervals of not more than one year, Conventions dealing more generally with medical examinations were adopted only 25 years later, i.e. in 1946: the one (No. 77) related to industry and the other (No. 78) related to non-industrial occupations and they have been ratified by 32 and 30 States respectively.

488. Convention No. 77 provides that children and young persons under 18 years[1] shall not be admitted to employment by an industrial undertaking unless they have been found fit for the work on which they are to be employed by a thorough medical examination. The fitness of a child or young person for the employment in which he is engaged shall be subject to medical supervision until he has attained the age of 18 years and the continued employment of a child or young person shall be subject to medical examination at intervals of not more than one year. In occupations which involve high risks medical examination and re-examinations for fitness for employment shall be required until at least the age of 21 years.[2] Medical examination should not involve the child or young person, or his parents, in any expense. The Convention also provides for measures for vocational guidance and physical and vocational rehabilitation of children and young persons found by medical examination to be unsuited to certain types of work or to have physical handicaps or limitations.

1. States which had no legislation on the matter at the date of ratification may substitute an age lower than 18, but not lower than 16.
2. In the cases provided in the footnote above the age of 21 may be replaced by the age of 19.

489. Convention No. 78 contains analogous provisions but applies to occupations other than industrial, agricultural and maritime. A Recommendation (No. 79) adopted the same year supplemented these two Conventions and clarified the scope of the regulations, the provisions concerning medical examination, the measures for persons found to be unfit or only partially fit for employment, the methods of enforcement, etc. More recently, a 1959 Convention (No. 113) concerning medical examination of fishermen – ratified by 20 States – and a 1965 Convention (No. 124) concerning medical examination of young persons for fitness for employment – ratified by 30 States – provided that medical examination and periodic re-examinations of persons under 21 years shall be required for the employment in these occupations.

490. On the whole, medical examination for fitness for employment of children and young persons is a subject which has given rise to great difficulties. At the present time, there is no general trend towards the acceptance of the international standards which were laid down in this field, although some twenty countries have ratified the two main conventions and a certain evolution is taking place among the countries which did not yet proceed to their ratification. The most important difficulties relate to the fact that these two conventions provide for medical examination for industrial or non-industrial occupations in general and not only for certain specific occupations. An additional difficulty is that they require that the medical examinations be repeated every year. These requirements come up against more limited provisions of national legislation, deficiencies in administrative procedures, shortage of medical staff and services, and finally the insufficient character of the measures taken for vocational guidance and physical and vocational rehabilitation of young persons.

491. It is also significant that the standard introduced more recently in the European Social Charter provides for medical examination only as regards certain occupations and does not require that such examination be repeated at fixed one-year intervals.

§4. Special Provisions Contained in Conventions of General Application

492. Apart from the conventions which deal specifically with the work of children and young persons, many other instruments of more general scope contain special provisions relating to young persons. In the field of general conditions of work, the conventions and recommendations relating to holidays with pay provide for a longer holiday for persons under 16 or 18 years as the case may be. As regards reduction of the hours of work, Recommendation No. 116 of 1962 advocates that priority be given to cases where the workers concerned consist mainly of young persons. Special provisions with a view to the protection of young persons are also contained in various conventions dealing with matters of safety and hygiene.[1] In the field of employment, reference was made[2] to the recommendations relating to vocational guidance, apprenticeship, and vocational training, which are of great importance for the development and the future of young persons. The Employment Service Convention, 1948 (No. 88) provides for special arrangements for juveniles within the framework of the employment and vocational guidance services. Several recommendations also dealt with the question of unemployment of young persons.[3] In the more special fields of forced labour (Convention No. 29 of 1930), of recruiting of indigenous workers (Convention No. 50 of 1936), of contracts of employment of indigenous workers (Convention No. 64 of 1939) and of penal sanctions for breaches of such contracts (Convention No. 65 of 1939), the relevant instruments contain provisions concerning the special protection of non-adult persons. Finally, as regards migrants, work of young persons is among the matters in respect of which the 1949 Convention (No. 97)[4] provided that the treatment of migrants should not be less favourable than that of nationals.

1. This is the case for lead poisoning (Recommendation No. 4 of 1919) of safety provisions in the building industry (Convention No. 62 of 1937), of use of white lead (Convention No. 13 of 1921), of protection against radiations (Convention No. 115 of 1960) and of maximum weight (Convention No. 127 of 1967).
2. See above No. 468.
3. See above No. 277.
4. See below No. 340.

§5. Other International Standards

493. The *International Covenant on Economic, Social and Cultural Rights* provides (Art. 10, para. 3) that 'special measures of protection and assistance should be taken on behalf of all children and young persons without any discrimination for reasons of parentage or other conditions. Children and young persons should be protected from economic and social exploitation. Their employment in work harmful to their morals or health or dangerous to life or likely to hamper their normal development should be punishable by law. States should also set age limits below which the paid employment of child labour should be prohibited and punishable by law'.

494. The United Nations also adopted in 1959 a *Declaration of the Rights of the Child*, the terms of which are very similar to the 1919 Constitutional provisions of the ILO. This Declaration affirms in particular that a child shall not be admitted to employment before an appropriate minimum age and that it 'shall in no case be caused or permitted to engage in any occupation or employment which would prejudice his health or education, or interfere with his physical, mental or moral development'.

495. The *European Social Charter* also contains provisions (Art. 7) relating to the right of children and young persons to protection. These provisions were based on the standards laid down in ILO conventions. Thus they set at 15 years the minimum age of admission to employment, subject to exceptions for children employed in prescribed light work without harm to their health, morals or education. A higher minimum age should be fixed with regard to prescribed occupations regarded as dangerous or unhealthy. In this connection, the workers representatives at the Tripartite Conference proposed that in such cases the minimum age should be specified, namely at 18 years, but the proposal was not generally accepted. Although the Consultative Assembly supported it, the more general text mentioned above was finally upheld. The Social Charter also provides that young persons who are still subject to compulsory education shall not be employed in such work as would deprive them of the full benefit of their education. As regards hours of work of persons under 16 years, they should be limited in accordance with the needs of their development, and particularly with their need for vocational training. Young workers and apprentices should also have the right to a fair wage or appropriate allowances. The time spent by young persons in vocational training during the normal working hours with the consent of the employer shall be treated as forming part of the working day. As regards holidays with pay, it has been already stated above[1] that according to the Social Charter employed persons of under 18 years of age shall be entitled not less than three weeks' annual holiday with pay. Furthermore, the Social Charter prohibits night work of persons under 18 years with the exception of certain occupations provided for by national laws or regulations. In the Appendix to the Charter it is specified that this provision will be considered as fulfilled if a State provides by law that the great majority of persons under 18 years shall not be employed in night work. As regards medical examination, the Social Charter does not go as far as the ILO conventions which deal with this matter. It provides merely for regular medical control of persons under 18 years 'employed in occupations prescribed by national laws or regulations'. At the Tripartite Conference proposals were made by the Belgian Government on the one hand, and on the other by the Workers, supported by the Government members for the Federal Republic of Germany, Austria and France, calling for this control to be extended to cover all workers aged under 18 years in order to ensure that their health is not endangered by their work. The proposal raised objections from certain governments which felt that medical examination was not necessary for all employment and pointed out that some countries had a free health service. Employers also expressed objections, and while the Consultative Assembly supported the Workers' proposal, the original text was not amended. Finally, the Social Charter contains a provision proposed by the Consultative Assembly and providing for 'special protection against physical and moral dangers to which children and young persons are exposed, and particularly against those resulting directly or indirectly from their work'. The Committee of Ministers of the Council of Europe has adopted, in February 1972, a Resolution (72)4 on the protection of young persons at work.

1. See above No. 372.

Chapter XII. Older Workers

496. In June 1979, the International Labour Conference will have on its agenda the question of older workers (work and retirement).

Chapter XIII. Special Categories of Workers

497. A certain number of Conventions or Recommendations deal with certain categories of workers on account of the special conditions of their work or of the protection of which they are in need. This applies in particular to seafarers and fishermen, workers in agriculture, indigenous workers and workers of non-metropolitan categories, civil servants, nursing personnel, etc.

§1. Seafarers and Fishermen

I. Seafarers

498. By reason of its nature and its history, maritime navigation is among the most international activities, while the work of seafarers has such a specific character that it had to be dealt with in a special way. From a formal point of view, the adoption of international standards in the field of maritime work follows special rules – and this raises the question of the applicability to seafarers of the international labour conventions of general scope. The entry into force of maritime conventions is also subject, in general, to special rules. As regards substance, more than fifty conventions and recommendations deal with the various aspects of maritime work[1] and most of them have entered into force.

1. For the first period of this international regulation of maritime work (1920–1936), see C. Wilfred Jenks, 'Contribution de l'Organisation internationale des Travail a l'élaboration d'un droit uniforme du travail maritime', in *Introduction à l'étude du droit comparé (Recueil d'études en l'honneur d'Edouard Lambert*, vol. II, Paris, 1938, pp. 870–883).

A. Special Procedure for the Framing of Standards Concerning Employment at Sea

499. The Commission on International Labour Legislation appointed by the 1919 Peace Conference, which prepared the original Constitution of the ILO, had adopted a resolution according to which 'the very special questions concerning the minimum conditions to be accorded to seamen might be dealt with at a special meeting of the International Labour Conference devoted exclusively to the affairs of seamen'. Since, the practice has been that the standards concerning maritime work are considered at special maritime sessions of the International Labour Conference after an advice has been given by the Joint Maritime Commission, which is composed of representatives of shipowners' and of seafarers' organizations and following a discussion of the matter by a tripartite Preparatory Technical Maritime Conference. There have been nine maritime sessions of the International Labour Conference until now, in 1920, 1926, 1929, 1936 (two sessions), 1946, 1958, 1970 and 1976.

B. The Question of the Applicability to Seafarers of International Labour Conventions of a General Scope

500. As standards concerning maritime work are adopted by special sessions of the International Labour Conference, the question sometimes arose of the extent to which the conventions of general scope which are adopted by the ordinary sessions of the Conference are also applicable to seafarers. General directives on the subject can be found in a resolution adopted by the International Labour Conference on 10 November 1921, according to which 'no Conventions or Recommendations shall apply to those employed in the Mercantile Marine unless they have been passed as a special maritime question on the agenda. All questions on maritime affairs put forward for consideration by Conferences should be previously considered by the Joint Maritime Commission of the International Labour Office.' There appears therefore to be a presumption that a convention or recommendation does not apply to employment at sea unless it has been adopted at a maritime session of the Conference or the question has been considered by the Joint Maritime Commission.[1] However this presumption is not an absolute one. In the course of the discussion of the above-mentioned resolution, it had been pointed out that a given session of the Conference has no power to bind future Conferences in this matter.[2] A Convention or Recommendation adopted by a general session of the Conference might by applicable to seafarers if it appears that this was the intention of the Conference when it adopted the instrument. Such an intention can have been clearly expressed by the Conference in the instrument itself, as in a number of general Conventions and Recommendations where it is expressly provided that they apply to maritime work.[3] This can also be implied from the general character of the terms used in the Convention and from the objective aimed at by the standard.[4] It should also be kept in mind that the reason for which Conventions applying to seafarers are adopted through a special procedure lies in the substantial differences which exist in many respects between conditions of work at sea and in other occupations. In the matters in which such a difference would not exist, there would be no justification for a Convention of general application not to cover seafarers. This view was recently confirmed by the fact that the Merchant Shipping (Minimum Standards) Convention, 1976 (No. 147) provides for the application in merchant ships of eleven Conventions, some of which – in particular the Freedom of Association Conventions (Nos. 87 and 98) – are of general character.[5]

1. See *Intern. Lab. Code*, p. 756.
2. *Rec. Proc. Conf.*, 1921, p. 262.
3. E.g. the Maternity Protection Convention (Revised), 1952 (No. 103). On the other hand, a number of instruments exclude maritime work from their scope.
4. Thus, the Freedom of Association Convention, 1948 (No. 87) refers to 'workers and employers, without distinction whatsoever'. Similarly, Conventions on matter such as forced labour and discrimination were clearly meant to be of general application.
5. See below No. 514.

C. Conditions for the Entry into Force of Maritime Conventions

501. The entry into force of maritime conventions was made subject to conditions which became progressively much stricter than for other international labour conventions. These conditions relate both to the number of States which have ratified the conventions concerned and the tonnage of their merchant marine. As will be said below,[1] international labour conventions generally enter into force, in accordance with their final clauses, when they have been ratified by two Member States of the ILO. A similar provision was also included in the first maritime conventions[2] and this formula is still used sometimes even in recent maritime conventions[3] when the matters dealt with do not raise the considerations of international competition which were taken into account in the other maritime instruments. However, since 1936, the conditions for the entry into force of maritime conventions became progressively more difficult. The explanation given was that, in an international field like maritime navigation 'governments needed to have some certainty that the convention would be ratified by other countries so that international competition might not be accentuated'.[4] In the first instance, the entry into force was made subject to the ratification of the convention by five States each of which has a mercantile marine tonnage of not less than one million tons.[5] Then, after repeated discussions, the formula became more complex and the conditions were the ratification by five,[6] seven[7] or nine[8] States from a list of 23 specified States and also that three,[9] four[10] or five[11] of the ratifying States have at least one million gross register tons of shipping each. Sometimes it was also required[12] that the aggregate tonnage of shipping by the ratifying countries is not less than 15 million tons. With the increase of the world tonnage, the formula changed a number of times and became still stricter. In 1970[13] the requirement was the ratification by 12 States having more than one million tons of shipping each, including at least four having each at least two million tons.

The most recent requirement, used in 1976,[14] is that the convention has been ratified 'by at least ten Members with a total share in world shipping gross tonnage of 25 per cent'. While some of the conventions containing this sort of clause state that such a 'provision is included for the purpose of facilitating and encouraging early ratification of the convention', these special conditions have clearly delayed and sometimes prevented the early entry into force of certain of these conventions. However, if one takes account of the fact that some of these instruments hâve been revised later, finally only two maritime conventions non revised since their adoption failed to enter into force as a result of the particularly strict conditions to which the entry into force was made subject: the Social Security (Seafarers) Convention, 1946 (No. 70), the revised Convention on Wages, Hours of Work and Manning (No. 109 of 1958), and the more recent convention on accommodation of crews (revised), 1970 (No. 133).[15]

1. See No. 583.
2. Conventions Nos. 7, 8 and 9 of 1920, Conventions Nos. 22 and 23 of 1926, three of the five conventions adopted at the 21st session (1936) and Convention No. 58 adopted at the 22nd session (1936).
3. E. g. Conventions No. 74 of 1946, No. 108 of 1958, No. 134 of 1970 and Nos. 145 and 146 of 1976.
4. *Rec. Proc. Conf.*, 21st and 22nd sessions, 1936, p. 228.
5. Conventions Nos. 54 and 57 of 1936.
6. Convention No. 71 of 1946.
7. Conventions Nos. 70, 73, 75 of 1946.
8. Conventions Nos. 68, 69, 72, 76 of 1946 and No. 109 of 1958.
9. Convention No. 71 of 1946.
10. Conventions Nos. 70, 73, 75 of 1946.
11. Conventions Nos. 68, 69, 72, 76 of 1946 and No. 109 of 1958.
12. Convention No. 76 of 1946 and No. 109 of 1958.
13. See Convention No. 133 of 1970.
14. Convention No. 147.
15. Convention No. 70 was ratified by seven States, Convention No. 109 by eight and Convention No. 133 by eleven. As for the last instrument in which this sort of clause was used, i.e. the Merchant Shipping (Minimum Standards) Convention, 1976 (No. 147), it is still too early to gauge what the effect of this clause may be, as the second ratification of the convention was received only in June 1978.

D. General Outline of the Standards Relating to Employment at Sea

502. Over 30 conventions and some 25 recommendations were adopted in the field of maritime work. They will be briefly reviewed below. A general question which has arisen in connection with these instruments is that of the criterion to follow to determine their scope as far as ships are concerned. In 1936 it was decided to adopt the criterion of the country in which the ship is registered, as the criteria of the nationality or of the flag could not appear to be satisfactory. The conventions and recommendations adopted over the years in the maritime field aimed at constituting progressively an *International Seafarers' Code*.[1] They dealt either with questions of a general character which had to be considered from the point of view of the special nature of employment at sea or with questions which are specific to such employment, e.g. unemployment in case of shipwreck or repatriation of seamen.

1. See *Intern. Lab. Code*, p. 755. In this connection the National Seamen's Codes Recommendation, 1920 (No. 9) advocated a clear and systematic codification of the national law in each country, in order that seamen of the world may have a better comprehension of their rights and obligations and that the task of establishing an International Sea-Men's Code may be advanced and facilitated.

503. In the first instance, many conventions related to the conditions for admission to employment at sea. This was in particular the case for *minimum age*, which was fixed at 14 years by Convention No. 7 of 1920, ratified by 48 States, then at 15 years by the revised Convention (No. 58 of 1936), ratified by 48 States, while Convention No. 15 of 1921, ratified by 63 States, had laid down the minimum age of 18 years for trimmers and stokers. This was also the case for *medical examination*, a first Convention (No. 16 of 1921), ratified by over 60 States, having provided for the medical examination of young persons, while at a later date a more ambitious – but less successful – Convention (No. 73 of 1946, ratified by 27 States) laid down the standard of medical examination of every person engaged for employment in a sea-going vessel, subject to certain exceptions. The more general question of the *protection of young seafarers* was dealt with in a recent Recommendation (No. 153 of 1976) which included provisions relating, *inter alia*, to objectives to be aimed at, hours of permitted duty and rest periods, repatriation, safety in work and health education, and opportunities for vocational guidance, education and vocational training.

504. Other conventions provide that, in order to perform certain duties on board ship, the persons concerned should hold a *certificate of competency or of qualification* to that effect, issued or approved by the public authority of the country where the vessel is registered. The conventions specify the conditions subject to which such certificates might be granted. They deal more particularly with the Officers' Competency Certificates (Convention No. 53 of 1936, ratified by 26 States), the certification of able seamen (Convention No. 74 of 1946, ratified by 20 States) and the certification of ships' cooks (Convention No. 69 of 1946, ratified by 24 States).

505. In the field of *vocational training* of seafarers, a first Recommendation (No. 77) of 1946 was more recently superseded by the detailed provisions of Recommendation No. 137 of 1976. As regards more generally the problems of *employment*, the placing of seamen was dealt with as early as 1920 by a Convention (No. 9, ratified by 33 States) which prohibits that the business of finding employment for seamen should be carried on as a commercial enterprise for pecuniary gain and that fees should be charged for finding employment for seamen. The Convention also provided for the establishment of an efficient system of public employment offices for finding employment for seamen without charge, and specified that such system might be organized either by representative associations of shipowners and seamen jointly under the control of a central authority, or by the State itself. In 1970, the maritime session of the Conference adopted a Recommendation (No. 139) concerning employment problems arising from technical developments on board ship; the question was considered from the point of view of manpower planning, of recruitment and placing, of training and retraining, of the regularity of employment and income and of international cooperation.

506. As regards *Seamen's Articles of Agreement*, there was an opposition between divergent views and while the compromise reached did not settle all the problems, the 1926 Convention (No. 22), which has been ratified by 48 States, was able to specify in detail the manner in which the articles of agreement should be concluded, to define the various types of agreements, to enumerate the particulars which they should contain and to indicate the conditions under which an agreement may be terminated. In this connection, the Convention provides that an agreement for an indefinite period may be terminated by either party in any port where the vessel loads or unloads, provided that the notice specified in the agreement shall have been given, which shall not be less than 24 hours. The Convention also defines the circumstances in which the seaman may claim his discharge. It also deals with the certificate which the seaman has the right to obtain.

507. More recently, in 1976, the maritime session of the Conference adopted a Convention (No. 145) and a Recommendation (No. 154) concerning continuity of employment of seafarers, which are based on the principle that it should be national policy in the various States to encourage all concerned to provide continuous or regular employment for qualified seafarers in so far as this is practicable and, in so doing, to provide shipowners with a stable and competent workforce.

508. Many other instruments related to the *conditions of work* of seamen. The question of *wages, hours of work and manning* has, as it has already been said, been dealt with in four conventions in succession, which were adopted in 1936, 1946, 1949 and 1958, after a first draft convention on hours of work failed by a very close vote to be adopted in 1920, at the Genoa Conference. In spite of these revisions and of the possibility given by the last of these instruments (Convention No. 109 of 1958) to exclude from its ratification Part II, relating to wages, which had raised the greatest difficulties as it fixed a minimum amount for the wages in dollars or pounds, the Convention has been ratified by eight States only and these ratifications do not yet meet the conditions set for its entry into force. As regards *minimum wages*, Convention No. 109 of 1958 was supplemented, in that same year, by a Recommendation (No. 109) which laid down amounts higher than those fixed in the Convention. In order to take account of the fact that the value of money generally has decreased since, the 1970 maritime session of the Conference adopted a resolution on 'the Minimum Basic Wage for Able Seamen' in which it considered that the figures of 42 British pounds and 100 dollars USA could be regarded as equivalent of those contained in the Recommendation. It envisaged that these figures be reviewed in future by the Joint Maritime Commission. In effect, in October 1976, the Joint Maritime Commission urged that the parties concerned should apply the figures of 78 pounds or 187 US dollars and more precisely, as provided in the Recommendation, whichever of these amounts may from time to time be the greater. As regards *hours of work* on board ship, Convention No. 109 laid down standards which were different for officers and ratings employed on the deck, engine-room and radio departments, and for persons employed in the catering department, according to whether the ship concerned is engaged in near trade or in distant trade, according to whether it is at sea or in port and according to whether the day concerned is the weekly day of rest or another day. Finally, as regards *manning*, the Convention provides that every vessel shall be sufficiently and efficiently manned for the purposes of ensuring the safety of life at sea, giving effect to the provisions on hours of work, preventing excessive strain upon the crew and minimizing the working of overtime.

509. Holidays with pay have been dealt with by a succession of conventions adopted respectively in 1936 (Convention No. 54), in 1946 (Convention No. 72), in 1949 (Convention No. 91, ratified by 21 States), when the standard had been 18 working days for masters and officers and 12 working days for other members of the crew, and finally in 1976 (Convention No. 146, which provides that the leave shall not be less than 30 calendar days for one year of service).

510. Numerous instruments were also adopted in the field of *safety and hygiene*, and, more generally, of the *conditions of life* of seamen, both on board and in the ports. Thus Convention No. 75 of 1946, revised by Convention No. 92 of 1949 – which was ratified by 28 States – contains detailed provisions about crew accommodation on board ship and supplementary provisions on this subject were included in Convention No. 133 of 1970 (ratified by 12 States but not yet in force). Other instruments adopted in 1970 were Recommendation (No. 141) concerning control of harmful noise in crew accommodation and working spaces on board ship and a Convention (No. 134) on prevention of occupational accidents to seafarers – which was ratified by 14 States – and was supplemented by a Recommendation (No. 142). Reference has already been made above[1] to the conventions concerning Marking of Weight (Packages Transported by Vessels) of 1929 and concerning Protection against Accidents (Dockers) (revised in 1932). In the field of hygiene, the Conference adopted in 1958, a Recommendation (No. 105) concerning Ships' Medicine Chests and a Recommendation (No. 106) concerning Medical Advice at Sea. The question of Food and Catering for Ships' Crews was also covered by a Convention (No. 68) of 1946, which was ratified by 19 States. Finally, recommendations on various aspects of the conditions of life of seamen were adopted over the years, such as the Recommendation on Seamen's Welfare in Ports, 1936 (No. 48), Recommendation on Social Conditions and Safety (Seafarers), 1958 (No. 108), Recommendation on Bedding, Mess Utensils, etc. (Ships Crews), 1946 (No. 78) and Recommendation on Seafarers' Welfare, 1970 (No. 138).

1. See above No. 388.

511. To facilitate freedom of movement for seamen, the Conference adopted, in 1958, a Convention (No. 108) on Seafarer's Identity Documents, which was ratified by 37 States. This instrument provides that each ratifying State shall issue to seafarers an identity document on the basis of which they shall be readmitted to the country where the document was issued and they shall be permitted the entry into a country for which the convention is in force for temporary short leave while the ship is in port, for the purpose of joining his ship or of passing in transit to joint his ship.

512. Quite a number of instruments were adopted in the field of *social security*. As early as 1920 a Recommendation (No. 10) advocated the establishment of a certificate of insurance against unemployment of seamen and a Convention (No. 8), ratified by 44 States, introduced a completely new rule providing for the payment of an indemnity of at least two months' wages to seamen in case of loss or foundering of the vessel. New standards, in certain respects, were also introduced in 1926 by Convention (No. 23) on repatriation of seamen – ratified by more than 30 States and by a Recommendation (No. 27) on repatriation of ship masters and apprentices. The Convention establishes the right of seamen who are landed during the term or on the expiration of their engagement to be taken back to their own country or to the port at which they were engaged, or to the port at which the voyage commenced. It specifies the cases in which the expenses of repatriation shall not be a charge on the seaman. In 1936 progress was made by the adoption of two conventions relating the one (No. 55) to the liability of the shipowner in case of sickness, injury or death of seamen and the other (No. 56) to sickness insurance for seamen; they were ratified by 14 and 12 States respectively. Finally in 1946 further progress in this field was achieved when the Seattle maritime session of the Conference adopted Convention (No. 70) concerning social security of seafarers (ratified by 7 States, but not yet in force) and Convention (No. 71) concerning seafarers' pensions, ratified by 10 States. At the same time recommendations were adopted on seafarers' social security agreements (No. 75) and medical care for seafarers' dependents (No. 76).

513. To ensure the observance of the legislation in the field of employment at sea, a Recommendation (No. 28) of 1926 dealt with the general principles for the *inspection* of the conditions of work of seamen.

514. An important development took place in 1976 in relation to the more general problem of *minimum standards* in merchant ships. Following discussions concerning substandard vessels, particularly those registered under flags of convenience, the maritime session of the Conference adopted a Convention (No. 147) concerning minimum standards in merchant ships and a Recommendation (No. 155) concerning the improvement of standards in merchant ships. The Convention provides, in particular, that States should have laws or regulations whose provisions should be substantially equivalent to eleven specified ILO conventions (some of them relating to maritime work and others of a more general character, such as those on freedom of association). The Convention authorizes States which have ratified it to examine complaints that a ship which has called in a port of its territory does not conform to the standards of the Convention. In such a case the State concerned may address a report to the government of the country in which the ship is registered, with a copy to the ILO, and it may take measures necessary to rectify any conditions on board which are clearly hazardous to safety or health. However, it should not unreasonably detain or delay the ship.

II. Fishermen

515. Conventions concerning seamen generally do not apply to fishermen. The 1921 Resolution quoted above[1] contained a provision to that effect and moreover various conventions, either relating to employment at sea,[2] or of a more general character,[3] exclude fishing vessels expressly or implicitly. This is not an absolute rule. Certain maritime conventions expressly apply to fishermen[4] and it may be considered that the conventions of general scope are applicable to fishermen in the same conditions as they do to seamen.[5] In these circumstances a number of instruments were adopted to take account of the special conditions of work of fishermen. One Recommendation (No. 7) dates back to 1920 and it deals with the limitation of hours of work in the fishing industry on the basis of the eight hours day and the forty-eight hours week but 'with such special provisions as may be necessary to meet the conditions peculiar to the fishing industry in each country.' Apart from this Recommendation the instruments relating to fishermen are of relatively recent date and they have been based, to a certain extent, to those concerning seamen.

1. No. 499.
2. See Conventions Nos. 22 and 23 of 1926 articles of agreement and on repatriation.
3. See Conventions Nos. 33 and 60 on minimum age (industry) of 1932 and 1937.
4. See Conventions Nos. 55, 56, 70 and 71 dealing with matters of social security of seamen.
5. See above No. 499.

516. Thus, in 1959, in the field of admission to employment, a Convention (No. 112), which has been ratified by more than 30 States, fixed at 15 years the minimum age for admission to employment for fishermen, while another Convention (No. 113) which has been ratified by 20 States, provided for the medical examination of fishermen of less than 21 years. The vocational training of fishermen was dealt with in a detailed Recommendation (No. 126) of 1966, and an equally detailed Convention (No. 125), which was adopted the same year but has been ratified by less than 10 countries, required the establishment by States of standards of qualification for certificates of competency entitling a person to perform the duties of skipper, mate or engineer on board a fishing vessel. As regards conditions of work, a Convention (No. 114) of 1959, which has been ratified by 19 States, dealt with Fishermen's Articles of Agreement on lines similar to those set out in the 1926 standard concerning seamen. Finally Convention No. 126 of 1966, which has been ratified by 13 States established precise requirements as regards accommodation on board fishing vessels, as this had been done by a 1949 convention in connection with sea-going vessels.

§2. Workers in Agriculture

517. The adoption of a number of standards concerning work in agriculture is mainly due to two different factors. In the first instance the national regulation of work in agriculture has been generally behind the legislation relating to industrial workers. Secondly, the economic and social conditions of agricultural work have special characteristics and sometimes do not allow the mere extension to agricultural workers of the labour legislation applying to industry. Thus the question of hours of work in agriculture was withdrawn, in 1921, from the agenda of the International Labour Conference and the extent to which recourse is had to family work in agriculture resulted, the same year, in the adoption of a Convention on minimum age in agriculture which was more flexible than the corresponding one concerning industry. In these circumstances, international standards adopted on agricultural work had two different objectives in view: in some cases, they only aimed at extending to agricultural work the rules applying to industry; in other cases, the aim was to frame rules which, while based on the standards laid down for industrial work, took into account the special features of work in agriculture. Apart from the Conventions which, in one way or another, have thus specifically dealt with work in agriculture certain Conventions of general scope also apply in this sector.

518. In the first group of cases, there are a certain number of Conventions which provide merely for the extension to agriculture of the benefit of laws and regulations which were initially applicable only to industrial workers. This was the purpose of two instruments adopted in 1921 and dealing with the rights of association and combination (Convention No. 11 which has been ratified by 100 States) and with workmen's compensation (Convention No. 12, which has been ratified by some 60 States). In other cases, instead of providing only for equality of treatment between workers in agriculture and those in industry, the Conventions relating to agriculture laid down some substantive rules, generally analogous to those established for industrial workers, but sometimes more flexible. Thus, two series of parallel instruments applying, on the one hand, to industry, and on the other hand to agriculture, were adopted in 1927 and 1933 in the fields of insurance against sickness, old-age, invalidity and for survivors. Similarly, in the field of minimum wage-fixing machinery, a Convention of 1951 (No. 99) and a supplementary Recommendation (No. 89) relating both to agriculture followed, with some variations, the pattern of the 1928 Convention (No. 26) and Recommendation (No. 30) which apply to industry and commerce.[1] In the field of holidays with pay, the differences between the Convention (No. 101) and the Recommendation (No. 93) of 1952 which relate to agriculture and the Convention (No. 52) and the Recommendation (No. 47) of 1935, which apply to industry and commerce, are greater, the main difference being that the Convention concerning agriculture did not lay down what the minimum duration of the holiday should be.[2] However, the general spirit is similar. It has also been noted[3] that, in the field of minimum age, the protection provided by Convention No. 10 of 1921 is clearly more limited than that which was laid down by the Conventions relating to industry. On the other hand, in connection with freedom of association, while the general instruments adopted in this field – such as Conventions Nos. 87 and 98 – apply to agricultural workers as to other categories of workers, it was felt necessary to supplement these general provisions by standards concerning more particularly the organizations of rural workers and aiming at facilitating their establishment and growth.[4]

1. See above Nos. 305–307.
2. See above No. 363.
3. See above No. 472.
4. See above Nos. 200–201.

519. A certain number of Recommendations also aimed either at extending to agricultural workers the benefit of legislation applicable to industrial workers. Most of these instruments date back to 1921, but a special mention can be made of a Recommendation of 1956 (No. 101) which deals in detail with vocational training in agriculture.

520. Standard-setting naturally raises the question of the measures which are necessary for the effective implementation of these standards. In this connection, the organization of a system of labour inspection in agriculture was provided for in a Convention of 1969 (No. 129), which has been ratified by some 20 States and was supplemented by a Recommendation (No. 133). These instruments[1] filled a gap which existed since the adoption, in 1947, of the general Convention concerning labour inspection, which applied only to industry and commerce.

1. See below Nos. 560 ss.

521. Standards have also been framed for two special categories of agricultural workers. As regards, first, plantation workers, the method followed has been to draft a Convention (No. 110 of 1958) composed of 12 parts dealing with different subjects of social policy. Each of these parts reproduces the provisions of other Conventions which have dealt with these subjects and States which ratify the Convention may, in accordance with a formula used already in Convention No. 102,[1] accept only 5 of these 12 parts. However, this Convention has been ratified by a limited number of States (10 altogether), the main reason being the extent of its scope. Standards were also adopted as regards tenants, share-croppers and similar categories of agricultural workers: a Recommendation of 1968 (No. 132) enunciated a great variety of measures aimed at the improvement of the conditions of life and work of these categories of workers.

1. See above No. 420.

§3. Indigenous Workers and Workers of Non-Metropolitan Territories

522. Indigenous workers and workers of non-metropolitan territories were

in particular need of protection because of the level of their development and of their political and social status. While differing in certain respects, these two categories are analogous to a great extent and they even sometimes coincide. The main difference is that *indigenous workers* can be found both in the metropolitan and in the non-metropolitan parts of a country. They are defined as belonging to the indigenous population of a dependent territory or to the dependent indigenous population of the home territory of a State Member of the ILO. *Workers of non-metropolitan territories* are simply those who reside in such territories. Separate Conventions have been framed for these two groups of workers. Special standards have also been adopted in favour of the indigenous and tribal populations.

I. Indigenous Workers

523. The main purpose of the Conventions and Recommendations which related to indigenous workers has been to protect them against exploitation and coercion. These instruments supplemented the measures taken in 1930 with the adoption of the first Convention concerning forced labour. They were adopted as from 1936 and they dealt with recruiting, contracts of employment, penal sanctions for breaches of contracts of employment and labour inspection.

A. Recruiting

524. As recruiting operations can give rise to abuses, the Recruiting of Indigenous Workers Convention, 1936 (No. 50), which has been ratified by some 30 States and declared applicable to some 20 non-metropolitan territories, required ratifying States to regulate the recruiting of indigenous workers and it laid down various standards aimed at avoiding the use of coercion, at protecting the communities against the repercussions of the withdrawal of too many adult males, at protecting non-adult persons against recruiting, at limiting the right of recruiting of public officers and at prohibiting its exercise by chiefs and other indigenous authorities. According to the Convention, no person or association shall engage in recruiting unless it has been licensed by the authorities. The Convention specifies the conditions under which licences should be issued and it specifies the obligations of the licencees. It provides that the authorities should exercise a certain supervision on recruiting operations and it lays down various guarantees as regards the medical examination of recruited workers, their transport, their repatriation, the advances of wages, etc. The Convention has been supplemented by a Recommendation of 1936 (No. 46), which advocates a number of measures aimed at hastening the progressive elimination of recruiting.

B. The Contracts of Employment

525. Two Conventions were adopted with a view to avoiding abuses in the conclusion of contracts of employment of indigenous workers. First, in 1939, a detailed Convention (No. 64) which has been ratified by 28 States and declared applicable to 20 non-metropolitan territories, provides that these contracts should be made in writing when they are made for a period of 6 months or more or when they stipulate conditions of employment which differ materially from those customary in the district. The Convention specifies the particulars which every contract should contain and it requires that it should be presented for attestation to an accredited public officer, who shall ascertain that certain conditions have been met. Every worker who enters into a contract should be medically examined. Non-adult persons should not enter into a contract. The Convention contains also provisions about the maximum period of service that may be stipulated in a contract and about the termination of the contract and the repatriation of the worker. A Recommendation (No. 58) adopted in 1939 at the same time as the Convention deals with the maximum length of written contracts of employment of indigenous workers.

526. A few years later, in 1947, a second Convention (No. 86) on the matter of contracts of employment of indigenous workers laid down standards about the maximum period of service which may be stipulated or implied in these contracts, whether written or oral. Such period shall not exceed 12 months, or – if the workers are accompanied by their families – two years, when the contract does not involve a long and expensive journey. Otherwise, the contract shall not exceed 2 or 3 years, according to the case. This Convention has been ratified by some 20 States and declared applicable to some 20 non-metropolitan territories.

C. Penal Sanctions for Breaches of Contracts of Employment

527. The penal sanctions for breaches of contracts of employment have been the subject of lively discussions between the two World Wars as they were considered by some to be a survival of bondage. Two Conventions were adopted in this field. Convention No. 65 of 1939, which has been ratified by some 30 States and declared applicable to more than 22 territories, provided that all such penal sanctions should be abolished progressively and as soon as possible and that their abolition should be immediate in the case of non-adult persons. In 1955, Convention No. 104, which has been ratified by 25 States and declared applicable to three territories, required the immediate abolition of this type of sanctions or their progressive abolition not later than one year from the date of ratification of the Convention. Moreover, with a view to abolishing discrimination between indigenous and non-indigenous workers, penal sanctions for breaches of contracts of employment not covered by the Convention which do not apply to non-indigenous workers shall be abolished for indigenous workers.

II. Workers in Non-Metropolitan Territories

528. The conditions of workers of non-metropolitan territories were already covered in several respects by the Conventions concerning indigenous workers. Moreover, certain standards of more general application and in particular those laid down in the 1930 Convention on Forced Labour[1] had been framed specially in the light of conditions prevailing in non-metropolitan territories and in fact exercised a considerable influence in these territories.[2] Finally, the implementation of Article 35 of the Constitution of the ILO[3] resulted in the progressive extension of the application of general Conventions to non-metropolitan territories. Nevertheless, it has also been felt necessary to frame certain standards relating particularly to the situation in non-metropolitan territories. Such a trend was initiated during the Second World War, and it led to the adoption, first, in 1944 and 1945, of Recommendations concerning social policy in dependent territories, and then, in 1947, of a series of Conventions concerning non-metropolitan territories, which played an important role, in particular in the development of social conditions in Africa.[4] The purpose of these instruments has been either to extend to the workers of non-metropolitan territories a number of standards of more general character, or to adopt special standards in respect of these workers; these were similar to or even ahead of the general standards. They dealt with social policy, right of association, labour inspection and labour standards.

1. See above Nos. 215 and f.
2. On this influence, see 'Aspects of Social Evolution in Present and Former Non-Metropolitan Territories', *Rep. Com. Exp.* 1961, p. 255.
3. See below No. 587.
4. See, in this connection, the message of President Senghor of Senegal to the International Labour Conference, *Rec. Proc. Conf.*, 53rd Session, 1969, p. 129.

A. Social Policy

529. Already in 1944 the ILO adopted a Recommendation (No. 70) concerning social policy in dependent territories which was based on the principle according to which States should take steps to promote the well-being and development of the peoples of such territories through the effective application of the general principles and the minimum standards set forth in the Recommendation and relating to various aspects of social policy. In 1945 another Recommendation (No. 74) included supplementary provisions on a series of other questions. Finally, in 1947 the question of social policy in non-metropolitan territories was dealt with in a Convention (No. 82) which, as indicated above,[1] has been revised in 1962 with a view to making its continued application and ratification possible for independent States.

1. See above No. 409.

B. Right of Association

530. As stated above,[1] the Right of Association (Non-Metropolitan Territories) Convention, 1947 (No. 84) has been the first instrument which included substantive provisions in this field. It was adopted a year before the general Convention on Freedom of Association (No. 87).

1. See above No. 169.

C. Labour Inspection

531. In 1947 also, at the same time as it adopted a general Convention (No. 81) on Labour Inspection, the International Labour Conference framed a special Convention (No. 85) on labour inspection in non-metropolitan territories, which reproduced certain provisions of the general Convention.[1] This Convention also had a great impact.

1. See above No. 563.

D. Labour Standards

532. Another instrument adopted in 1947 has been the Labour Standards (Non-Metropolitan Territories) Convention (No. 83). This Convention did not itself introduce any new standards. Its aim was to allow States to make, as regards a number of Conventions which were appended to this text, declarations of application to non-metropolitan territories analogous to those provided for by Article 35 of the Constitution of the ILO,[1] even if the State concerned had not ratified the Convention in question for its home territory. It took a long time for this Convention to enter into force. While two ratifications only were required for its entry into force and the first ratification, from the United Kingdom, was received in 1950, it was not until 1973 that the second ratification (by Australia) was communicated and the Convention therefore entered into force the following year in accordance with the usual final clauses.[2] However this delay does not mean that the Convention had no effect during a quarter of a century. In fact, when the United Kingdom ratified the Convention, it made a great number of declarations of application of the Conventions listed in this instrument to the various territories for which it was responsible. These declarations did not become effective until Convention No. 83 came into force. However, when many of these territories reached their independence, the new States declared themselves bound, in most of these cases, by the declarations made on their behalf. The declarations were therefore transformed into ratifications in the name of the new member States and Convention No. 83 could thus attain, to a certain extent, the objective at which it was aimed. More recently, the entry into force of the Convention resulted in more than 100 declarations of application of the Conventions concerned being still registered in the name of various territories.

1. See below No. 587.
2. See below No. 583.

III. Indigenous and Tribal Populations

533. In 1957, the International Labour Conference adopted a Convention (No. 107) – which has been ratified by 27 States – and a Recommendation covering a wide range of subjects in respect of indigenous and other tribal and semi-tribal populations. These instruments went much beyond the questions of labour as such. They were framed with the co-operation of the United Nations and the Specialized Agencies concerned – which are also called upon to co-operate in promoting their application – and they deal with all aspects of the conditions of life of these populations. In order to promote concerted and simultaneous action in respect of all the factors which have maintained these populations on the fringe of their respective national communities and have prevented them from sharing in the progress of these communities, these instruments include a variety of provisions which aim at assuring 'the progress of the populations concerned, their progressive integration into their respective national communities and the improvement of their living and working conditions'.[1] Thus, the Convention and Recommendation in question deal not only with recruiting and conditions of employment, vocational training, handicrafts and rural industries, and social security, but also with wider questions, such as citizenship rights, cultural and religious values, customs and institutions, ownership over the lands, health, social control and criminal penalties, education and means of communication, etc. In recent years, the question of the revision of the Convention in order to take account of new conceptions, and in particular to avoid policies of systematic integration, has been raised in certain quarters.

1. Preamble of Convention No. 107.

§4. Public Employees

534. While some doubts were expressed, when the ILO was established, as to whether the Organization was expected to deal with the conditions of work of civil servants, or more generally of public employees it soon appeared that the competence of the ILO in this area could not be denied, even if the conditions of work of civil servants were regulated by public law and if the application of a given international standard was to be ensured by different sets of national rules for different categories of workers. In fact some of the Conventions adopted by the ILO are applicable to civil servants as well as to other workers, in particular in the field of freedom of association, equal remuneration and discrimination in employment and occupation while it is specified in many other Conventions that they apply to the workers of both public and private establishments. On the other hand, in a Convention like the Right to Organize and Collective Bargaining Convention, 1949 (No. 98), it has been specified that 'the Convention does not deal with the position of public servants engaged in the administration of the State'.

535. In 1978, the Conference adopted a Convention (No. 151) and a Recommendation (No. 159) relating to Labour Relations in the Public Service. The Convention, as indicated above,[1] relates to protection against acts of anti-union discrimination and against acts of interference by a public authority, to the facilities to be afforded to the representatives of public employees' organizations, to procedures for determining terms and conditions of employment, to settlement of disputes and to civil and political rights.

1. For more details, see No. 202 above.

§5. Nursing Personnel

536. As, in recent years, serious problems were met as regards the employment of nursing personnel, standards relating to the employment and conditions of work and life of this personnel have been framed by the ILO in co-operation with the World Health Organization. As a result, the International Labour Conference adopted, in 1977, a Nursing Personnel Convention (No. 149) which was supplemented by a Recommendation (No. 157). The Convention contains a number of basic provisions relating, in particular, to the adoption and application of national policies concerning nursing services and personnel, to the basic requirements regarding nursing education and training, to the determination of conditions of employment and work and to equality of treatment with conditions of work of other workers in the country. The Recommendation is much more detailed and its various parts relate, in particular, to national policies concerning nursing services and nursing personnel, education and training, practice of nursing profession, participation, career development, remuneration, working time and rest periods, occupational health protection, social security, special employment arrangements, nursing services and international co-operation. An Annex to the Recommendation contains suggestions concerning practical application.

Chapter XIV. Foreign and Migrant Workers

537. The protection of foreign workers has been, as already indicated, considered from the outset as one of the main functions of the ILO. The Preamble of its Constitution states that one of the tasks of the ILO shall be the 'protection of the interests of workers when employed in countries other than their own'. In fact, foreign and in particular migrant workers are often isolated in countries with whose laws and customs they are not familiar, they are more likely to be exploited and are often unable to defend their interests effectively. It is therefore natural that the ILO should devote special attention to their protection. To this effect, a number of Conventions have been adopted dealing specifically with matters relating to foreign workers. In addition, some Conventions of a more general scope contain special provisions applying to this category of workers. Finally, it will be seen that international labour Conventions which do not contain any express provision on the subject are generally also applicable to foreign workers.

§1. Conventions Dealing Specifically with the Situation of Foreign and Migrant Workers

538. A first group of Conventions dealing specifically with the situation of foreign and migrant workers relate to *social security*.[1] Three Conventions were adopted in this field: the Equality of Treatment (Accident Compensation) Convention, 1925 (No. 19), the Maintenance of Migrants' Pension Rights Convention, 1935 (No. 48) and the Equality of Treatment (Social Security) Convention, 1962 (No. 118). These Conventions are based on the principle of reciprocity,[2] i.e. each State which has ratified one of them is bound to apply it only to the nationals of States which have also ratified it.

1. See above Nos. 416–421.
2. See Jean Morellet, 'La notion de réciprocité dans les traités de travail et les conventions internationales du travail', *Revue de droit international privé*, 1931, pp. 642 and ff.; Jacques Secrétan, 'International Labour Conventions as a Means of Assuring Identity of Treatment for National and Foreign Workers on a Basis of Reciprocity', I.L.R., June 1933.

539. Contrary to this first group of instruments, a more general Convention – the Migration for Employment Convention (Revised), 1949 (No. 97) – which has been ratified by 33 States, is applicable generally to migrant workers 'without discrimination in respect of nationality, race, religion or sex', and ratifying States are bound to apply it even to nationals of States which have not ratified it. The Convention includes, in the first instance, a series of provisions relating to migrations, in particular as regards the maintenance of free service to assist migrants for employment and to provide them with accurate information. States should also, as far as possible, take steps against misleading propaganda relating to emigration and immigration. Measures should be taken as appropriate to facilitate the departure, journey and reception of migrants. The Convention also provides for the maintenance of appropriate medical services responsible for migrants for employment and the members of their families.

540. A second series of provisions relates to equality of treatment. States which have ratified the Convention should apply – without any discrimination, as stated above – to immigrants lawfully within their territory treatment no less favourable than that which it applies to its own nationals in respect of a number of matters, such as:

a. in so far as such matters are regulated by laws or regulations or are subject to the control of administrative authorities, remuneration, hours of work, overtime arrangements, holidays with pay, restrictions on home work, minimum age for employment, apprenticeship and training, women's work

and the work of young persons, membership of trade unions and enjoyment of the benefits of collective bargaining, accommodation;
b. social security, with two limitations;
c. employment taxes, dues or contributions payable in respect of the person employed and
d. legal proceedings relating to the above matters.

The Convention also contains provisions concerning co-operation between the employment services and other services connected with migration. It specifies that the services rendered by the public employment service to migrants for employment should be rendered free. It prohibits that a migrant who has been admitted on a permanent basis and the members of his family who have been authorized to accompany him be returned to their territory of origin because the migrant is unable to follow his occupation by reason of illness contracted or injury sustained subsequent to entry. The States bound by the Convention should permit, taking into account the limits allowed by national laws and regulations concerning export and import of currency, the transfer of such part of the earnings and savings of the migrant as the migrant may desire. The Convention is accompanied by three Annexes and ratifying States may exclude from their ratification any or all these Annexes. The two first Annexes relate to recruitment, placing and conditions of labour of migrants for employment recruited under (or otherwise than under) government-sponsored arrangements for group transfer. The third one relates to the importation of personal effects, tools and equipment of migrants for employment. Finally, the Convention has been supplemented by a Recommendation (No. 86) which contains more detailed provisions on the general policy of States to develop and utilize all possibilities of employment, on the free service to be provided to assist migrants, on intermediaries who undertake the recruitment, on the selection of migrants for employment, on the reunification of families, on the removal of restrictions to employment of the migrant and his wife and children after a regular residence of 5 years, on refraining from removing a migrant from the territory on account of his lack of means or the state of the employment market, on the benefits to be granted to nationals when they return to their State of origin. The Recommendation has as an Annex a Model Agreement on temporary and permanent migration for employment, including migration of refugees and displaced persons.

541. In the course of more recent years, increased attention was paid to migrant workers. Following the adoption of detailed resolutions in 1971 and 1972, the International Labour Conference framed, in 1975, a Convention (No. 143) concerning migrations in abusive conditions and the promotion of equality of opportunity and treatment of migrant workers, and a supplementary Recommendation (No. 143) on this subject. The Convention includes a first part relating to migrations in abusive conditions, which aims at suppressing such migrations as well as the illegal employment of migrant workers and provides for various measures in this connection. Part II deals with equality of opportunity and treatment for migrant workers and their families. It also provides for the reunification of families. As regards free choice of employment, it authorizes States to make it subject to the condition that the migrant worker has resided lawfully in the territory for the purpose of employment for a period not exceeding two years (or less, when the first work contract has to be of less than two years). The Convention also authorizes States to restrict access to limited categories or functions where this is necessary in the interests of the State. When ratifying the Convention, States can exclude either of the two Parties. Only six States have ratified the Convention until now. The Recommendation contains more detailed provisions on equality of opportunity and treatment, social policy (in particular, reunification of families, protection of the health of migrant workers, social services) and employment and residence.

542. In connection with migrants, reference should also be made to a 1926 Convention (No. 21) concerning the simplification of the inspection of emigrants on board ship which has been ratified by 31 countries. In this respect, the question of the competence of the ILO to deal with such matters had been raised but, in 1926, the International Labour Conference pronounced itself in the affirmative. The Convention was supplemented by a Recommendation (No. 26) concerning the protection of emigrant women and girls on board ship, also adopted in 1926.

543. Moreover, in 1955, a Recommendation (No. 100) aimed at the protection of migrant workers in underdeveloped countries and territories.

§2. General Conventions Containing a Special Provision on Foreign Workers

544. Apart from the Conventions which deal specifically with the situation of foreign workers, special provisions applying to this category of workers are to be found in some twenty Conventions of a more general scope. In certain cases such provisions merely aim at making it clear that the benefits for which they provide more generally should be granted to foreign workers also. This is done, in particular, by an express provision that the standard in question should be applied 'irrespective of nationality' or 'without distinction as to nationality' or more generally to 'all persons employed' or 'every person employed'.[1] Such Conventions should then apply to all foreign workers, even if they are nationals of countries which have not ratified them. This is the case, in particular, of several social insurance or social security Conventions.[2] It is exceptional that such Conventions apply only to nationals of countries which have ratified the Convention concerned[3] and still more that a State bound by the Convention would be authorized to exclude any foreign worker.[4] However many Conventions,[5] while applying to all foreign workers, allow for a certain difference of treatment – but not the complete exclusion – depending on whether the problem concerns a foreigner who is resident in the country or who is a national of a State having ratified the Convention and depending on the origin of the funds (public funds or contributory insurance).

1. E.g. Conventions (Nos. 3 and 103) on maternity protection 1919 and 1952, Convention on Shipowners' Liability (Sick and Injured Seamen) 1936 (No. 55), Convention on Seafarers' Social Security, 1946 (No. 70), Convention concerning Plantations, 1958 (No. 110).
2. See previous footnote and also Conventions (No. 121) concerning Employment Injury Benefits, of 1964, and (No. 130) concerning Medical Care and Sickness Benefits, of 1969.
3. Convention (No. 2) concerning Unemployment, 1921. See also Convention (No. 9) concerning Placing of Seamen, 1920, which provides that the facilities for employment of seamen shall be available for the seamen of all countries which ratify the Convention and where the industrial conditions are generally the same. It was however also noted that certain special Conventions are based on the principle of reciprocity.
4. The only Convention authorizing such an exception is Convention (No. 71) concerning Seafarers' Pensions, of 1946.
5. Conventions Nos. 35 to 40, No. 44 and No. 102.

§3. Conventions which Do not Contain Any Provision on Foreign Workers

545. Most international labour Conventions do not contain any provision concerning their application to foreign workers. However, the general terms in which a great number of these Conventions are drafted, the preparatory work which sometimes is clear in this connection, and the actual aim of this type of Conventions lead to the conclusion that they should also be applicable to foreign workers. As regards the terms used in Conventions, they sometimes include expressions such as 'workers . . . without distinction whatsoever'[1] and their general character, as well as preparatory work, clearly show that, when adopting the Convention concerned, the International Labour Conference intended to exclude expressly any distinction as to nationality.[2] In other Conventions,[3] the expression used is that they are applicable to 'all persons employed' and the supervisory bodies of the ILO considered that such an expression 'does not allow for any exception on the grounds of nationality'.[4] More generally, the application of international labour Conventions to foreign workers follows from the nature of the objectives of this type of Conventions. Contrary to the bilateral or multilateral labour treaties, which are based on the notion of reciprocity, it has been underlined[5] that the aim of international labour Conventions is, in most cases, to establish, in countries which ratify them, legal schemes of general application. Moreover, if one excepts social security, these Conventions deal with questions which are of such a general scope (such as hours of work, weekly rest, safety and hygiene, etc.) that one can hardly imagine how distinctions based on nationality could be made in practice, as the measures provided in the Conventions should naturally be applied to all the workers of an undertaking. In conclusion, and with the exception of some Conventions whose terms indicate the intention to exclude foreign workers,[6] the great majority of international labour Conventions are of general application and do not allow limitations based on the nationality of protected persons.[7] The equality between foreigners and nationals which they imply is generally absolute and they are only exceptionally based on equality subject to reciprocity.

1. Convention No. 87.

2. See *Intern. Lab. Code*, note 3 under art. 857 (p. 681); Jenks, *The International Protection of Trade Union Freedom*, London, 1957, pp. 25 and 243–244; see also above No. 174.
3. E.g. Convention No. 8.
4. *Rep. Com. Exp*. 1956, p. 31.
5. Jean Morellet, *op. cit.*, p. 644. See also Secrétan, *op. cit.*
6. In this connection, it was explained (above No. 245) that, in the case of the Discrimination (Employment and Occupation) Convention, 1958 (No. 111), the expression 'distinction . . . made on the basis of national extraction' does not refer to foreigners, but to nationals of a foreign origin.
7. See also 'Comparative analysis of the International Covenants on Human Rights and International Labour Conventions and Recommendation', O.B., Vol. LII, 1969, No. 2, para. 18.

§4. Other International Standards

546. The *International Covenant on Economic, Social and Cultural Rights* is far from being clear about its application to foreigners. In the first instance, it provides (Art. 2, para. 2), according to a formula which had also been used by the Universal Declaration of Human Rights, that the rights enunciated in the Covenant will be exercised without discrimination of any kind *inter alia* as to 'national origin', a term which differs from that of nationality, as it normally concerns nationals who are of foreign origin. The Covenant also refers to 'other status' but if this expression were to cover nationality, *inter alia*, one might wonder why the term 'nationality' has not been expressly used. However, the following provision (Art. 2, para. 3) provides that 'developing countries, with due regard to human rights and their national economy, may determine to what extent they would guarantee the economic rights recognized in the . . . Covenant to non-nationals'. *A contrario*, one might be led to think that as regards social rights, on the one hand, and developed countries, on the other, the Covenant would apply to foreigners. However, this is not conclusive.[1] Apart from the question of legal interpretation itself, a difficulty of substance lies in the very wide range of the matters dealt with in the Covenant, and about which the automatic and general application to foreigners would appear to be as difficult in some cases (e.g. right to work) as their exclusion would be unthinkable in others (e.g. hours of work, industrial safety and hygiene).

1. Thus, Egon Schwelb, in 'Some Aspects of the International Covenants on Human Rights of December 1966', *International Protection of Human Rights, Nobel Symposium 7*, edited by A. Eide and A. Schou, Stockholm, 1968, p. 10, considers that the Covenant does not prohibit discrimination based on nationality.

547. Regional, and in particular European instruments, are generally based on the notion of reciprocity. Thus, the Appendix to the European Social Charter provides that 'without prejudice to Art. 12 para. 4 and Art. 13 para. 4,[1] persons covered by Articles 1 to 17 include foreigners only insofar as they are nationals of other Contracting Parties lawfully residing or working regularly within the territory of the Contracting Party concerned, subject to the understanding that these articles are to be interpreted in the light of the provisions of

Articles 18 and 19. This interpretation would not prejudice the extension of similar facilities to other persons by any of the Contracting Parties'.

1. Art. 12 para. 4 relates to bilateral or multilateral agreements providing for equality of treatment in the field of social security – on the basis of reciprocity – and Art. 13 para. 4 relates to equality of treatment – also on the basis of reciprocity – under the European Convention on Social and Medical Assistance of 1953.

548. Articles 18 and 19 have been understood by the supervisory bodies under the European Social Charter as applying only to nationals of Contracting Parties. Article 18 relates to the right to engage in a gainful occupation in the territory of other contracting parties. It provides for the undertaking of contracting parties to apply existing regulations in a spirit of liberality, to simplify existing formalities and to reduce or abolish chancery dues and other charges payable by foreign workers or their employers and to liberalize regulations governing the employment of foreign workers. It also refers to the recognition by States of the right of their nationals to leave the country to engage in a gainful occupation in the territories of the other Contracting Parties.

549. Article 19 of the Social Charter relates to the right of migrant workers and their families to protection and assistance. It reproduces to a large extent the gist of ILO Convention No. 97,[1] in particular as regards the obligation to maintain services to assist migrant workers, the adoption of measures to facilitate the departure, journey and reception of such workers, the co-operation between social services in emigration and immigration countries, the equal treatment of migrant workers lawfully within the territory and nationals in respect of different matters (remuneration, working conditions, membership of trade unions and enjoyment of benefits of collective bargaining, accommodation, employment taxes, dues or contributions payable in respect of employed persons, legal proceedings relating to such matters) and the transfer, within limits, of the earnings and savings of these workers. The Charter does not refer, as Convention No. 97 does, to equal treatment in respect of social security. In other respects it goes beyond Convention No. 97. Thus, it provides that States should facilitate as far as possible the reunification of the family of a foreign worker permitted to establish himself in the territory (and the family is defined in the Appendix to the Charter as meaning at least the wife and dependent children under the age of 21 years). A similar provision was contained in the ILO Recommendation No. 86 of 1949 and has since been included in Convention No. 143 of 1975, but in the latter case with a wider definition of the family (spouse, dependent children – without limitation of age – father and mother). The Charter also provides that foreign workers lawfully residing in a country should not be expelled unless they endanger national security or offend against public interest or morality. ILO Recommendation No. 151 also contains provisions designed to limit the cases of expulsion of foreign workers. Finally, the Charter specifies that the protection and assistance provided for in that article should be extended to self-employed migrant workers insofar as such measures apply.

1. See above No. 539.

550. As regards the *European Code of Social Security* which has been framed on the basis of ILO Convention No. 102 and entered into force in 1968, it does not include a provision analogous to that which, in Convention No. 102 deals with equal treatment of non-national residents.

551. Finally, more recently, in November 1977, States Members of the Council of Europe signed a *European Convention on the Legal Status of Migrant Workers*. The Convention would apply to workers who are nationals of Council of Europe member States and it deals with a great variety of matters (forms of recruitment, medical examination and vocational test, right of exit, right to admission, administrative formalities, formalities and procedure relating to work contract, information, travel, work permit, residence permit, reception, recovery of sums due in respect of maintenance, family reunion, housing, pre-training, schooling, linguistic training, vocational training and retraining, teaching of the migrant worker's mother tongue, conditions of work, transfer of savings, social security, social and medical assistance, industrial accidents and occupational diseases, industrial hygiene, inspection of working conditions, death, taxation of earnings, expiry of contract and discharge, re-employment, right of access to the courts and administrative authorities in the receiving State, use of employment services, exercise of the right to organize, participation in the affairs of the undertaking, return home, conservation of acquired rights). The Convention specifies that it shall not prejudice the provisions of laws or treaties, conventions, etc. under which more favourable treatment has been or would be accorded to the persons protected by the Convention. As regards the application of the Convention, the latter provides for the establishment of a consultative committee which would be constituted by a representative of each contracting party and which would report to the Committee of Ministers of the Council of Europe. The Convention would enter into force when it is ratified, accepted or approved by five member States of the Council of Europe.

Chapter XV. Labour Administration

552. The adoption in a country of labour laws and regulations might be ineffective if that country does not have also at its disposal a competent and efficient labour administration, entrusted with the task of following the development of the social situation, of supervising the implementation of the legislation and of ensuring the operation of the existing machinery. International standards have been adopted as regards various aspects of labour administration. Reference has already been made to the organization of a public employment service.[1] The present chapter will deal with the standards relating to labour inspection, labour administration as such, labour statistics and tripartite consultation relating to standards.

1. See above No. 289.

§1. Labour Inspection

I. General Outline

553. The need for inspection services entrusted with the task of supervising the implementation of labour legislation has been felt quite soon and the establishment of such services has generally followed, but sometimes with a certain delay, the adoption of the first labour laws.[1] At the international level, the question of labour inspection was raised in various conferences and congresses[2] and, when the ILO was set up, it figured among the general principles listed in Article 427 of the Treaty of Versailles. It was stated there that 'Each State should make provision for a system of inspection in which women should take part, in order to ensure the enforcement of the laws and regulations for the protection of the employed.'

1. The first of these services was established in the United Kingdom in 1833.
2. The Berlin Conference of 1890, in particular, made a recommendation in this connection.

554. The first instrument to be adopted in this field has been, in 1919, a Recommendation on Labour Inspection (Health Services) (No. 5). It was followed, a few years later, by a more general and more detailed instrument, i.e. the Labour Inspection Recommendation, 1923 (No. 20) which already foreshadowed the Convention which was going to be adopted a quarter of a century later. In the course of the following years, Recommendations were adopted as regards labour inspection in specific occupations – such as seafarers (Recommendation No. 28 of 1926) and building (Recommendation No. 54 of 1937) – and provisions relating to labour inspection were included in instruments dealing with specialized fields (such as minimum wage-fixing machinery (Recommendation No. 30 of 1928) and prevention of industrial accidents (Recommendation No. 31 of 1929)). However, the need for a general Convention on this matter became increasingly evident, in order to give a greater efficiency to the standard-setting activities of the ILO in this field.

555. The question of the organization of labour inspection was placed on the agenda of the session of the Conference which was to take place in 1940, but which could not be held because of the outbreak of the war. However a useful preparatory work had been made and the question was taken up again in 1947, when the Labour Inspection Convention (No. 81) was adopted. This Convention became the fundamental instrument in this field. The Conference adopted at the same time two Recommendations, the first of which (No. 81) was supplementary to the general Convention, and the second (No. 82) dealt with labour inspection in mining and transport undertakings. It also adopted a Convention (No. 85) concerning Labour Inspectorates in Non-Metropolitan Territories. As Convention No. 81 related to industry and commerce only, a separate Convention, supplemented by a Recommendation, had to be adopted in 1969 to provide for a labour inspection in agriculture. Apart from these various instruments, numerous Conventions[1] dealing with substantive matters contain provisions which call for the establishment of an appropriate system of inspection in order to ensure their effective enforcement. Finally, many resolutions on labour inspection have been adopted by ILO conferences or committees.

1. See, e.g., Conventions No. 101 of 1952, Nos. 106 and 107 of 1957, No. 119 of 1963, No. 120 of 1964, Nos. 123 and 124 of 1965 and No. 125 of 1966.

II. Labour Inspection in Industry and Commerce

A. Convention No. 81 of 1947

556. Convention No. 81 of 1947 is now the basic international standard in the field of labour inspection in industry and commerce.

Scope. In Part I, the Convention applies mainly to industrial workplaces in respect of which legal provisions relating to conditions of work and the protection of workers while engaged in their work are enforceable by labour inspectors. Mining and transport undertakings may be exempted, but this possibility of exemptions was not utilized by ratifying States. As regards commercial undertakings, Part II provides that States shall maintain a system of labour inspection in accordance with the provisions on labour inspection in industry, in so far as they are applicable. However, any State which ratifies the Convention may exclude Part II from its acceptance of the Convention.

Functions of inspection. Each ratifying State should maintain a system of labour inspection in industrial workplaces, which shall have as its functions to secure the enforcement of the legal provisions relating to conditions of work and the protection of workers, to supply technical information and advice to employers and workers and to bring to the notice of the competent authority defects or abuses not specifically covered by existing legal provisions. The Convention adds that any further duties which may be entrusted to labour inspectors should not be such as to interfere with the effective discharge of their primary duties or to prejudice in any way the authority and impartiality which are necessary to inspectors in their relations with employers and workers.

Organization, functioning and composition of inspection services. The Convention lays down the principle that labour inspection shall be placed under the supervision of a central authority. The authorities should promote effective co-operation between the inspection services and other governmental services and public or private institutions, as well as collaboration with employers and workers or their organizations. The inspection staff should be composed of public officials whose status and conditions of service are such that they are assured of stability of employment and are independent of changes of government and of improper external influences. Labour inspectors should be recruited with sole regard to their qualifications. They should be adequately trained. Both men and women should be eligible for appointment. Qualified technical experts and specialists should be associated in the work of inspection. The number of labour inspectors should be sufficient to secure the effective discharge of the duties of the inspectorate and they should have at their disposal the necessary material means. The competent authority should furnish them with local offices and the necessary transport facilities, and reimburse them any travelling and incidental expenses.

Powers of inspectors. The Convention specifies the powers which should be granted to inspectors: to enter freely at any hour of the day or night any workplace liable to inspection; to enter by day any premises which they may have reasonable cause to believe to be liable to inspection; to carry out any necessary examination, test or enquiry, to interrogate, alone or in presence of witnesses, the employer or the staff of the undertaking; to require the production of any books, registers and documents the keeping of which is prescribed by law; to enforce the posting of notices required by legal provisions and to take samples of materials and substances used. Inspectors should be empowered to take steps with a view to remedying defects observed which constitute a threat to the health or safety of the workers. They should be empowered to make orders requiring necessary alterations to the installation or plant to be carried out within a specified time limit or measures with immediate executory force in the event of imminent danger. Where this procedure is not compatible with national practice, inspectors should have the right to apply to the competent authority for the issue of orders or for the initiation of measures with immediate executory force.

Industrial accidents and occupation diseases. Labour inspection should be notified of industrial accidents and occupational diseases.

Obligations of inspectors. Labour inspectors should be bound by a number of obligations: they should not have any interest in the undertakings under their supervision; they should not reveal any manufacturing or commercial secrets or working processes which may come to their knowledge in the course of their duties and they should treat as absolutely confidential the source of any complaint.

Frequency of inspections. Workplaces should be inspected as often and as thoroughly as is necessary.

Discretionary power of inspectors. The Convention leaves to the discretion of labour inspectors to give warning and advice instead of instituting or recommending proceedings.

Sanctions. Adequate penalties for violations of legal provisions and for obstructing labour inspectors should be provided for by national legislation and effectively enforced.

Inspection reports. Labour inspectors should submit periodical reports to the central inspection authority and that authority should publish an annual general report on the subjects and with the statistics specified by the Convention.

B. The 1947 Recommendations

557. Recommendation No. 81, which supplements the 1947 Convention contains a number of suggestions on the preventive duties of labour inspectorates, the collaboration of employers and workers in regard to health and safety, labour disputes and annual reports on inspection. Finally, Recommendation No. 82 on labour inspection in mining and transport undertakings, also adopted in 1947, advocates that States should apply to these undertakings appropriate systems of labour inspection.

C. Problems of Ratification and of Application of Convention No. 81

558. Convention No. 81 has been ratified by 94 States; 17 of these States have excluded Part II relating to commerce. Various types of difficulties have prevented or delayed further ratifications or raised problems of application: the lack of qualified staff or of sufficient material means and the insufficient structure of administration have been the main obstacles, mainly in developing countries. In the developed world, the functions of technical information, the general organization of inspection and specialization are among the most frequent problems. Sometimes, the difficulties encountered are of a legal character. They relate, in certain cases, to the limited competence of labour inspection, to the lack of stability for the employment of inspectors or to the federal structure of the country. A problem peculiar to socialist countries of Eastern Europe lies in the fact that inspection duties are exercised, to a great extent, by members of trade unions, while the Convention provides that the inspection staff should be composed of public officials. It was however pointed out in this connection that the purpose of the Convention was to ensure to inspectors stability and independence in employment. If the status of public officials appeared more appropriate to this end, other formulae which would ensure the same guarantees may also be considered satisfactory.[1] Other difficulties relate to the functions of conciliator or arbitrator in labour disputes which are entrusted to inspectors. This is not recommended by Recommendation No. 81, but these functions would be incompatible with the Convention only to the extent to which they would prevent inspectors to fulfil their main duties. Finally, in a number of countries, the powers recognized to inspectors are more limited than those provided in the Convention. In spite of these difficulties, the modification of national laws and practice to adapt them to the international standard made good progress in many countries and the ratification of the Convention has reached an impressive figure. The principle of the institution of labour inspection services has become now an almost universal reality, but the degree of development of these services varies considerably from one country to another. In this evolution, the role of the ILO standards has been strengthened by the increasing technical co-operation which the ILO supplies to many countries in all continents.

1. *Rep. Com. Exp*. 1964, p. 222, paras. 99–100; *ibid*. 1969, p. 214. para. 127.

III. Labour Inspection for Seamen

559. Three years after the adoption of Recommendation (No. 20) on Labour Inspection, the Conference adopted, in 1926, a Recommendation (No. 28) on Labour Inspection of the conditions of work of seamen. This instrument followed in many respects the principles of Recommendation No. 20, while taking into account the special features of maritime navigation, in particular as regards the right of inspectors to visit vessels, the right to prohibit a vessel from leaving port in serious cases and the right to grant exemption in special cases.

IV. Labour Inspection in Agriculture

560. In the field of *plantations*, the main provisions of Convention No. 81 of 1947 had already been introduced in Convention No. 110 and Recommendation No. 110 of 1958. However, as regards labour inspection in *agriculture* more generally, a Convention (No. 129) and a Recommendation (No. 133) dealing with the matter as a whole were adopted only in 1969. These instruments were based to a large extent on the standards established in 1947 for industry and commerce, but they take account of the experience acquired and they also introduce certain innovations. After having laid down the basic obligation for States which would ratify it to maintain a system of labour inspection in agriculture, the Convention provides for the optional extension of the system to various categories of workers or persons who are not wage-earners such as tenants who do not engage outside help, sharecroppers and similar categories, persons participating in a collective economic enterprise, such as members of a co-operative, and members of the family of the operator of the undertaking. The Convention specifies that labour inspectors may be granted advisory or enforcement functions regarding legal provisions relating to conditions of life – and not only conditions of work – of workers and their families. As regards the composition of the labour inspection staff, while maintaining the rule according to which it should be composed of public officials, the Convention permits the inclusion of officials or representatives of occupational organizations, whose activities would supplement those of public inspection staff; these persons should be assured of stability of tenure and be independent of improper external influences. Another new provision was that, on the occasion of an inspection, the inspector should in principle notify not only the employer but also the workers or their representatives, of his presence, unless such a notification might be prejudicial to the performance of his duties. The defects noted should be immediately made known to the employer and the representatives of the workers. As regards the powers of inspectors, the Convention specifies that inspectors shall not enter the private home of the operator of the undertaking except with his consent or with a special authorization issued by the competent authority. The various duties of the labour inspection services should include their association in the preventive control of new plant, new materials or substances and new methods which appear likely to constitute a threat to health or safety. As far as possible, inspectors should be associated with any inquiry on the spot into the causes of the most serious occupational accidents or diseases. In other respects, the Convention is analogous to Convention No. 81. It has been ratified by some 20 States.

561. Recommendation No. 133 advocates that, when national conditions permit, the functions of labour inspectorate should include collaboration with the competent technical services with a view to helping the agricultural producer to improve his holding and the conditions of life and work of the persons working on it, and also that labour inspectorates should be associated in the enforcement of legal provisions on training of workers, social services, co-operatives and compulsory school attendance. Moreover, while maintaining the principle that the functions of labour inspectors in agriculture should not include that of acting as conciliator or arbitrator in proceedings concerning labour disputes, the Convention provides that, where no special bodies for this purpose exist in agriculture, labour inspectors may be called upon as a temporary measure to act as conciliators. The Recommendation also specifies the qualifications required for labour inspectors in agriculture and the training they should receive, and contains provisions on the working of inspectorates. It finally advocates education campaigns and lists the measures which such action could include.

V. Labour Inspection in Non-Metropolitan Territories

562. In 1939 a Recommendation (No. 59) on labour inspectorates (indigenous workers) had advocated that States concerned should establish labour inspection services in any territories where such services did not already exist. In 1947, at the same time as the general Convention (No. 81) on labour inspection, a special Convention (No. 85) was adopted for non-metropolitan territories. Somewhat less detailed than the general Convention, the special text reproduces its fundamental provisions as regards suitable training of inspectors, facilities for workers and their representatives for communicating freely with the inspectors, frequency of inspections, functions, powers and obligations of inspectors. Convention No. 85 has been ratified by the five main States responsible for non-metropolitan territories and has been declared applicable to 57 territories. Subsequently, most of these territories became independent and they have either ratified the general Convention (No. 81) or declared that, until they are in a position to do so, they remain bound by Convention No. 85. The latter Convention is still applicable without modification in 15 territories, while Convention No. 81 is applicable to 18 territories. The application of the standards on labour inspection in non-metropolitan territories was faced with a number of difficulties: sometimes the problems were of technical nature, as in the case of the powers of inspectors or of the establishment and publication of an annual inspection report. However the main problems were those of the number of inspectors, their training and the available financial resources.

VI. Other International Standards

563. The only other international provision on labour inspection appears in the *European Social Charter*. It consists of a paragraph providing merely that 'Each Contracting Party shall maintain a system of labour inspection appropriate to national conditions' (Art. 20, para. 5). As this article is contained in Part III, relating to undertakings – and not in Part II which contains the substantive provisions – it is compulsory for any State which has ratified the Charter. However, it does not specify the rules governing labour inspection.

§2. Labour Administration

564. In 1978, the Conference adopted a Convention (No. 150) and a Recommendation (No. 158) on Labour Administration. The Convention provides that States should, in a manner appropriate to national conditions, ensure the organization and effective operation in its territory of a system of labour administration, the functions and responsibilities of which are properly co-ordinated. Arrangements should be made to secure, within such a system, consultation, co-operation and negotiation between the public authorities and the most representative organizations of employers and workers. The Convention defines the main responsibilities which should be assumed by the competent bodies within the system of labour administration, and it specifies that the staff of that system shall be composed of persons who are suitably qualified for the activities to which they are assigned, who have access to training necessary for such activities and who are independent of improper external influences. Such staff should have the status, the material means and the financial resources necessary for the effective performance of their duties. The Recommendation which supplements the Convention contains more detailed information on the role, the functions (as regards labour standards, labour relations, employment and research) and the organization (co-ordination, resources and staff, internal organization and field services) of the national system of labour administration.

§3. Labour Statistics

565. One of the functions of the International Labour Office is, under the Constitution of the Organization (Art. 10), the collection and distribution of information on conditions of industrial life and labour, and this relates in particular to labour statistics. Moreover, without such statistics it is hardly possible to have a clear view of the labour situation in a country. However, in order to be of real use and to be comparable, statistics have to be compiled on the basis of sound and uniform methods and to relate to the same type of data. It therefore appeared necessary to establish international standards on labour statistics. In the framing of such standards, the international Conferences of labour statisticians, which have been organized by the ILO, played an important role. Since the first one, which was held in 1923, there have been twelve such conferences. The fifth conference prepared a draft which constituted the basis of Convention on Statistics of Wages and Hours of Work, 1938 (No. 63). Convention No. 63 provides for the compilation and the publication, at quarterly, six-monthly and yearly intervals, of statistics of wages and hours of work and the communication of such statistics to the ILO, which publishes a Yearbook and a quarterly Bulletin of Labour Statistics. Apart from a general part, the Convention comprises three parts indicating with what the statistics should precisely deal, i.e. average earnings and hours actually worked in mining and manufacturing industries (Part II), time rates of wages and of normal hours of work in mining and manufacturing industries (Part III) and wages and hours of work in agriculture. States can exclude from their ratification one or two of these parts (but not both Parts II and III). The Convention has been ratified by 33 States and its revision has been suggested by the International Labour Conference in 1973.

§4. Tripartite Consultation Relating to Standards

566. The effect to be given to international labour standards depends to a great extent from the interest with which they are received at the national level. The Constitution of the ILO already contains rules, such as those on submission to competent authorities[1] which aim at bringing them to the attention of State authorities at the highest level. In 1976, a Convention (No. 144) and a Recommendation (No. 152) were adopted to provide for the establishment of tripartite consultations aimed at promoting the implementation of international labour standards. Thus, the Convention requires ratifying States to operate procedures which ensure effective consultations between representatives of the government, of employers and of workers with respect to various matters concerning the activities of the ILO (replies to questionnaires concerning items on the agenda of the Conference and government comments on proposed texts, proposals to be made to the competent authority in connection with ILO standards, re-examination at appropriate intervals of unratified Conventions and of Recommendations to which effect has not yet been given, questions arising out of reports to be made to the ILO on the application of ratified Conventions, possible denunciations). Such consultations should be undertaken at least once a year. When appropriate, an annual report should be issued on the working of these procedures. Until now, this recent Convention has been ratified by 6 States.

1. See below Nos. 569 ff.

Chapter XVI. The Review of Existing Standards

567. As existing ILO Conventions and Recommendations have been adopted over a period of sixty years, it has been decided in 1976 to review them with a view to determining the extent to which they still responded to present needs and thinking. To this effect, the Governing Body established a Working Party which went through the whole body of existing standards and took into account a general consultation of ILO States Members as well as of international and national employers' and workers' organizations. The Working Party proceeded to classify existing Conventions and Recommendations and those which are being envisaged in four categories:

1. existing instruments, ratification and application of which should be promoted on a priority basis;
2. existing instruments, revision of which would be appropriate;
3. other existing instruments;
4. subjects concerning which the formulation of new instruments should be considered.

While this exercise has not yet been completed, it may already be said that the reports already submitted by the Working Party suggest that several Conventions and Recommendations should be revised and that the formulation of new instruments should be considered for a considerable number of subjects.

Part II. The Implementation of International Labour Standards

Chapter I. Obligations in Respect of Standards

568. In a general way, international labour standards are binding only on those States which have ratified ILO Conventions. In addition, the Constitution of the ILO, which is binding on all States Members, creates certain obligations for them, irrespective of whether or not they have ratified a particular Convention. These are the obligation to submit the Conventions and Recommendations before the national 'competent authority', the obligation to respect certain fundamental principles and the obligation to supply reports on unratified Conventions and on Recommendations.

§1. The Obligation to Submit Conventions and Recommendations to Competent Authorities

569. When the system of international labour standards was set up, in 1919, a general desire to make ILO Conventions particularly effective and to give them a greater impact than traditional diplomatic treaties led to the introduction, in the Constitution of the ILO (now Article 19, paras. 5 to 7), of a rule which was new to international law. This rule represented a compromise between the position of those delegations which wanted Conventions to have a mandatory character as soon as they were adopted and those which argued in favour of national sovereignty and the competence of parliaments. Under the rule,[1] the member States of the ILO are under the obligation to bring Conventions and Recommendations, within one year or exceptionally 18 months from their adoption by the Conference, before the national 'authorities within whose competence the matter lies, for the enactment of legislation or other action'. In the case of Conventions, the States which obtain the consent of the competent authority have to communicate the formal ratification of the Convention to the ILO and to 'take such action as may be necessary to make effective' its provisions. In the case of Recommendations, States have to inform the ILO of the measures taken. The rule was strengthened in some respects, when the ILO Constitution was amended in 1946, by the introduction of an obligation on States Members to inform the Director-General of the ILO of the measures taken to bring competent authorities, giving particulars of these authorities and of the action taken by them, a provision which has since enabled the ILO to exercise close supervision over the fulfilment of this obligation. The significance of the rule has been highlighted by the preparatory work as well as the findings of the bodies responsible for supervising its application.

1. See Valticos, *Droit international du travail*, pp. 521–532, and *idem, The International Labour Organization and National Parliaments, Inter-Parliamentary Bulletin*, 1969 no. I, pp. 16–31.

570. As regards the 'competent authority', the term clearly refers to the legislative authority of the country – in other words, the authority competent to bring the legislation into conformity with the Convention or Recommendation concerned, i.e. normally the Parliament.[1] Special or borderline cases may arise, for instance where legislative power is vested in the government, where a more limited body than the full assembly exercises certain legislative functions, or where the matters dealt with in a Convention or Recommendation do not call for parliamentary action, but can be given effect by the executive authorities. In this latter case it would be possible to comply with the provisions of the ILO Constitution in the strict sense simply by bringing the instrument before the executive authority competent to take the necessary action. The supervisory bodies have, however, expressed the view on several occasions that in order to give full effect to ILO Constitution Article 19, which is also designed to enlighten public opinion, it would be desirable that all Conventions and Recommendations should also be brought before the legislative authority, thus affording to a parliamentary assembly an opportunity of considering these instruments.

1. See in this connection the memorandum on 'The Nature of the Competent Authority Contemplated by Article 19 of the Constitution of the International Labour Organisation' (O.B. 1944, pp. 205–221). The supervisory bodies of the ILO have also frequently expressed a similar view. See recently *Rep. Com. Exp*. 1978, pp. 32–44.

571. The implications of this obligation have occasionally been misunderstood. While governments are indeed required to bring all Conventions and Recommendations before the competent authorities, they are free to make such proposals concerning them as they may deem appropriate, that is to say negative as well as positive proposals. What is important is that the instrument should be submitted to the legislative authority in every case, and not merely when it appears possible to ratify a Convention or to give effect to a Recommendation. The purpose of the rule is to ensure that Conventions and Recommendations are not 'buried or set aside without due consideration'[1] by national administrations, but that Parliaments are given an opportunity of debating the question and of deciding on whatever action they consider should be taken on ILO instruments. Accordingly, when the instrument is brought before Parliament, it would be accompanied by a message or by proposals by the government concerning any action which can be taken on it.

1. R. Ago, 'La codification du droit international et les problèmes de sa réalisation', *Recueil d'études de droit international, Hommage à Paul Guggenheim*, Geneva, 1968, p. 118.

572. The ILO Constitution also includes special provisions on this matter for Federal States (Art. 19 para. 7). They lay down that in respect of Conventions and Recommendations which the federal government regards as appropriate under its constitutional system for federal action, the obligations of the federal State are the same as those of non-federal States. In respect of instruments which, in whole or in part, call for action by the constituent states, provinces or cantons, the federal government must make effective arrangements for the reference of such Conventions and Recommendations not later than 18 months from their adoption by the Conference to the appropriate federal, state, provincial or cantonal authorities for the enactment of legislation or other action. The federal government should also arrange for periodical consultations between the federal and the state, provincial or cantonal authorities with a view to promoting within the federal State co-ordinated action to give effect to the provisions of such Conventions and Recommendations. Finally, the federal government must inform the ILO of the measures taken to bring such Conventions and Recommendations before the appropriate authorities with particulars of the authorities regarded as appropriate and the action taken by them. This provision, and more generally the more or less direct effect of international labour standards, raises the question whether labour matters are or are not within the exclusive competence of the federal authority under the constitutional system of each federal State. There are only a limited number of federal States – including, however, some of the largest – in which labour matters do not fall within the exclusive competence of the federal authority.[1] Among these States some, such as Australia and Canada, have introduced a system of periodical consultations between federal authorities and the authorities of the constituent units, as a result of which they have been able to ratify some ILO Conventions which were not within the exclusive competence of the federal authority.

1. See a study of the matter in *Rep. Com. Exp.* 1966, pp. 181–192. On the general problem of Federal States in relation to ILO Conventions, see *Int. Lab. Code*, pp. LXXIX–LXXXI and Art. 278 n. 315. See also Taylor, *Federal States and Labor Treaties* (New York 1935) and Landy, *The Effectiveness of International Supervision. Thirty Years of ILO Experience*, London and New York, 1966, pp. 108–114. Concerning certain ratifications of Conventions by Canada the legislation for the implementation of which has been declared by the Judicial Committee of the Privy Council to be *ultra vires* the constitutional authority of the Dominion Parliament (Attorney-General for Canada v. Attorney-General for Ontario, 1937, A.C. 326), see Jenks, *The Present Status of the Bennett Ratifications of International Labour Conventions*, 15 Can. Bar Rev. pp. 464–477 (1937). More generally, see Sorensen, 'Federal States and the International Protection of Human Rights', A.J.I.L, pp. 195–218.

573. Generally speaking, the application of the rule concerning the submission of Conventions and Recommendations to the competent authorities has run up against difficulties and even resistance, and still does so; it is, however, now widely applied, especially in countries with democratic parliamentary regimes. It has undoubtedly been an important factor in securing the thousands of ratifications of ILO Conventions which now exist.

§2. The Obligation to Respect Certain Fundamental Principles

574. While States Members of the ILO are formally bound only by the Conventions they have ratified, it has been held that by reason of the fact that they have accepted the ILO Constitution they are bound to observe certain fundamental principles laid down in the Constitution and in particular that of freedom of association.[1] Similarly, the International Labour Conference has held that the South African Government's policy of *apartheid* is incompatible with the Declaration of Philadelphia which the Government of that country undertook to observe in accepting the ILO Constitution, and in June 1964 the Conference condemned that policy and submitted a detailed plan for its elimination in labour matters.[2]

1. See above Nos. 164 ss and below No. 631.
2. See *Apartheid in Labour Matters*, ILO, Geneva, 1966, and the special reports on apartheid submitted by the Director-General to the Conference annually since 1965.

§3. The Obligation to Supply Reports on Unratified Conventions and on Recommendations

575. Although they have no substantive obligations in respect of Conventions they have not ratified, any more than in respect of Recommendations, which are not open for ratification, member States are under the obligation to report on them in virtue of ILO Constitution Art. 19 para. 5–7. This provision requires them to make such reports on Conventions they have not ratified and on Recommendations as may be requested by the Governing Body of the ILO. In these reports they should:

a. indicate the position of their law and practice in regard to the matters dealt with in these instruments;
b. show the extent to which effect has been given or is proposed to be given to any of the provisions of the said instruments and
c. state the difficulties which prevent or delay the ratification of the Convention or the application of the Recommendation.

Governments also have to communicate copies of these reports to the representative organizations of employers and workers in their countries. On the basis of this obligation, the Governing Body requests reports on one or more Conventions and Recommendations every year, and these reports are examined by the supervisory bodies.[1]

1. See below No. 607 ss.

Chapter II. Ratification of Conventions and Ensuing Obligations and Effect

§1. Ratification of Conventions

I. The Ratification: Concept and Procedure

576. It is by ratifying a Convention that a State assumes the international obligation to give effect to it. In the case of ILO Conventions, ratification is the formal act whereby a State Member of the ILO communicates to the

Director-General of the International Labour Office its undertaking to give effect to a particular Convention (Art. 19 para. 5(d) of the Constitution of the ILO). At the outset, and as a result of the special character of ILO Conventions, the nature of their ratification gave rise to some discussion, in the light of Scelle's views on this point,[1] but that stage is now long past. The special nature of these ratifications, which do not require either previous signatures or the exchange of instruments of ratification, appeared unusual also to the French Government which, however, finally accepted this new procedure in 1924.[2]

1. See above No. 74.
2. See Scelle, *op. cit.*, pp. 179–181; Troclet, *Législation sociale internationale*, Brussels, 1952, pp. 539 and s.; Valticos, *Droit international du travail*, no. 601, p. 534.

577. The ratification of an ILO Convention cannot be accompanied by reservations. This is because of the tripartite composition of the Conference by which the Conventions are adopted, so that not only the States which are the formal parties have a vested interest in them; more generally, reservations would be incompatible with the whole object of Conventions.[1]

1. See Jenks, 'Les instruments internationaux à caractère collectif', *Rec. Cours*, 1939–III, pp. 472–473 and the ILO Memorandum of 12 January 1951 to the International Court of Justice, *I.C.J. Pleadings* 'Reservations to the Convention on the Prevention and Punishment of the Crime of Genocide' 216–282; see also Report of the International Law Commission to the General Assembly Covering the Work of its Third Session (May-July 1951): United Nations General Assembly, Official Documents, VIth Session, Suppl. No. 9. Doc. A/1858, para. 20; *Intern. Lab. Code*, p. XCIX-CIV; O. B. 1951, pp. 274–288.

578. There have, however, been some ten cases of conditional ratifications, especially during the early years of the Organization's existence, making the entry into force of the Convention for the State concerned contingent on its ratification by certain other States. This practice has not been followed for a long time now.

579. Under the terms of some Conventions, ratification must be accompanied by a declaration stating the choice made by the member State where an option is offered between obligations of varying strictness, or the precise level of the standard it undertakes to observe, or again whether it wishes to avail itself of certain possible exceptions.

580. Ratifications are registered by the Director-General of the International Labour Office, who notifies member States and informs the Secretary-General of the United Nations for the purpose of their registration in accordance with the United Nations Charter Art. 102.

II. Present State of Ratifications

581. International labour Conventions have been the subject of more than 4,600 ratifications. In addition, over 1,200 declarations of application have been registered in respect of 40 non-metropolitan territories. There is considerable variation in the number of ratifications from country to country and from one Convention to another. Of the 136 member States of the Organization, 15 have ratified more than 60 Conventions each, 26 from 40 to 60, 56 from 20 to 39, 27 from 10 to 19, 8 less than 10 and the remaining four none yet. The average number of ratification per member State is 56 in the case of Western European countries, 47 for Eastern European countries, 39 for American countries, 25 for African countries, 18 for Asian countries, and 32 for Oceania (Australia, Fiji, New Zealand and Papua New Guinea). The number of ratifications also varies widely from one Convention to another; 19 Conventions have received more 60 ratifications, 21 from 40 to 60, 45 from 20 to 39, 29 from 10 to 19, and 37 less than 10. The six Conventions dealing directly with fundamental rights (freedom of association, forced labour and discrimination) have each received an average of 100 ratifications.

III. State Succession

582. Newly independent States which have become members of the ILO have almost unanimously followed the practice of confirming that they continue to be bound by the obligations previously assumed on their behalf by the States which were responsible for their international relations. This practice[1] has resulted in the registration of some 953 ratifications representing the confirmation by 57 States of obligations previously assumed on behalf of the territories they constituted before attaining their independence or the country of which they formed part before becoming separate States. It was vigorously encouraged by the ILO, and in particular by its first African Regional Conference, held in 1960.

1. On this practice see Jenks, 'State Succession in Respect of Law-making Treaties', *B.Y.B.I.L.* 1952, pp. 105–144; Wolf, 'Les conventions internationales du travail et la succession d'Etat', *Ann*. 1961, pp. 742–751; O'Connell, *State Succession in Municipal Law and in International Law*, vol. II, Cambridge (England), 1967, pp. 202–204.

§2. Entry into Force of Conventions

583. Every ILO Convention includes in its final articles provisions concerning its entry into force. The coming into force of the Convention is conditional on the receipt of a minimum number of ratifications, usually two. In the case of some Conventions, particularly maritime Conventions, a larger number of ratifications is required.[1] In the other cases, the model clause current since 1928 provides that the Convention shall come into force 12 months after the registration of the second ratification. For States ratifying after a Convention has initially come into force, the usual period is 12 months after registration of the ratification.

1. See above No. 501.

§3. Denunciation of Conventions

584. The final articles of Conventions also specify the conditions for their denunciation. The wording used since 1932 is that a Convention may be denounced during the year following the expiration of each ten-year period after it first came into force. As of July 1978, there have been 199 denunciations in all since the system of ILO Conventions was introduced in 1919. These denunciations are of two types. Most of them (171) apply to Conventions which the State concerned has ratified in an amended form. As already stated,[1] ratification of a Convention which revises an earlier one automatically entails denunciation of the earlier one in the cases of all Conventions adopted since 1929. The Conventions adopted before 1929 do not include a final article to this effect and their denunciation requires a special act. The second type of denunciation has no connection with any revision of a Convention. There have been only 28 such outright denunciations as against more than 4,500 ratifications.

1. See above No. 110.

§4. The Obligation to Implement Ratified Conventions

I. Nature of the Necessary Implementing Measures

585. A State which ratifies a Convention binds itself to take such action as may be necessary to make effective the provisions of such Convention (Article 19 para. 5 (d) of the Constitution). As already explained, this does not mean that legislative measures will necessarily be required to give effect to a Convention, but what is essential is that the provisions of a Convention should be fully applied; in regard to the manner of application both the Constitution of the Organization and the terms of the individual Conventions deliberately leave a wide measure of discretion to each country.[1] The extent to which legislative measures may be necessary therefore depends on the subject of the particular Convention, on any explicit provisions it may contain with regard to the measures of application required, and lastly, on the legal system of each country, as labour matters are dealt with generally by legislation in many countries while in others they are traditionally governed by custom or collective agreements.[2]

1. See the opinion given by the International Labour Office to the Irish and United States Governments, *Intern. Lab. Code*, art. 342 n. 464, pp. 277–278, and art. 1082 n. 352, pp. 863–864. See also Valticos, 'Conventions internationales du travail et droit interne', *Rev. crit.*, 1966, pp. 277 and s.
2. See however Kahn-Freund, 'The Shifting Frontiers of the Law. Law and Custom in Labour Relations', in *Current Legal Problems*, London, 1969. More generally on this subject, see Valticos, *Droit international du travail*, pp. 544–546.

II. International Labour Standards as Minimum Standards

586. The obligation to implement ratified Conventions must be interpreted in the light of the fact that international labour standards, which are designed to improve the conditions of the workers, are minimum standards. To prevent any misunderstanding on this point, the ILO Constitution (Art. 19 para. 8) provides that 'in no case shall the adoption of any Convention or Recommendation by the Conference, or the ratification of any Convention by any Member, be deemed to affect any law, award, custom or agreement which ensures more favourable conditions to the workers concerned than those provided for in the Convention or Recommendation'. The implications of this provision have been examined on several occasions. It has been pointed out, for instance, that it 'does not impose any obligation to maintain standards higher than those prescribed by the Convention'.[1] It has also been considered that it is 'applicable to provisions which go beyond the requirements of a Convention without contradicting them'.[2]

1. See O.B. 1938, p. 33. See also O.B. 1932, p. 51.
2. On this point, see Report of the Committee to Consider the Representation submitted by the General Confederation of Italian Agriculture Concerning the Application of the Employment Service Convention, 1948 (No. 88) by Italy: O.B. 1972, p. 147, para. 83.

III. Obligations in Respect of Non-Metropolitan Territories

587. Under Art. 35 of the Constitution of the ILO, countries which are responsible for the international relations of non-metropolitan territories have three main obligations: first, the basic obligation to apply the Conventions they ratify to all their territories except where the subject-matter of the Convention is within the self-governing powers of the territory or is inapplicable owing to the local conditions or subject to such modifications as may be necessary to adapt the Convention to local conditions; secondly, the obligation to make, as soon as possible after ratification, a declaration indicating the extent to which they undertake that the provisions of the Convention shall be applied; and lastly, the obligation to report annually on the position in all their territories, including those to which the ratified Conventions have not been declared applicable. Over 1,100 declarations of application without modification, as well as over 100 declarations with certain modifications, have been registered to date in respect of 40 territories which still exist. It has been indicated (No. 582) that by virtue of State succession the new States have in some 890 cases confirmed the obligations assumed on their behalf, under such declarations, by the States formerly responsible for their international relations.

588. An amendment to the Constitution adopted in 1964, but not yet in force, provides for the replacement of Art. 35 by a more general provision aiming at 'promoting the universal application of Conventions to all peoples, including those who have not yet attained a full measure of self-government'.

IV. The Effect of War, *Force Majeure* and Emergency

589. Some Conventions include a clause providing that the application of their provisions may be suspended by the government concerned in the case of war or events constituting a danger to national security, or *force majeure*, or in the public interest because of particularly serious circumstances. In the rare cases in which recourse has been had to this provision, the supervisory bodies have placed a strict interpretation upon it and have asked for particulars of the exceptions made thereunder. They have drawn a clear distinction between times of war and times of peace, and in times of peace have on several occasions refused to accept certain difficulties put forward by governments as constituting a case of *force majeure* under the terms of the Convention concerned.[1] However, most of the Conventions contain no special clause of this kind, and the supervisory bodies have expressed the view that a state of emergency cannot justify suspension of the obligations arising out of ratification, and that in any case a plea of emergency has to be appraised by an impartial authority at the international level and the State concerned is not the sole judge of the issue.[2]

1. See *Rep. Com. Exp.* 1955, p. 69 and *Rep. Conf. Com.* 1961, p. 563.
2. See Report of the Commission appointed under Art. 26 of the Constitution of the ILO to examine the Complaints concerning the Observance by Greece of the Freedom of Association Conventions: O.B. 1971, pp. 24–26, para. 102–112.

590. As for the effect of war, the position both of the ILO and of national legal authorities is that because of the nature of International Labour Conventions war cannot have the effect of cancelling the obligations they entail but such obligations may simply be suspended for the duration of the war between belligerents on opposite sides.[1]

1. See Valticos, *Droit international du travail*, No. 621, pp. 551–552 and references cited.

V. The Obligation to Supply Reports

591. Every State is required to make an annual report to the ILO on the measures which it has taken to give effect to the provisions of Conventions which it has ratified (ILO Constitution, Art. 22). Since 1959, detailed reports under this article have been due normally only every two years, unless owing to the seriousness and persistence of the divergences noted the supervisory bodies ask for a detailed annual report. In view of the continuing increase of the number of reports, the Governing Body of the ILO decided in November 1976 to introduce a greater degree of flexibility and a further spacing-out in reporting arrangements. As from 1977, reports are normally requested at four-yearly intervals, with a number of safeguards to ensure an effective system of supervision. The two-year periodicity has been maintained for some important Conventions, in particular those relating to fundamental human rights. The two reports following the first report after ratification should also normally be requested at two-yearly intervals. A general report has to be submitted each year on Conventions for which detailed reports are not due. In cases in which there are serious problems of application reports can be requested earlier than the year in which they would normally be due. The same may be done when observations on the application of a ratified Convention are made by a national or international organization of employers or workers, etc.[1]

1. See ILO Governing Body document G.B.201/14/32, November 1976.

592. As regards their contents, ILO Constitution (Art. 22) provides that the reports of governments shall be made in such a form and shall contain such particulars as the Governing Body may request. The Governing Body of the ILO accordingly adopts for each Convention a form of report containing questions on a certain number of points. States are also required to communicate copies of their reports to the representative organizations of employers and workers of their country (ILO Constitution, Art. 23 para. 2).

§5. The Incorporation of International Conventions into National Law as a Result of Ratification and the Conflict between International and National Rules

I. Incorporation of International Conventions into National Law

593. Apart from its effects at the international level, the ratification of a Convention can produce immediate effects at the national level, in a number of countries which follow the so-called monistic system. In these countries, by the very fact of ratification of a treaty (and this applies to international labour Conventions also), the publication or promulgation of a ratified treaty makes it part of national law and directly enforceable at the national level. This is provided for by the constitutional provisions of certain countries (for instance France, the Netherlands, Switzerland, several countries in Africa, the United States, Mexico and other Latin-American countries) or has been decided by case-law (for instance Belgium, Luxemburg). In other countries it results from the practice frequently adopted of including in the act authorizing ratification of a treaty a clause specifying that the treaty shall be enforceable in national law (for instance, the Federal Republic of Germany, Italy). Under some of these systems the treaty thus incorporated in national legislation is assimilated in every respect to ordinary law, whereas in others it is accorded overriding authority by the Constitution or by the decisions of the courts, a point which will be dealt with later. The question of such incorporation and of the conflict it may involve on the national plane between international standards and ordinary legislation is one aspect of the broader question of the relationship between treaties and law, which has been the subject of a large number of works in the field of international law.[1] It is a question which has often arisen in connection with labour law because of the large number of instruments in that particular field.[2] In the groups of countries mentioned above where the ratification of a treaty entails its incorporation in national law, international standards may be regarded as a direct source of law.[3]

1. It is not possible to give even a selected bibliography on this broader question here. By way of example, see O'Connell, *International Law* I, 2nd ed, London, 1970, pp. 38–79; Waelbroeck, *Traités internationaux et droit interne dans les pays du Marché Commun*, Brussels and Paris, 1969; Rousseau, *Droit international public*, vol. I, Paris, 1970, pp. 172–174; de Visscher, 'Cours général de droit international public', *Rec. Cours*, 1972–II, pp. 24–43.
2. See Berenstein, *La ratification des conventions internationales du travail et la législation interne*, Friedens-Warte, 1955, pp. 136–165; Valticos, 'Conventions internationales du travail et droit interne', *Rev. Crit.*, 1955, No. 2, pp. 251–288; *idem*, 'Les conventions internationales du travail devant le juge français', *Rev. crit.*, 1964, No. 1, pp. 41–72; *idem*, 'Droit international du travail et droit interne français', *Travaux du Comité français de droit international privé*, 1973–1975, Paris, 1977, pp. 11–37.
3. On the situation in the six original States Members of the European Economic Community in particular, see Boldt, Durand a.o., *Les sources du droit du travail*, Communauté européenne du Charbon et de l'Acier, Droit du travail, Vol. I, Luxemburg 1962, and Waelbroeck, *op. cit.*

II. The Question of Self-Executing Standards

594. To be effectively applied in countries of the type described above, or relied upon before the courts, or, in the event of conflict, regarded as amending contrary legislation, a treaty must not be drafted in terms creating merely an international obligation of the ratifying State. Its provisions must be self-executing – that is to say, they must be so drâfted as to allow of their direct application in national law. Many of the provisions of international labour Conventions are not self-executing and require supplementary laws or regulations for their application. This applies in particular to instruments laying down 'programmatic' standards which cannot give rise directly to individual rights, the implementation of which can be claimed by the beneficiaries, but consist of a general description of objectives and represent programmes for action by governments which may be carried out by different methods and over a period of time. These are the so-called promotional Conventions.[1] The position is similar in the case of Conventions requiring the setting up and maintenance by the State of certain services or institutions (social security, employment services, labour inspection, statistics), or the establishment of machinery for consultation with employers' and workers' organizations, or the taking of certain measures, in respect of industrial health and safety for instance, of which the Convention gives a general description, or again the introduction of a system of supervision and penalties. Another type of provisions which fall within the non self-executing group are those which establish a rule of law, but do so in such general terms that closer definition by the State is needed before it can be effectively implemented by national law. The question whether a standard is self-executing or not does not, moreover, depend solely on its subject-matter; the answer may also vary from one country to another according to the ease with which a given provision lends itself to incorporation in the particular legal system.

1. The Conventions concerned are primarily those on employment policy, social policy, and discrimination in employment.

595. From the point of view of the discharge of international obligations by States ratifying such instruments, it has been pointed out that the mere incorporation into national law of ratified Conventions whose provisions are not self-executing does not discharge the international obligations of the ratifying State.[1]

1. See *Rep. Com. Exp.* 1963, pp. 8–12; *ibidem*, 1970, p. 8.

596. In other cases, however, a number of provisions of international labour Conventions have been regarded as directly applicable in national law by virtue of the fact that they are self-contained and guarantee a right to individuals or organizations in sufficiently clear and precise terms (provisions fixing a minimum age, providing for freedom of association, equal rights for certain categories of workers in relation to others), or lay down a prohibition (for instance, in respect of night work or forced labour). The courts of law or authorities of a number of countries have taken this view on various occasions, particularly in Brazil,[1] France,[2] the Federal Republic of Germany,[3] Italy,[4] Japan,[5] Madagascar,[6] Spain,[7] Switzerland[8] and the United States.[9] Similar decisions have been given in several other African and Latin American countries.[10]

1. See, as regards the Holidays with Pay Convention, 1936 (No. 52), Decree No. 546 of 7 October 1976, *D.O.* 18 October 1976, p. 13801.
2. See in particular Cass. Req. 27 February 1934, D.H. 1934, p. 203, S. 1935. I.I. and note Niboyet; Cass. Civ., 28 March 1962, D. 1963. J. 578, and *Rev. Crit. d.i.p.* 1964, pp. 41 ss; Conseil d'Etat, 25 July 1975, *Rev. Crit. d.i.p.* 1976, pp. 60–63 with note Valticos.
3. See BSG, 14 February 1964, AP § 37 AVAVG No. 2.
4. There have been a number of decisions of Italian courts relating to Conventions ratified by Italy (e.g. Pretura Biella, 14 January 1963, *Riv. dir. lav.* 1963, p. 220, *I.L.R.,* vol, 91 pp. 210–231, p. 219, 1965 and App. Turin 29 May 1964, *Riv. giur. lav. previd. soc.* 1964, pp. 339), but the question was clearly settled, in particular, by opinion No. 228/73 of 20 February 1973 of the Council of State (quoted in the decree and the circular referred to below), which held that the Night Work (Women) Convention (Revised), 1948, (No. 89) had been incorporated in internal law by Act No. 1305 of 2 August 1952 which not only authorized ratification of the Convention but expressly put it into full execution. The Council of State concluded that this had entailed the abrogation of a contrary provision of an earlier law. A Ministerial Decree of 5 July 1973 (*G.U.* 26 July 1973, No. 192, p. 5298) and a Ministry of Labour Circular No. 208 of 19 September 1973 (Notiziario della Conferazione dell' Industria Italiana, 1973, p. 1562), drew the appropriate conclusions.
5. Supreme Court, 2 April 1969, *Rodo Horei Tsushin* 1969 II, No. 2.
6. See Supreme Court, 19 April 1969, *Penant* 1971, p. 224.
7. See González Velasco, 'A proposito de un convenio de la OIT applicado por el Tribunal Central de Trabajo', *Rev. Pol. Soc.* 108, 1975, pp. 129–135.
8. See *Rec. Proc. Conf.* 1973, p. 548; Berenstein, *op. cit.,* and Valticos, 'Les effets des conventions internationales du travail en Suisse', *Mélanges Société suisse de juristes*, Geneva, 1976, pp. 327–345.
9. Warren v. United States, 340 US, 523, 1951.
10. See Gonidec, *Cours de droit du travail africain et malgache*, Paris, 1966, p. 31; for Mexico, *Rec. Proc. Conf.* 1952, p. 492 and 1953, pp. 372–373, and for Guatemala *Rec. Proc. Conf.* 1961, pp. 591 and 609.

III. The Conflict between the Incorporated International Standards and Ordinary Laws

597. When the terms of an international labour Convention are incorporated in national legislation and are self-executing, there may be conflict between that standard and the provisions of an ordinary law. The courts do indeed usually try first to reconcile the terms of the international Convention with those of the national law. This is relatively easy in the case of bilateral agreements, but not in the case of Conventions designed to introduce generally applicable labour conditions.

598. In the event of conflict, one relevant consideration is the fact that international labour standards represent minimum standards.[1] If, however, the ratified Convention provides for a higher level of protection than that established by national legislation the solution of the conflict depends upon the fact whether the conflicting law is earlier or later than the ratification of the Convention and its incorporation into national law.

1. See above No. 586.

A. Conflict with Earlier Law

599. The first case presents no major difficulties. As the courts of several countries have ruled on various occasions, a Convention which by virtue of its ratification and publication has acquired the force of national law repeals or amends any earlier enactment which may be contrary to its provisions. This is simply a consequence of the rule *lex posterior derogat priori*, and it is not necessary to bring in the notion of the primacy of treaties, referred to later (unless complications were to arise as a result of the earlier law being regarded as more specific).

600. While this type of conflict does not as a rule involve any special legal problems, it does raise some practical questions. The ILO Committee of Experts has stressed on various occasions that 'even when the automatic incorporation of a ratified Convention in internal law involves the implicit repeal or amendment of earlier legislation, it is generally desirable, in order to make all persons concerned aware of amendments thus introduced and to avoid any uncertainty as regards the position in law, that appropriate publicity be given; the surest solution still consists in bringing the legislation formally into harmony with the Convention.'[1] In this connection the new French Labour Code of 1973 is of interest; it provides that the text of the provisions of international labour Conventions which are applicable in French internal law shall be appended to the Code.[2]

1. See *Rep. Com. Exp*. 1963, p. 23 and 1974, p. 8.
2. Act No. 73–4 of 2 January 1973, Art. 5.

B. Conflict with Later Law

601. The internal legal problems are more complicated in cases where a ratified Convention which has been incorporated into national law conflicts with a law promulgated after the ratification. A distinction must then be drawn between two groups of countries.

602. In the first group of countries, treaties, when ratified and published, have primacy over ordinary laws, whether such primacy is laid down in the national Constitution (France, various French-speaking African countries, the Netherlands) or is established by case law (Belgium, since a decision of the Court of Cassation of 27 May 1971,[1] Luxembourg, Switzerland, according to prevailing trends). In principle, the Convention should then prevail even over the later law. Particularly in France, there was some doubt on this point. Opinion was divided as to the true effect of the constitutional provision recognizing that treaties have 'an authority above that of (national) law'.[2] In particular it was doubtful whether, without a judicial power to examine the constitutionality of laws, a judge may refuse to apply a law which is contrary to an earlier ratified treaty, as this might be considered tantamount to a ruling that such a law infringes upon the constitutional principle of primacy of treaties. The courts had often based their decisions on the constitutional provisions concerning the primacy of treaties, but the case law had not been really conclusive[3] until a decision of the *Court de cassation* of 24 May 1975[4] which confirmed the power of the judiciary to recognize to ratified treaties precedence over later laws.

1. Pas. 1971. I, p. 886, J.T. 1971, p. 470.
2. Art. 55 of the French Constitution of 1958.
3. For France see above footnote under No. 596 and Valticos, 'Les conventions internationales du travail devant le juge français', *op. cit.,* pp. 64–67.
4. D. 1975, p. 497, *Clunet* 1975, p. 801, *Rev. crit.,* 1976, p. 347.

603. In the second group of countries, of which the United States is the most representative example, treaties are incorporated in municipal law by virtue either of the Constitution or of an Executive Order included in the ratifying law and are put on the same footing as ordinary laws.[1] Consequently, and as a result of the operation of general rules of interpretation governing conflict of statutory provisions, the later law will prevail over the treaty in internal law (but this will involve the international responsibility of the State concerned).

1. On the effect of the constitutional system of this group of countries on the ratification of international labour Conventions, see Report of the Commission appointed under Article 26 of the Constitution of the ILO to examine the complaint filed by the Government of Portugal concerning the Observance by the Government of Liberia of the Forced Labour Convention, 1930 (No. 29): *O.B.* 1963, No. 2, Suppl. II, par. 401–406, pp. 158–161.

C. European Communities

604. The principles outlined above are applicable to Conventions and agreements of the traditional type involving no element of supra-nationality. The question of conflict between international and national rules, however, arises in different terms in cases involving the regulatory powers of the European Communities. In the latter cases the possibility of conflict is reduced, if not entirely eliminated, by the fact that the regulations, regarded as quasi-legislative measures, are directly applicable in the national law of the member States.[1] Moreover, under the Treaty of Rome (Art. 177) the courts of these States may, and in certain cases must, refer a case in which the compatibility of a national provision with a Communities regulation is doubtful to the Court of Justice of the Communities for decision.

1. See Pescatore, 'Droit communautaire et droit national selon la jurisprudence de la Cour de Justice des Communautés européennes', D. 1969, Chr. p. 179 ss.; Ganshof van der Meersch, 'Le droit communautaire et ses rapports avec les droits des Etats Membres', *Idem.* and Waelbroeck, *Droit des Communautés européennes*, Brussels, 1969, pp. 41–79; Constantinides and Mêgret, *Le droit de la CEE et l'ordre juridique des Etats Membres*, Paris, 1967.

D. European Social Charter

605. In contrast to the preceding cases, the authors of the European Social Charter seem to have wished to avoid any interpenetration between the provisions of the international instrument and the internal law of States that ratify it. The Appendix to the Charter includes a provision specifying, in connection with Part III, that 'it is understood that the Charter contains legal obligations of an international character, the application of which is submitted solely to the supervision provided for in Part IV thereof', that is, solely to the international supervision provided for by the Charter. The purpose of this provision appears to have been to withdraw the supervision of the application of the Charter from national jurisdictions, and the intentions of the parties on this point cannot be disregarded.[1] Problems may nevertheless arise for the courts in countries where, by virtue of the national Constitution, a treaty which has been ratified and published is incorporated in national law and should be able to be invoked before the courts. However, the problem is not of great practical importance, since most of the provisions of the Charter do not appear to be self-executing.

1. See Wengler, 'Réflexions sur l'application du droit international public par les tribunaux internes', *Rev. gén. dr. int.* 1968, p. 950. More generally see de Visscher, *op. cit.*, pp. 27–28, 32.

Chapter III. The General Supervisory Machinery of the ILO: (I) the Examination of Periodical Reports

606. The ILO has established a diversified system of supervision which has been developed over the years.[1] The procedures fall into two main groups: *ex officio* supervision based on the examination of the periodical reports of governments, and supervision based on the submission of complaints. The present chapter will deal with the former method, which constitutes the regular supervisory machinery.

1. See Valticos, 'Un système de contrôle international: la mise en oeuvre des conventions internationales du travail', *Recueil Cours,* 1968–I, pp. 315–407; *Droit international du travail,* pp. 561–599 and *Mise à jour*, pp. 93–98 and *Derecho Internacional del Trabajo* préc., pp. 500–544; Wolf, 'Aspects judiciaires de la protection internationale des droits de l'homme', *Human Rights Journal* 1971, pp. 773–838.

607. The reports furnished by governments on the application of Conventions ratified by them,[1] on the effect given to unratified Conventions and/or Recommendations[2] and on the submission of these instruments to the competent authorities[3] are examined by the supervisory bodies set up for the purpose by the ILO. These are two in a number.

1. See above Nos. 591–592.
2. See above No. 575.
3. See above No. 569.

§1. The Committee of Experts on the Application of Conventions and Recommendations

608. The main supervisory body, from the legal point of view, is the Committee of Experts on the Application of Conventions and Recommendations, set up in 1927, which is composed of experts of recognized competence who are completely independent of governments and appointed in their personal capacity. This independence is underlined by the fact that its members are appointed by the Governing Body on the proposal of the Director-General of the International Labour Office, and not of the governments of their home countries. They are selected from among persons with the highest qualifications in the legal and social fields, as a rule from the judiciary (several of them are or have been chief justices), from the field of education (professors of international law, labour law, etc.) or among former statesmen. The Committee's fundamental principles, as it has itself stressed on a number of occasions and in particular in 1969 and 1977[1] 'call for impartiality and objectivity in pointing out the extent to which it appears that the position in each State is in conformity with the terms of the Conventions and obligations which that State has undertaken by virtue of the Constitution of the ILO'. These principles also stress that the members of the Committee 'must accomplish their task in complete independence as regards all member States'. The Committee also stressed that 'its function is to determine whether the requirements of a given Convention are being met, whatever the economic and social conditions existing in a given country. Subject only to any derogations which are expressly permitted by the Convention itself, these requirements remain constant and uniform for all countries. In carrying out this work the Committee is guided by the standards laid down in the Convention alone, mindful, however, of the fact that the modes of implementation may be different in different States. These are international standards, and the manner in which their implementation is evaluated must be uniform and must not be affected by concepts derived from any particular social and economic system.'[2]

1. See in particular *Rep. Com. Exp.* 1969, p. 19; 1971, p. 6 and 1977, p. 13.
2. See *Rep. Com. Exp.* 1977, p. 11.

609. The Committee of Experts now comprises 18 members who come from the various regions of the world. The scope of its appraisal depends on the terms of the individual Conventions. It is necessarily somewhat wide, as indicated above,[1] in the case of Conventions which lay down standards in general terms (for instance, in respect of forced labour or of freedom of association), since in such cases the Committee cannot determine the conformity of national legislation without forming a conclusion as to the precise meaning to be attached to the international standards. The body of opinions which has evolved in the course of time has acquired considerable weight. The Committee also has wide discretion in the case of Conventions providing for the progressive application of a principle with due regard to the methods customarily applied in the country concerned (for instance, in respect of equal remuneration, discrimination in employment and employment policy); in such cases the function of the Committee is to consider, year after year, whether the measures adopted are genuinely consistent with the dynamic nature of the Convention and with national conditions.

1. See above Nos. 92, 94–96.

610. The Committee's procedure is based on documentary evidence. It appraises the position in the light of the reports of governments, laws and regulations, and any other relevant material (for instance, observations by employers' and workers' organizations), and also of the governments' replies to any comments made by the Committee.

611. The Committee's comments may be individual or may take the form of a comprehensive study. Individual comments are submitted when the Committee is considering the fulfilment by each State of its international obligations towards the ILO, that is to say in respect of the implementation of ratified Conventions and of the discharge of the obligation to bring Conventions and Recommendations before the competent authorities. These comments may be in two different forms: in the most important cases they take the form of *observations* on a discrepancy that has been noted (the text of such observations is included in the Committee's printed report), the other form being that of *requests* which are communicated directly to the government concerned in order that it may reply to them in its next report. In 1977, as it appears from its report for that year, the Committee of Experts made some 400 observations and 800 direct requests in respect of the application of ratified Conventions.

612. In addition to these two types of individual comments, the Committee of Experts makes a general study every year of one particular subject, on the basis of reports requested from all States on the Conventions and Recommendations relevant to that subject, whether or not they have ratified the Conventions concerned. The object of such studies is to elucidate the position in respect of the selected subject in each State, to appraise the difficulties which may be encountered in the application of the relevant instruments, and, where appropriate, to suggest means of overcoming them. Studies of this kind covered, in 1973, the Conventions dealing with Freedom of Association (No. 87 of 1948 and No. 98 of 1949), in 1974 the Recommendation concerning Termination of Employment (No. 119 of 1963), in 1975 the instruments relating to Equal Remuneration (Convention No. 100 and Recommendation No. 90 of 1951), and in 1979 the Conventions (Nos. 29 and 105) relating to Forced Labour.

§2. The Conference Committee on the Application of Conventions and Recommendations

613. The second body composing the supervisory machinery is the Committee on the Application of Conventions and Recommendations set up by the International Labour Conference at each of its annual sessions and consisting of representatives of governments and of national organizations of employers and workers. This Committee takes as the basis of its work the report of the Committee of Experts, selecting the cases dealt with in the report which it regards as the most important. It invites the governments concerned to furnish explanations in respect of the discrepancies noted and the measures taken or contemplated by them to remove such discrepancies. The replies, written or oral, of governments sometimes give rise to detailed discussion. The discussion and conclusions of the Committee are summarized in a report which is transmitted to the Conference and is then discussed in plenary sitting.

614. Among the matters with which it deals in this way, the Committee draws attention, in its general report, by means of a list established in the light of certain criteria, to cases 'where governments apparently encountered serious difficulties in discharging their obligations under the ILO Constitution or under Conventions they had ratified'. In this connection the Committee has emphasized at times that its functions were different from those of a tribunal and that the inclusion of a country in the list was not to be construed as amounting to a sort of sanction; nevertheless sometimes it gives rise to sharp discussions. More recently, since 1976, the Conference Committee also devotes special paragraphs in its general report to discussions which it had about some important cases.

§3. Direct Contracts with Governments

615. The fact that the Committee of Experts proceeds on the basis of documentary material and the nature and limited duration of the discussions in the Conference Committee have sometimes been the cause of prolonged controversies with governments; in some cases the procedure has not allowed of a full appreciation of the questions raised. Accordingly, a new procedure consisting of 'direct contacts' with governments was introduced in 1968. This procedure, which follows certain guidelines laid down by the supervisory bodies in their reports[1] is resorted to at the request or with the agreement of the government concerned in cases where special difficulties of sufficient magnitude have been encountered in giving effect to ratified Conventions. Its object is to establish a broader and more fruitful dialogue with governments. It involves full discussion in the country concerned between a representative of the Director-General of the International Labour Office, who may be either an independent person or an appropriate ILO official, and the government authorities; contact is also made at the same time with the national organizations of employers and workers. While this procedure is in progress, consideration of the case by the supervisory bodies is suspended for a reasonable period (normally not more than a year) so that account can be taken of its results, but the functions and responsibilities of the Committee of Experts and the Conference Committee are in no way limited by the procedure of direct contacts, the primary purpose of which is to promote a better implementation of Conventions. From 1969 to 1978 this procedure was resorted to by more than 25 countries, chiefly in Latin America, but also in Africa, Asia and Europe, to deal with some 350 cases. The results on the whole have been definitely positive and recourse to it is made on an increasing scale.

1. See in particular *Rep. Com. Exp.* 1973, pp. 16–17.

§4. The Main Difficulties Encountered

616. The first type of difficulty encountered by the Committee of Experts is connected with the accurate appraisal of national situations. This occasionally raises juridical problems, such as that of the incorporation of a ratified Convention into national law and the eventual necessity of supplementary measures to ensure its application,[1] or the application of Conventions by means of collective agreements. In the case of a supervisory procedure based on documentary material, however, the major difficulty is to appraise the application of Conventions not only at the legislative level but also in practice. There are certain indirect means which can at least give some indications in this respect: governments are required by the forms of report to furnish information on the practical application of the instrument (legal decisions, particulars of the authorities responsible for the enforcement of the relevant national legislation, information on methods of inspection and supervision, extracts from inspectors' reports, various kinds of statistics, etc.), and for their part, national organizations of employers and workers may submit observations on the application of Conventions in their respective countries. Until recently, the last-mentioned possibility was little used, but latterly greater advantage has been taken of it by workers' organizations.

1. See above Nos. 594–595.

617. A second series of difficulties is connected with the bringing of national legislation into conformity with the international standard. The difficulties encountered in this sphere are many and varied: they may be connected with the economic and social conditions of the country, with administrative problems, with more or less serious political obstacles, with constitutional problems (as in the case of federal States), and so forth.

§5. The Results Obtained

618. As regards the reports due by governments, the proportion received in the last ten years averages 80 per cent at the time of the Committee of Experts' session and 87 per cent at the time of the meeting of the Conference Committee. The practical results obtained by the supervisory machinery have been the subject of systematic studies[1] which show an appreciable degree of effectiveness. The Committee of Experts itself reported in 1978 that during the past 15 years there had been progress in some 1,200 cases concerning more than 150 countries. In all these instances the governments had taken action on the observations made by the Committee and had adopted measures to bring their legislation into conformity with ratified Conventions. These cases of progress are distributed over all regions of the world, including many of the developing countries. Moreover, a number of cases of 'invisible' or less obvious progress have been noted which can be attributed directly to the operation of the machinery for promoting the implementation of international labour standards. The very existence of a vigilant system of supervision has played a preventive part in encouraging States to take the necessary measures of application in good time or discouraging them from adopting measures which would have conflicted with ratified Conventions. In a more general way, the fact that supervision in the broader sense extends to non-ratified Conventions and to Recommendations, and particularly the details given in the general studies of the Committee of Experts and the discussions in the Conference Committee, have often stimulated the interest of governments, clarified doubtful points and led States to review the possibility of taking action on the instruments concerned.

1. See Landy, *The Effectiveness of International Supervision, op. cit.; idem*, 'The Influence of International Labour Standards – Possibilities and Performance', *I.L.R.* June 1970, pp. 555–604.

619. The effect of international labour standards is not, of course, limited to cases in which the supervisory machinery operates to ensure their implementation. Quite apart from the influence of these quasi-judicial bodies, the standards have more generally served as a kind of international common law permanently available to governments as a source of guidance, and to a greater or lesser extent they have affected the situation in the great majority of countries, whatever the prevailing conditions or stage of development.[1] For instance, it has been pointed out that the labour codes of virtually all the African States have the Conventions and Recommendations of the ILO as their common denominator.[2] Regional instruments such as the European Social Charter of 1961 and the Arab Labour Standards Convention of 1967[3] are also largely based on ILO standards.

1. For a general study of the influence of standards, see *The Impact of International Labour Conventions and Recommendations*, ILO, Geneva, 1976. As regards individual countries, see in *I.L.R.* articles on the influence of Conventions in Belgium (by Troclet and Vogel-Polsky) in Nov. 1968; Cameroon (by Ayissi Mvodo and Le Faou) in Aug.-Sept. 1973: Colombia (by Plata Castilla) in Febr. 1969; France (by J. Morellet) in April 1970; Federal Republic of Germany (by Schnorr) in Dec. 1974; Greece (by Valticos) in June 1955; India (by Menon) in June 1956; Ireland (by Cashell) in July 1972; Italy (by Riva-Sanseverino) in June 1961; Nigeria, in July 1960; Norway (by Dahl) in Sept. 1964; Poland (by Rosner) in Nov. 1965; Switzerland (by Berenstein) in June 1958; in Tunisia (by Abdeljaouad) in March 1965; in the United Kingdom (by Johnston) in May 1968; in Yugoslavia (by Pesić) in Nov. 1967.
2. See statment of a high official of the Organization of African Unity, quoted in Landy, *Influence, op. cit.*, p. 566.
3. See above Nos. 134 and 141.

Chapter IV. The General Supervisory Machinery of the ILO: (II) the Examination of Complaints

620. The Constitution of the ILO makes provision for two kinds of complaints which may set in motion contentious proceedings concerning the application of a ratified Convention: complaints properly so-called, and representations.

§1. Complaints

621. The complaints procedure proper, provided for under Articles 26–34 of the Constitution of the ILO is the most formal type of supervisory procedure in the ILO. A complaint may be filed by any member State 'if it is not satisfied that any other Member is securing the effective observance of any Convention which both have ratified'. It is not required that the State filing the complaint, or any of its nationals, should have suffered any direct prejudice. The complaints procedure may also be initiated by the Governing Body of the ILO either of its own motion or on receipt of a complaint from a delegate to the International Labour Conference.

622. When a complaint has been filed, the Governing Body of the ILO may appoint a Commission of Inquiry to make a thorough examination of the matter. Each member State is required to place at the disposal of the Commission any information in its possession on the question at issue. When the Commission of Inquiry has fully considered the matter, it prepares a report embodying its findings on all questions of fact relevant to determining the issue, together with its recommendations as to the steps to be taken to meet the complaint. The governments concerned are required to state within a period of three months whether or not they accept the Commission's recommendations, and if not, whether they propose to refer the complaint to the International

Court of Justice, whose decision shall be final. If a member State fails to carry out the recommendations of the Commission of Inquiry or of the International Court of Justice within the specified time-limit, the Governing Body may recommend to the Conference such action as it may consider expedient to secure compliance with the recommendations.

623. The complaints procedure was set in motion for the first time on the initiative of a member State in 1961, when the government of Ghana filed a complaint concerning the application by Portugal of the Abolition of Forced Labour Convention, 1957 (No. 105) in its African territories. A few months later a second complaint was filed, by Portugal concerning the application by Liberia of the Forced Labour Convention, 1930 (No. 29). The procedure followed was similar in both cases.[1] The Governing Body set up Commissions of Inquiry, each composed of three members who were appointed on the proposal of the Director-General of the International Labour Office. These members were personalities of the highest standing appointed in their personal capacity. Both the Governing Body and the Commissions themselves stressed their independent character and the judicial nature of their functions. The members were required to make a solemn declaration in the same terms as that of judges of the International Court of Justice, undertaking to perform their duties 'honourable, faithfully, impartially and conscientiously'.

1. See the reports of the two Commissions: *O.B.* 1962, No. 2, Suppl. II and *O.B.* 1963, No. 2, Suppl. II.

624. The Commissions of Inquiry asked both parties for detailed information and also gave other governments, employers' and workers' international organizations, and certain non-governmental organizations an opportunity of providing relevant information. They heard witnesses, some called by the parties and some by the Commission itself. In connection with the first complaint, the Commission visited Angola and Mozambique and collected first-hand information from the authorities, heads of undertakings and a large number of workers (interviewed without the presence of the authorities or of representatives of undertakings). The reports of the Commissions included a number of recommendations to the governments concerned. These were accepted by the parties in each case, and the governments concerned subsequently took various steps to give effect to them.

625. In 1968 a complaint was filed by a number of workers' delegates to the Conference concerning the application by Greece of the Freedom of Association Conventions, and a similar procedure was followed.[1] At a certain stage of the proceedings, the government withdrew its co-operation with the Commission because of objections as regards the hearing of a witness. Therefore, the Commission did not pursue the question of a possible visit to the country concerned, and it prepared its report on the basis of the information received and the evidence adduced. In its report, the Commission drew attention to the relation between trade union rights and civil liberties and it recalled the 1970 Conference Resolution.

1. See the report of the Commission, *O.B.* 1971, No. 2, Special Supplement.

626. In June 1974, following the adoption of a Resolution on the matter by the International Labour Conference, a Commission of Inquiry was appointed to consider the application by Chile of the Hours of Work (Industry) Convention, 1919 (No. 1) and the Discrimination (Employment and Occupation) Convention, 1958 (No. 111). The Commission proceeded on the same lines as the earlier ones. It also acted in the capacity of Fact-Finding and Conciliation Commission in the field of freedom of association.[1]

1. See below No. 638.

627. In these various cases the Committee of Experts on the Application of Conventions and Recommendations was entrusted with the task of regularly following up the action taken by the governments concerned to comply with the recommendations of the Commission of Inquiry. The chief characteristics of these procedures are the independent nature of the body appointed to consider the complaints, the steps taken to ensure impartiality, the thoroughness of the inquiries undertaken, the principle that the investigation of such complaints involves the public interest and that the Commissions must themselves take steps to obtain full and impartial information, and the provision made for regular follow-up procedure after the complaint as such has been disposed of. As concerns results, it has been noted that in the various cases in which a Commission of Inquiry has made recommendations, the governments concerned have generally taken legislative or other action along the lines suggested (at least to a certain extent). The parties have accepted the Commission's recommendations in every case and have never appealed against them to the International Court of Justice. With respect to its nature, the complaints procedure is quasi-judicial, its primary purpose being to ascertain whether the situation in a given country is in conformity with international obligations assumed, but Commissions of Inquiry are also required to make recommendations for remedying any deficiencies observed.

628. In some recent cases, the submission of Article 26 complaints was not followed by the constitution of a Commission of Inquiry. This happened in the case of a complaint submitted in October 1976 by the Government of France against the Government of Panama on the grounds that the latter did not ensure the defrayal of expense for medical care to a foreign seaman as provided by the Shipowners' Liability (Sick and Injured Seamen) Convention, 1936 (No. 55). One month later, before even a Commission of Inquiry was established, the Government of Panama stated that the necessary steps for such a payment had already been taken. Two further complaints by France against Panama about the observance of maritime Conventions were filed in June 1978.

629. In other recent cases, complaints were submitted, in 1975, 1976 and 1977, by workers' delegates at the Conference in connection with the application of the Freedom of Association Conventions by Uruguay, Bolivia and Argentina, but these complaints have been considered in the first instance in the framework of the special procedure on freedom of association.[1]

1. See below Nos. 632 ss.

§2. Representations

630. The second type of contentious procedure provided for by the ILO Constitution (Art. 24–25) is that of representations. A representation may be made by an employers' or workers' organization on the ground that a State has failed to secure in any respect the effective observance of a Convention to which it is a party (Art. 24). This type of complaint is governed by precise rules providing, in brief, for the representation to be considered in the first place by a committee of three members from the ILO Governing Body and subsequently by the Governing Body as a whole.[1] Not more than 13 such representations in all have been made to the ILO, and only six within the past 25 years, five by workers' organizations and one by an employers' organization. This is probably due to the fact that other procedures are available to enable employers' and workers' organizations to put foward their views (reports on the application of Conventions, special machinery for complaints in respect of freedom of association). However, in recent years there has been an increase in the number of representations received and in the importance of the questions at issue, which related in particular to discrimination in employment.

1. It was in connection with such a representation that in 1938 the Governing Body established a principle which has since been confirmed in respect of various other procedures, namely that withdrawal of the representation by the complainant organization does not automatically entail the termination of the case. See *Intern. Lab. Code*, art. 1492 No. 562 and *O.B.* 1938, pp. 60–61. This rule was based on the fear that pressure might be brought to bear on the complainant organization and also on the fact that the public interest is involved in the procedure.

Chapter V. The Special Machinery in the Field of Freedom of Association[1]

631. Special machinery in the field of freedom of association for trade union purposes was set up by the ILO in 1950 following an agreement with the Economic and Social Council of the United Nations.[2] It is based on the submission of complaints by governments or by employers' or workers' organizations, the latter case being the most frequent. Complaints under this procedure may be made even against States which have not ratified the 1948 and 1949 Freedom of Association Conventions (Nos. 87 and 98). This is because the ILO Constitution, which the States Members of the Organization have accepted, lays down the principle of freedom of association; it has therefore been held that this principle should be observed by all States Members by virtue of their membership of the Organization alone.[3] The general view was that, even though the more detailed standards of the ILO Conventions in the field of freedom of association cannot be imposed on States which have not ratified the relevant Conventions, the Organization is entitled to promote the implementation of this constitutional principle by means such as investigation and conciliation. The machinery set up in this field comprises two different bodies.

1. See Jenks, *The International Protection of Trade Union Freedom,* London, 1957; idem., 'The International Protection of Trade Union Rights' in *The International Protection of Human Rights*, ed. by Evan Luard, London, 1967, pp. 210–247; von Potobsky, 'Normas internacionales, libertad sindical y derecho colectivo del trabajo' in Deveali, *Tratado de derecho del trabajo*, vol. V, Buenos Aires, 1966, pp. 597–609; idem, 'Protection of Trade Union Rights – Twenty years' work by the Committee on Freedom of Association', *I.L.R.*, April 1972, pp. 69–83; Cassese, 'Il controllo internazionale sul rispetto della libertà sindacale nel quadro delle attuali tendenze in materia di protezione internazionale dei diritti dell'uomo', *Communicazioni e Studi*, Vol. XII, Milan, 1966, pp. 293–418; Valticos, 'La protection internationale de la liberté syndicale vingt-cinq ans après', *Human Rights Journal*, Vol. VII–1, 1974, pp. 5–39; idem, 'Les méthodes de la protection internationale de la liberté syndicale', *Rec. Cours*, 1975–I, pp. 77–138.
2. Resolution 277(X) of 17 February 1950 of the Council.
3. This was stated, in particular, by the Second European Regional Conference of the ILO in a Resolution adopted on 23 January 1974 (*O.B.* vol. LVII, 1974, p. 152).

§1. The Committee on Freedom of Association

632. The first of these bodies is the Committee on Freedom of Association.[1] This Committee is appointed by the Governing Body of the ILO from among its own members and comprises nine members – three representatives each of governments, employers and workers. Since it was first set up in 1951 the Committee has had only two chairmen, the present one being Professor Roberto Ago, who has served since 1961. The Committee usually proceeds on documentary evidence supplied both by the complainant and the government against which the complaint is directed. In a number of cases an independent personality or an ILO official has, at the request or with the consent of the government concerned, visited the country to have discussions with the authorities and the occupational organizations, establish the facts, sometimes meet detained trade unionists and report back to the Committee. Thus increasing resort is had, in this field also, to the procedure of 'direct contacts' mentioned above.[2] This has been done, at the request or with the agreement of the governments concerned, in a number of countries (Jordan in 1974, Uruguay in 1975, Bolivia in 1976, Chile in 1978). The reports of the Committee, which as a rule are unanimous, are made to the Governing Body of the ILO. They contain the findings of the Committee on the cases submitted to it and, where appropriate, recommendations to the governments concerned. The Governing Body has generally endorsed such recommendations without discussion. Cases of considerable importance have sometimes given rise to discussion before the approval of the Committee's recommendations.

1. See in particular von Potobsky, *op. cit.,* in *I.L.R.*, April 1972.
2. See above No. 615.

633. Since it was first set up, the Committee has dealt with over 900 cases affecting a wide range of aspects of freedom of association: legislation contrary to the principles of freedom of association, action taken by governments such as dissolution of trade unions, arrest of trade union leaders, intervention in trade union activities, etc. The Committee has based its examination of cases referred to it on the general principles of freedom of association and has been guided by the provisions of the Conventions adopted in this field. In disposing of hundreds of cases it has, as already indicated,[1] gradually built up an impressive body of opinion.

1. See above Nos. 121–123.

634. The results of the work of the Freedom of Association Committee has been very uneven. In a number of cases the States concerned have taken account of the Committee's recommendations by amending their legislation, releasing trade union leaders from prison, granting pardons, etc. In other cases the recommendations have had no effect, or at least no immediate effect. Arrangements are made for following up the action taken by governments on the Committee's recommendations. Apart from the results obtained in specific cases dealt with by the Committee, the procedure has had the effect of placing on governments a general obligation to account for their actions in the field of freedom of association. It has also exercised a preventive influence on the action of the public authorities.

§2. The Fact-Finding and Conciliation Commission

635. The most formal part of the machinery for the protection of freedom of association is the Fact-Finding and Conciliation Commission.[1] This Commission is composed of independent personalities appointed by the Governing Body of the ILO on the proposal of the Director-General of the International Labour Office. In principle, a case may not be referred to the Commission without the consent of the government concerned. In the first years which followed the establishment of the procedure, some governments[2] which had been requested by the Governing Body to give their consent to the referral to the Commission of cases relating to their countries, refused to do so. Measures of publicity were then taken in connection with these cases.

1. See Valticos, 'La Commission d'investigation et de conciliation en matière de liberté syndicale et le mécanisme de protection internationale de la liberté syndicale', *Ann*. 1967, pp. 445–468.
2. Czechoslovakia, Hungary and the USSR.

636. The first case referred to the Commission, with the agreement of the government concerned, was, in 1964, a complaint by the General Council of Trade Unions of Japan concerning trade union rights in the public sector in Japan. The procedure was similar to that followed in the case of formal complaints.[1] Three independent members were appointed to examine the case, and after requesting information from the parties and from the international and national organizations of employers and workers, the Commission heard a number of witnesses, some of whom had been called by itself, then went to Japan, where it held discussions in private with representatives of the complainant organization and of the government. It submitted to the parties certain proposals which were accepted, and as a result the Government of Japan ratified the Freedom of Association and Protection of the Right to Organize

Convention, 1947 (No. 87) and exchanges of views began between the authorities and the trade unions. The Commission made a full report including its conclusions and recommendations,[2] and this was accepted by the complainant organization and the government as a basis for the progressive settlement of the pending issues. Other cases have since been referred to the Commission, such as one concerning Greece in 1965 and another concerning Lesotho, which is a Member of the United Nations and not of the ILO, but the government of which gave its consent to the procedure. In that case the Chairman of the Commission appointed to examine the complaint visited the country, with a member of the secretariat, and he had discussions with the authorities and trade union leaders, one of whom was in prison. The report of the Commission was transmitted by the Governing Body to the United Nations in 1975.

1. See above Nos. 622–624.
2. See *O.B.*, 1966, No. 1, Special Supplement.

637. An important development has been the Governing Body's decision of June 1974 to refer to the Commission, with the consent of the government concerned, various complaints concerning the trade union situation in Chile; three independent members were appointed to the Commission to deal with the case, the president being a former President of the International Court of Justice. In October 1974, the Commission met in Geneva to hear witnesses called by the principal complainants (the three big international workers' organizations) and by the government. In November-December 1974 it visited Chile, after arrangements had been made to ensure the facilities and safeguards necessary for the carrying out of its mandate, as in the case of earlier similar visits.[1] In Chile, the Commission travelled to different regions, visited a number of undertakings, and had discussions with the authorities, prominent persons, representatives of numerous trade unions, a number of trade union leaders (including some in detention), workers who had been dismissed, professors, lawyers, churchmen, etc. The report of the Commission dealt both with trade union matters and with questions of human rights and civil liberties which are closely linked with the excercise of trade union rights.[2] When the report was discussed, in May 1975, the representative of the Chilean government accepted its recommendations, while making some observations. The Governing Body appealed to the government to give effect to the recommendations and asked it, at various intervals, to supply detailed reports on the steps. The reports are examined by the Freedom of Association Committee and by the Governing Body and the question is regularly followed and discussed by the organs of the ILO.

1. See below No. 694.
2. See *The Trade Union Situation in Chile*. Report of the Fact-Finding and Conciliation Commission, Geneva, 1975; Valticos, 'Un double type d'enquête au Chili', *Ann.* 1975, pp. 483–502.

638. In 1978, following a complaint against the USA about trade union matters in Puerto-Rico – and as the US is no longer a Member of the ILO[1] – the Economic and Social Council of the United Nations decided, under the established procedure and with the consent of the US Government, to refer the case to the ILO Fact-finding and Conciliation Commission.

1. See above No. 30.

Chapter VI. Special Studies and Inquiries, Promotional Measures and Technical Co-operation

§1. Special Studies and Inquiries

I. Freedom of Association

639. Apart from the supervisory procedures proper, studies and inquiries of varying scope have been undertaken by the ILO from time to time.[1] Most of them have been concerned with freedom of association. In some cases they were carried out by missions of ILO officials who visited countries at the request of the governments concerned to collect full and impartial information on situations which had been the subject of criticism on the international level (in Hungary in 1920, in Venezuela in 1949). Sometimes the study has covered the country's labour problems as a whole, though triggered off by complaints concerning the trade union situation (e.g. in Greece in 1947). Sometimes it has extended to all member States or to a certain number of them. Thus, in 1955, a committee of independent persons under the chairmanship of Lord McNair, former President of the International Court of Justice, was appointed to examine the extent of the freedom of employers' and workers' organizations from government domination or control.[2] Later, from 1958 to 1963, the Governing Body set up machinery to determine the real facts about the trade union situation in member States. Teams of ILO officials went on mission to various countries (United States, USSR, United Kingdom, Sweden, Malaysia, Burma) on the invitation of the governments concerned, and drew up detailed reports which attempted to give a full picture of the situation in the respective countries without expressing any judgment upon it.[3]

1. See Valticos, 'L'inspection internationale dans le droit international du travail' in *L'inspection internationale* (ed. by Fischer and Vignes), Brussels, 1976, pp. 379–437.
2. See Report of the Committee on Freedom of Employers' and Workers' Organizations: *O.B.* XXXIX, 1956, No. 9, pp. 475–599.
3. See reports published by the International Labour Office on the trade union situation in the United States (1960), the USSR (1960), the United Kingdom (1961), Sweden (1961), Burma (1962) and Malaya (1962).

640. In 1967, in pursuance of a request by the government of Spain, which had not ratified the Freedom of Association Conventions, the Governing Body of the ILO appointed a Study Group to examine the labour and trade union situation in Spain,[1] composed of three independent persons appointed by the Governing Body on the proposal of the Director-General. In this case the procedure was not of a contentious type, although complaints concerning the trade union situation in Spain had been examined earlier by the Freedom of Association Committee. The Governing Body specified that the study should be carried out 'in the light of the principles laid down in the Constitution of the ILO' and the Study Group stated that it had been guided, in particular, by the principle – which is part of the ILO Constitution – that 'freedom of expression and of association are essential to sustained progress'. The members of the Group also indicated that 'while they have no judicial powers, their responsibility has to be discharged in a judicial manner and they have to be guided throughout by the duty to record their findings without fear or favour'.[2] The procedure was based, *mutatis mutandis*, on that of the Commissions of Inquiry and the Fact-Finding and Conciliation Commission. A preliminary agreement in precise terms was concluded between the Director-General and the Spanish government providing all necessary safeguards to enable the Study Group to discharge its task with full freedom and impartiality. It provided, *inter alia*, that the group would enjoy complete freedom of movement and would be entitled to undertake private talks and interviews at which no witness would be present, and that no person who had been in contact with the group might for that reason be subjected to coercion, sanctions or punishment at any time.

1. See the Committee's Report: *The Labour and Trade Union Situation in Spain*, ILO, Geneva, 1969, and Valticos, 'Une nouvelle expérience de protection des droits de l'homme: le groupe d'étude de l'OIT chargé d'examiner la situation en matière de travail et en matière syndicale en Espagne', *Ann.*, 1970, pp. 567–570.
2. Committee's Report quoted above, p. 8, para. 26.

641. The Group met in Geneva to hear representatives of the government and of the three big international workers' organizations, and in March 1969 visited Spain, where it divided its time between official visits and interviews (in particular interviews with ministers, officials, the highest judicial authorities, and employers' and workers' representatives of the Trade Union Organization and visits to various undertakings chosen by the Group) and private visits and interviews with more than 100 persons, ranging from the highest ecclesiastical authorities and public figures politically opposed to the government, university professors in labour law and lawyers specializing in the defence of trade unionists, to members of works councils, trade unionists in detention, and ordinary workers. The final report of the Study Group contains detailed description of the situation in Spain as well as some considerations directed towards the future. The Group drew particular attention to the fact that in the course of its consultations a consensus of opinion had emerged as to the conditions which the trade union law should fulfil and it listed those conditions. In conclusion, it also pointed out that there are unequivocal world standards in labour and trade union matters and in respect of the civil liberties which are revelant to trade union rights, and that 'no State is bound contractually by any of these standards unless it has ratified the appropriate instrument, but no State can escape comparison with them'.[1] The Governing Body decided to adopt, as suggested in the report, every measure to ensure its most widespread diffusion, and in fact the report was widely distributed both in Spain and outside Spain. A few years later, following the political change which took place in Spain, a completely new legislation, based on the ILO standards on freedom of association was enacted in Spain, in April 1977 and, the same month, the Conventions on Freedom of Association (Nos. 87 and 98) were ratified by the Spanish Government.

1. *Idem*, p. 297, para. 1264.

II. Forced Labour

642. In the field of forced labour, special procedures for investigation and study were in use from 1921 in collaboration with the League of Nations. After the Second World War, the work of an *ad hoc* Committee on Forced Labour set up jointly in 1951 by the ILO and the United Nations and continued by an ILO Committee on Forced Labour up to 1959 led to the adoption in 1957 of the Abolition of Forced Labour Convention (No.105).

III. Discrimination

643. In the field of discrimination, the Governing Body of the ILO approved in 1973 a formula for special surveys on situations connected with the elimination of discrimination in employment with a view to promoting the implementation of the Discrimination (Employment and Occupation) Convention, 1958 (No. 111).

644. Moreover, on an *ad hoc* basis, a mission of ILO officials visited Israel and the occupied territories in April 1978 to consider the various aspects of equality of opportunity and treatment of the Arab workers of these territories as regards employment, conditions of work and social benefits as well as trade union activities related to their employment both in Israel and in the occupied territories. The mission was guided in its work by the principles and objectives laid down in the Constitution of the ILO (Declaration of Philadelphia) and in the Discrimination (Employment and Occupation) Convention and Recommendation (No. 111), as in other instruments concerning the fundamental rights of workers such as the Freedom of Association and Protection of the Right to Organize Convention, 1948 (No. 87). The findings and suggestions of the mission were contained in its report,[1] which was submitted to the 64th Session of the International Labour Conference.

1. See this report in *Action Taken on the Resolutions Adopted by the International Labour Conference at its 59th to 63rd Sessions, Supplement to the Report of the Director-General*, International Labour Conference, 64th Session, 1978, pp. 24–32.

§2. Promotional Measures: Information, Education and Training

645. Implementation of ILO standards is also sought by means of various educational and training measures. Regional seminars for labour officials are held every year with a view to promoting a better understanding and functioning of ILO procedures relating to international labour standards. Seminars for trade union representatives are also held from time to time on a regional or universal basis to inform them of the part they are entitled to play in the supervisory procedures, publications are made in the framework of the Workers' Education Programme.[1] In 1978, a documentary film on international labour standards was produced by the ILO in English and French. The film describes the ILO's standard-setting and supervisory procedures, and includes interviews inter alia with government, employer and worker representatives on various aspects of these procedures. In more specific matters, regional seminars in the field of freedom of association have been held for labour administrators, judges and specialized professors.[2] Regional tripartite seminars are also organized systematically to consider the problems which arise in the field of equality of opportunity and treatment in the region concerned.[3] They are part of a wider programme of practical action designed to combat discrimination in employment. Many publications have been made under this programme.[4]

1. See in particular *International Labour Standards, A Workers' Education Manual*, ILO, Geneva, 1978.
2. Mexico, 6–14 October 1976. See *Principios y normas de la OIT sobre libertad sindical*, Geneva, 1976, and Report on the First Symposium on Freedom of Association in Latin America (COL/LS/AL-D.1) (201st Session of the Governing Body of the ILO, November 1976).
3. See *Equality of Opportunity in Employment in Asia: Problems and Policies*, Report and Documents of a Regional Seminar (Manila, 2–11 December 1969), ILO, Geneva, 1970; *Equality of Opportunity in Employment in the American Region: Problems and Policies*, Report and Documents of a Regional Symposium (Panama, 1–12 October 1973, ILO, Geneva, 1974; *Equality of Opportunity and Treatment in Employment in the European Region: Problems and Policies,* Report and Documents of a Regional Symposium (Geneva, 21–29 April 1975), ILO, Geneva, 1975; *Equality of Opportunity and Treatment in Employment in Africa: Problems and Policies*, Report of a Regional Symposium (Dakar, 19–29 September 1977), ILO, Geneva, 1977.
4. See, e.g., *Fighting Discrimination in Employment and Occupation. A Workers' Education Manual*, ILO, Geneva, 1968; *ILO's Action against Discrimination in Employment*, ILO, Geneva, 1968; *Equality in Respect of Employment under Legislation and other National Standards*, ILO, Geneva, 1967; *Special National Procedures concerning Non-Discrimination in Employment – A Practical Guide*, ILO, Geneva, 1975; *Labour and Discrimination in Namibia*, ILO, Geneva, 1977; *Labour Conditions and Discrimination in Southern Rhodesia* (Zimbabwe), ILO, Geneva, 1978; *The ILO and Apartheid*, Geneva, 1977.

§3. Technical Co-operation and World Employment Programme

646. The ILO Constitution (Art. 10 para. 2b) provides that the International Labour Office 'shall accord to governments, at their request, all appropriate assistance within its power in connection with the framing of laws and regulations on the basis of the decisions of the Conference'. Since 1950 the scope of the technical co-operation offered to countries by the ILO jointly with the United Nations has expanded very considerably.[1] It may serve as a means of helping governments to reach the level of international standards and thus to ratify Conventions or to remove discrepancies observed in the application of ratified Conventions. In this respect international labour standards provide guidance for the experts and for the staff of the ILO in their technical co-operation work, and there are arrangements to ensure that these experts are fully briefed on standards aspects relevant to their work and that their recommendations take full account of these aspects.

1. The total expenditure of the ILO on technical co-operation during the period 1950–1977 amounted to some US $487 million. In 1977 it exceeded US $48 million.

647. In the specific field of employment, the ILO launched in 1969 a programme based on the standards contained in the Employment Policy Convention and Recommendation, 1964 (No. 122), with a view to helping countries to attain the highest possible level of productive employment. As part of this programme, missions organized by the ILO have visited a number of countries in Africa, America and Asia at the request of the governments concerned and have submitted recommendations to the governments. In June 1976, a Tripartite World Conference on Employment, Income Distribution and Social Progress and the International Division of Labour was convened by the ILO. The Conference adopted a detailed Declaration of Principles and Programme of Action on these matters. It sets as the objective of national action and international co-operation the promotion of employment and the satisfaction of the basic needs of each country's population, defined in terms both of minimum family requirements and the provision of essential public services. These activities in the field of employment involved a combination of the ILO's various means of action (standard-setting, research, meetings and operational activities).

Chapter VII. Main Characteristics of the Supervisory System

648. The supervisory system of the ILO is based primarily on provisions of the ILO Constitution, but these have served as the starting point for progressive developments. The initial aim of supervision was to ensure the discharge by States of obligations arising out of the ratification of Conventions, but this was subsequently extended to promoting the implementation of ILO standards even where no formal obligations existed. The search for effectiveness has led to the introduction of a wide variety of procedures, ranging from the examination of documentary material to visits or inspections in different forms. The relative importance of procedures based on documentary examination and on on-the-spot visits evidently depends on the nature of the questions at issue (for example, whether they concern legislation or factual situations). While designed to meet particular situations and needs, these various procedures are nevertheless complementary to each other.

649. Generally speaking, the system comprises several elements: a specialized secretariat to assist the supervisory bodies by providing detailed objective analyses of the available documentary material; a body composed of independent personalities charged with the task of appraising the extent to which national situations conform to international standards;[1] the policy-making bodies of the ILO (Governing Body and International Labour Conference) on which the various interests involved, both governmental and non-governmental, are represented, and which seek in co-operation with the governments concerned to find solutions to the problems raised; and lastly, discreet action by the Director-General or senior officials of the International Labour Office aimed at persuasion or clarification of problems for the benefit of the governments or parties concerned and various types of 'direct contacts' to clarify the problems and seek solutions to existing difficulties.

1. The genuine independence of the members of the supervisory bodies is a fundamental principle of the ILO system (see Jenks, *The International Protection of Trade Union Rights, op. cit.*, pp. 239–240).

650. The operation of all the supervisory machinery is guided by certain common principles: a striving for exactitude in establishing the facts, impartiality in appraising situations, firmness on the principles and obligations at issue, boldness combined with a sense of proportion and realism, and the will to achieve positive results through constructive mutual discussion.[1]

1. On this point see Jenks, 'Human Rights, Social Justice and Peace – The Broader Significance of the ILO Experience', in *International Protection of Human Rights*, Proceedings of the Seventh Nobel Symposium, Oslo, September 1967, ed. by Eide and Schou, Stockholm, 1968, pp. 227–260; Valticos, 'Un système de contrôle international: la mise en oeuvre des conventions internationales du travail', *op. cit.*, pp. 386–388; idem, 'L'inspection internationale dans le droit international du travail', *op. cit.*, pp. 428–437.

651. The supervisory procedures of the ILO are foremost among international systems of supervision and it has often been suggested that they might be taken as models by other international organizations, either in respect of the system as a whole[1] or in respect of particular rules, such as those relating to submission to the competent authorities or reporting on non-ratified Conventions,[2] or again, the machinery for the protection of freedom of association.[3] For various reasons, the whole complex of these characteristics cannot be found or introduced in other international organizations, but there is no doubt that ILO procedures have influenced, to a greater or lesser extent the systems organized by other organizations belonging to the United Nations family and the Council of Europe.[4]

1. Scelle, *Précis de droit des gens*, vol II, Paris, 1934, p. 521; Lord McNair, *The Expansion of International Law,* Jerusalem, 1962; Earl Warren, 'It's Time to Implement the Declaration of Human Rights', 59 *American Bar Association Journal*, pp. 1257–1260, 1973. See also House Comm. on Foreign Affairs, 93rd Cong., 2nd Sess., *Human Rights in the World Community – A Call for U.S. Leadership*, 1974.
2. R. Ago, 'La codification du droit international et les problèmes de sa réalisation', *op. cit.*, pp. 117 ss.
3. Cassese, *op. cit.*; Vellas, 'L'évolution de la compétence de l'OIT et l'affaire de la liberté syndicale au Japon', *Droit social,* 1967, p. 362; see also Carey a.o., Report of the Committee on Publications of the Department of State and the United Nations, *A.J.I.L*, 1970, No. 4, pp. 293–314, 309.
4. Jenks, *Social Justice in the Law of Nations. The ILO Impact after Fifty Years*, London, 1970, pp. 33 ss; Valticos, 'Les systèmes de contrôle non judiciaire des instruments internationaux relatifs aux droits de l'homme', *Mélanges Modinos*, Paris, 1968, pp. 331–356; idem, *Droit international du travail*, pp. 600–607.

Chapter VIII. Supervisory Machinery Established by Other International Organizations

652. In respect of instruments adopted by international organizations other than the ILO, and in particular the United Nations, the Council of Europe and the European Communities,[1] more or less elaborate supervisory procedures have been introduced. In the first two of these cases, provisions for implementation are not included in the constituent Charter of the Organization, but only in each of the separate instruments. The result is a variety of formulas, each instrument prescribing a different kind of implementation system. A second consequence is that there are no obligations (such as an obligation to report) on States which have not ratified the instruments concerned.

1. A joint ILO-UNESCO procedure has also been set up in connection with the Recommendation concerning the Status of Teachers (see above No. 126) to follow up its implementation on the basis of reports from governments. Such reports were examined by a Committee of 12 independent experts in 1970 and in 1976. The Committee's reports were issued by the ILO and UNESCO.

§1. United Nations Instruments

653. As regards the International Covenants on Human Rights,[1] the Covenant on Economic, Social and Cultural Rights provides (Art. 16–20) that States which are parties to it shall submit reports on its implementation; such reports shall be presented in stages[2] and may be transmitted by the Economic and social Council to the Human Rights Commission.[3] The Commission and the Council itself may make recommendations 'of a general nature' (Art. 19 and 21). Copies of the reports must be sent to the specialized agencies, such as the ILO, in so far as they relate to questions within their competence. Where relevant information has previously been furnished to the United Nations or to a specialized agency, States Parties can merely provide a reference to that information. Under arrangements with the Economic and Social Council, the specialized agencies may report on the progress made in achieving the observance of those provisions of the Covenant which fall within the scope of their activities, including particulars of the decisions and recommendations on such implementation adopted by their competent organs. The specialized agencies may also submit observations on any general recommendations of the Human Rights Commission. In the ILO, the Committee of Experts on the Application of Conventions and Recommendations[4] has been entrusted with the task of examining reports under this Covenant and reporting to the Economic and Social Council. The Committee first undertook this work at its session in March 1978, when it examined reports from nine States on measures taken to implement Articles 6 to 9 of the Covenant and prepared a report which was transmitted to the Economic and Social Council at its session in April–May 1978.[5] In the case of the Covenant on Civil and Political Rights, provision is made (Art. 28–45) not only for the submission of reports, but also for the setting up of a special body, the Human Rights Committee, to examine them.[6] This body has been established and started its work in 1977.

1. See above No. 129.
2. By Resolution 1988(LX) of 11 May 1976 (UN document E/RES/1988(LX) of 14 May 1976), the Economic and Social Council provided for a programme of reporting in three stages, at two-yearly intervals, and also made arrangements for the implementation of the system of reporting under the Covenant.
3. By the above-mentioned resolution 1988(LX), the Economic and Social Council decided that a sessional working group of the Council should be established whenever reports are due for consideration by the Council, to assist it in the consideration of such reports.
4. See Nos. 608 ss. The decision to entrust this task to the Committee of Experts was taken by the Governing Body of the ILO at its 201st Session (November 1976) in response to a request addressed to the specialized agencies by the Economic and Social Council in its resolution 1988(LX) to submit reports to it, as provided for in the Covenant.
5. Document E/1978/27.
6. On the supervisory arrangements provided for in the Covenant, see Jenks, 'The United Nations Covenants on Human Rights Come to Life', *Recueil Paul Guggenheim*, Geneva, 1968, pp. 765–773; Capotorti, 'The International Measures of Implementation included in the Covenants on Human Rights', in *International Protection of Human Rights*, ed. by Eide and Schou, Stockholm, 1968, pp. 131–148; Schwelb, 'Civil and Political Rights – The International Measures of Implementation', 62 A.J.I.L., 1968, pp. 827–868; *idem*, 'Some Aspects of the Measures of Implementation of the International Covenant on Economic, Social and Cultural Rights', *Revue des droits de l'homme/Human Rights Journal*, 1968, pp. 363–377; and *idem*, 'Entry into force of the International Covenants on Human Rights', 70 A.J.I.L., 1976, pp. 511–519.

654. Similar arrangements for supervision have been made in the case of the Convention for the Elimination of All Forms of Racial Discrimination:[1] they began to function in 1969.

1. See above No. 131.

§2. Council of Europe Instruments

I. European Social Charter

655. As regards Council of Europe instruments,[1] the arrangements for supervision of the European Social Charter (Art. 21–29) are largely based on the ILO system, though differing in certain respects.[2] Governments are required to submit two-yearly reports on the application of those provisions of the Charter which they have accepted (and States which have ratified the Charter may also be asked to submit reports on provisions which they have not accepted, but no use has yet been made of this provision). The reports are examined by a Committee of seven members appointed by the Committee of Ministers from a list of independent experts nominated by the contracting parties. A representative of the ILO participates in a consultative capacity in the deliberations of this Committee of Independent Experts. The reports from the governments and the conclusions of the Committee of Independent Experts are examined by a Governmental Committee, which invites not more than two international organizations of employers and two international trade union organizations to be represented by observers in a consultative capacity at its meetings. The Consultative Assembly is also called upon to communicate its views on the conclusions of the Committee of Independent Experts. Finally, the Committee of Ministers may, by a majority of two-thirds, make recommendations to each contracting party.

1. See above Nos. 134 ss.
2. See Kahn-Freund, 'The European Social Charter', *European Law and the Individual*, ed. by Jacobs, Amsterdam, 1976, pp. 181–211; Wiebringhaus, 'Première mise en oeuvre du systeme de contrôle instauré par la Charte sociale européenne', *Ann.*, 1968, pp. 784–789; *idem*, 'L'état d'application de la Charte sociale européenne', *Ann.* 1973, pp. 928–940; Valticos, *Droit international du travail*, p. 604, No. 4, and see 'The European Social Charter and International Labour Standards', *I.L.R.*, December 1961, pp. 464–469; Valticos, 'Mise en parallèle des actions et des mécanismes de contrôle au niveau du Conseil de l'Europe et de l'Organisation internationale du Travail', in *La Charte sociale européenne*, Brussels, 1978.

656. These supervisory arrangements began to operate after the Charter came into force in 1965. By 1978, five sets of very detailed conclusions had been adopted by the Committee of Independent Experts. Certain difficulties have been experienced, due primarily to the reluctance of the Governmental Committee and of the Committee of Ministers to endorse some of the initial conclusions and proposals of the Committee of Independent Experts. Contrary to these proposals, no recommendations have yet been made to States. There were also delays in the procedure subsequent to the submission of the reports of the Committee of Independent Experts. Steps have, however, been taken by several countries to give effect to some of the Committee's conclusions.

II. European Social Security Code

657. The system established by the European Social Security Code provides for the reports by the contracting parties to be examined in the first place by the competent ILO body (i.e. the Committee of Experts on the Application of Conventions and Recommendations). The latter's conclusions are to be submitted to the Council of Europe, whose Committee of Ministers will then determine, by a two-thirds majority, whether each contracting party has discharged the obligations arising out of the Code (Art. 74). This system has been functioning regularly since 1969, when the Code came into force.

§3. The Instruments of the European Communities

658. As regards the various instruments concerning labour introduced by the European Communities (the Treaties setting up the Communities themselves and various special instruments) suffice it to recall here that they have such effects as the general legal system of the Communities assigns to each of them. In some cases, therefore, it is the 'supranational' procedure that applies, its principal instrument being the *regulation*, which is directly enforceable in the internal legal system of the member States and is used in the matters of free movement, social security of migrant workers, and the European Social Fund –

that is, in the field of employment generally –; it is occasionally supplemented by *directives*, which are mandatory as regards their objectives but not as regards the formal means for attaining them. In other cases, the procedure is that of non-mandatory co-operation, of which the principal instrument is the *recommendation*, often used to promote social harmonization in various fields, such as conditions of employment, social security, equal remuneration, etc. In the case of mandatory provisions, disputes may normally be referred by the Commission to the Court of Justice of the Communities. In addition, the courts of the member States, under the Treaty of Rome (Art. 177), may refer to the Court of Justice of the Communities questions concerning the interpretation of the Treaty or the validity or interpretation of measures taken by the institutions of the Communities, and the Court has in fact handed down a large number of decisions concerning social security. With regard to recommendations and other texts which are not binding, States are invited to take action along the lines suggested and to report periodically, for instance every two years, on the action they have taken.

Concluding Remarks: the Outlook for the Future

659. While the present body of international labour standards already comprises over 300 instruments and covers a large part of the field of labour law, it can be expected that international standard-setting will be pursued for the years to come. First, needs and conceptions change with the years and some of the oldest instruments will have to be reworked to be adatped to contemporary needs. Secondly, new questions arise which will call for the adoption of international standards, to meet the need for greater material security and welfare, but also the need for freedom, equality and participation. As said above (No. 567), the Working Party of the ILO Governing Body which is examining international labour standards has identified a number of instruments which are in need of revision and of subjects on which the preparation of new standards should be considered. A great area thus remains to be covered by international labour law. In framing new instruments, it can be expected that recourse to flexibility devices will be pursued and even intensified, e.g. in the form of Conventions laying down general principles which are supplemented by Recommendations providing guidance on methods of implementation, and of Conventions containing provisions for their progressive application, such as those which can be ratified by parts.

660. Among the growing number of instruments which will thus constitute the body of international labour law, it is likely that attention will be primarily concentrated on a limited number of them, whose ratification and application will be promoted on a priority basis.

661. Finally, as regards the implementation of international labour standards, it will no doubt be guided by the trends which became apparent during recent years, i.e. the development of the role of non-governmental (employers' and workers') organizations, a search for increased efficiency coupled with a simplification of procedures, a continued use of discreet methods of discussion between the governments concerned and representatives of the Director-General, but also, in serious cases, resort to the formal procedures of complaint and representation. As in the past, its efficiency will depend both on the methods used and on the spirit in which these methods will be put into operation, with a view to permit an objective examination of cases.

Index

The numbers given are paragraph numbers.

CPSIA information can be obtained at www.ICGtesting.com
Printed in the USA